Diplomatic Correspondent

Diplomatic Correspondent

BY

THOMAS BARMAN

THE MACMILLAN COMPANY

New York

Library of Congress Catalog Card Number: 69–11208

First American Edition 1969

First published in Great Britain in 1968
by Hamish Hamilton Ltd., London

The Macmillan Company, New York

Printed in Great Britain

To My Father

CONTENTS

FOREWORD

THIS BOOK would not have been written without the prompting and bullying of friends in the BBC. When I retired from my post as diplomatic correspondent after twenty-one years, Mr. Roger Lazar asked me to prepare a talk on my life in journalism, and promised to devote to it the whole of that well-known half-hour programme called 'From Our Own Correspondent'. I doubted and hesitated but finally gave way to overwhelming pressure. The consequences surprised and delighted me. The talk aroused some interest; and some people took the trouble to write to the BBC to say so. When its text was published in full in *The Listener* on 5 January 1967, other and equally pleasant letters followed. It was then suggested to me that perhaps I had enough material to expand my talk into a book. I have never kept a diary; but I have hoarded notes on some of the interesting events that I have been able to observe at close quarters, and also some newspaper cuttings. I did not file them in an orderly fashion: they were left in cupboards in the office and at home, or in old trunks, or just on some handy shelf out of reach of cleaners and other tidy persons. When I began sorting out all these odd bits of paper, I found past events springing to life in my mind. Some of them became as vivid as if they had happened yesterday instead of forty years ago. I cannot claim copybook accuracy for all the quotations that are given in this book; but I believe the sense of what appears is in accordance with what was said at the time.

To Mr. Lazar, then, and his assistant, Miss Paddy O'Keeffe, I owe a very special debt: not only for encouraging me to write this book but for their help and friendship over the years. My gratitude goes out also to Miss Jennifer Howard, the most self-effacing of secretaries, for typing and re-typing from an untidy and no doubt almost illegible manuscript; and to Miss Carol Bellchambers for checking dates and references. Willing helpers in the BBC Library and its News Information Department smoothed away many difficulties. To old friends on *The Times* I am also under an obligation. Their patient response to my questions brought back memories of happy days in Printing House Square.

THOMAS BARMAN

THE DIPLOMATIC CORRESPONDENT'S WORLD

THERE WAS no place for journalists in the respectable world of diplomacy of half a century ago. Before the First World War, they were not allowed inside the Foreign Office until the doorkeeper had first satisfied himself that there was a bit of news that could be fed to them. If senior officials had decided that there was nothing they wanted to say, the journalists waiting in the courtyard would be sent away and told to try again another day. In the early nineteen-twenties there came a change. The ordinary newspaper-reading public began to take an interest in the conduct of foreign policy; but since many Foreign Office people remained suspicious of the press and therefore uncooperative, journalists had to get their diplomatic news from other sources: from foreign capitals, perhaps, or from the representatives of foreign governments in London. This could mean that the British view was not adequately reflected in the columns of the daily press, even in those cases where British interests were directly involved; and that was something the politicians soon came to regard as unfortunate. Lord Curzon, the Foreign Secretary at the time, decided that something had to be done. He instructed his Assistant Private-Secretary to act as a sort of liaison officer between the press and the Foreign Office, and to make sure that His Lordship was given a good press while telling the journalists as little as possible. These liaison arrangements were gradually formalized and institutionalized in the News Department which came to handle all contacts with the press, British, Commonwealth and foreign, on behalf of the Foreign Secretary and his staff.

The News Department is at its best when Foreign Secretaries are allowed to do their work without constant interference by the Prime Minister of the day. It is paralysed when the head of the

Government becomes too publicity-conscious and too certain that he alone knows how foreign policy should be conducted. When Neville Chamberlain was at No. 10 Downing Street, and again when Anthony Eden was there, and during the early days of the Wilson Government, the channels of communication between the Foreign Office and the press were choked with publicity blurbs. But in spite of these occasional failures the system has worked reasonably well over a period of forty years or so.

But it seems to me that it is now on the point of breaking down. Relations between Foreign Secretaries and diplomatic correspondents are not as close as they had become over the years. There are, I think, two reasons for this. In the first place, relations between politicians and the public have been revolutionized by television. The politician gains no kudos out of a private talk with a handful of journalists; like Lord Curzon, he wants publicity. But he wants it in vast quantities, and only television can satisfy his insatiable appetite. His dearest wish is to be seen and heard on the television screen in disputations with 'television personalities'. When a Foreign Secretary arrives at London Airport after a long flight from Washington or Moscow, the first thing he looks for is the television camera: family, friends, senior officials with urgent messages—all are of secondary importance. Unshaved and unkempt, he insists upon being filmed; and he would feel cheated if he were not. No great harm is done so long as the politician who is being interviewed deals only with home affairs. But in foreign affairs, his statements and even his facial expression can have disastrous effects. Where the situation calls for the still small voice, the television camera tempts the star performer into boisterous gestures, into throwing boulders rather than fitting bits and pieces into a fine mosaic. A Foreign Secretary who comes back to London after quiet talks with political leaders in Washington or in Moscow, during the course of which he may have put over with success the British point of view on some problem or other, will undo all the good he has achieved if he responds to the camera's wicked invitation to tell an exciting story. If he boasts of having persuaded the Americans or the Russians to become more reasonable, about South-East Asia for instance, or about nuclear disarmament, a humiliating disavowal from one capital or another may follow within the hour. Yet if he says nothing at all in public, he feels that his 'public image' will suffer. So he may aim at a sort

PART ONE

A DECADE OF FEAR 1929–1939

CHAPTER 1

THE DOOR to international journalism was opened for me by one of the greatest financial swindles of this century. I had long been fascinated by the personalities of the great financial manipulators—men like J. Pierpont Morgan, Hugo Stinnes and Ivar Kreuger, to take three names at random. The greatest of them combine the skill of the politician with the flair of the gambler and the vision of the prophet. Many bankers are as easily victimized by them as clergymen's widows, retired colonels and other unworldly people. Some are no more than robber barons; others have played a constructive part in history. They tend to flourish in times of financial disorder; and if their operations provide them with huge profits and great political power, at least for a time, they also help to postpone or even to ward off altogether the evil day of economic breakdown. Professor Ure's *The Origin of Tyranny*, published in the early nineteen-twenties, seemed to me to have a direct bearing upon the problems of the time: I was especially fascinated by the earlier chapters in his book. He observed that the seventh and sixth century B.C. Greek rulers were the first men to realize the political possibilities of the conditions created by the introduction of the new coinage. To a large extent, he wrote, they owed their new position as rulers to a financial supremacy which they had established before they attained to supreme political power in their several states. So in the financial chaos between the two world wars, I began to look at the records and careers of men who might conceivably play the same sort of part on the political scene as the Greek tyrants had done, or the Medici of Florence, or the early Rothschilds. I came across the name of Hugo Stinnes and digested every scrap of information about him that came my way. I still have a lot of dog-eared notes about him lying at the bottom of an old trunk. But he was a dull fellow, vulgar and ill-mannered; and he fell far short of my financial ideal.

And then I had the good fortune to meet Ivar Kreuger, who was known for a time as the Swedish-Match King. His comings and goings had become of interest to newspapers all over the world, and especially to *The Financial Times* to which I had become a regular contributor from Scandinavia in the late nineteen-twenties. I saw in Kreuger a man who might succeed by his skilful financial techniques in bringing some kind of order and stability to the world. He emerged into prominence at a time when the Transfer Problem had become a fashionable term; a term used in those days to describe the difficulties that arose when payments had to be made across the foreign exchanges to meet such obligations as war debts, reparations, or ordinary commercial debts by countries that were not earning an adequate surplus of exports over imports to meet the demands of their creditors, mainly in the United States. When the difficulties reappeared after the Second World War, we spoke of the dollar shortage, and not of the transfer problem. We had Marshall Aid instead of private enterprise credits and loans. Governments undertook the salvage work instead of allowing it to be done by banks and finance houses. In the 'twenties, Kreuger provided the foreign exchange where it was needed—in Poland, in France, in Germany —against the security of a match monopoly, and usually with an undertaking by the debtor governments to tax cigarette-lighters in such a way as to make them more expensive to use than matches. If you were optimistic you believed that he was helping to solve the transfer problem. If you were pessimistic, or just hard-headed, like members of the House of Wallenberg in Stockholm or Morgans in New York, you were convinced that his methods were mere palliatives and that the whole adventure would end in disaster.

I wrote an enthusiastic article about him and his constructive role in history for *The Fortnightly Review*. It appeared in December 1931. It made a favourable impression on H. G. Wells who made a brief reference to it in his *Work, Wealth and Happiness of Mankind* published early in 1932. Wells observed that I had written in 'glowing terms of the advent of the organized money power'. But he went on to point out that there were many 'difficulties in the way of accepting this forecast of a benevolent oligarchy—or if you prefer it—an aristocracy of finance'. I had indeed written in very glowing terms. To me, Kreuger represented the hope that the West would eventually recover. It is hard to remember, now, how widespread was the feeling of despair in the years 1931 and 1932 about which Arnold Toynbee has written that 'men and women all over the world were seriously contemplating and frankly discussing the possibility that the Western system of society might break down and cease to work'. Maynard Keynes, as recorded in Harold Nicolson's diary, also thought that a general breakdown was inevitable. From this fate, I hoped, the methods and techniques of Ivar Kreuger might yet save us.

I must add here that I had no stake in the Kreuger empire. I have never owned a share in my life; my financial ambitions have never soared beyond a deposit in a respectable building society. The only advantage I derived from my acquaintance with Kreuger took the shape of an expensive-looking writing desk. It embarrassed me a great deal, that desk. It so happened that when we moved into a new flat in Stockholm, the only bit of furniture in it was a handsome desk and its accompanying chair. It was not mine; and I did not know how it got there. An hour or two later, I discovered how it came to be in my flat. It was a present from Ivar Kreuger. It was the same sort of desk as used by senior officials in the Swedish Match building in Stockholm. I did not like this at all; but was quite certain that I could not just send it back. So I reported the affair to the Editor of *The Financial Times*, and his reply came very quickly. I do not now remember the precise words he used, but in effect he said something like this: 'If you don't know what to do with the desk, send it to me.' So I kept it. I got rid of the cumbersome thing during the war and was paid £20 for it.

Three and a half months after the publication of my enthusiastic article in *The Fortnightly Review*, Ivar Kreuger committed suicide. I was asked by *The Times* to write his obituary notice; and I wrote of him in very favourable terms. I was not alone in so doing. The whole world paid tribute to him. *The Economist* described his death as a Greek Tragedy. 'Here was no mere gambler on a gigantic scale in the world's bourses', it wrote, 'no mere promoter in quest of personal profit at the expense of sucking dry the enterprises to which he laid his hand. By the death of Kreuger the world has lost a man of great constructive intelligence and wide vision, who planned boldly and who for once seemed about to combine with the profits of private enterprise a real contribution to the welfare of the world'. This picture of a universal benefactor soon gave way to another. A fortnight after his death, Ivar Kreuger was openly accused of having falsified his accounts. By early April, it was officially confirmed that he had been guilty of the grossest frauds; that he had forged securities on a gigantic scale; and that he had swindled investors to the tune of some £250 millions.

There had been rumours, in 1931, that things were going wrong. People who knew him said that he looked more pallid than usual. He began seeing shadows in the dark, at times and in places where no one else could see them. Very early in 1932 came the first report that he had committed suicide. It was untrue. When, early in March, it actually happened, and the news was telephoned to me I refused to believe it. I thought it was just another rumour. I found it harder still to accept the stories of fraud and forgery, spread with assiduous *schadenfreude* by his rivals and competitors who, as soon as the great man had gone, summoned up the courage to speak openly of their early doubts and fears. I was dismayed by all these frightful revelations. But what *surprised* me was the carelessness and the gullibility of some of the men who had lent him great sums of money—other people's money of which they were the custodians—without asking the obvious questions, without apparently checking the accounts, without inspecting—or causing to be inspected—the assets listed in the balance sheets of his many concerns and enterprises. I concluded that the middle-men in the world of high finance, the agents and the half-commission men and the so-called bankers—or banksters as they came to be known during the great depression—were an irresponsible lot, with a low-grade intellect hidden behind a bland and opulent manner, whose main asset was a talent for nosing out easy profits, just as a well-trained pig has a talent for smelling out truffles. It is a view that I have not abandoned. It is a view, incidentally, that caused me to be turned down for a job on *The Times* that might eventually have led to the City Editor's chair.

Looking back now upon that notorious affair, I suppose I could have been a good deal more suspicious, a good deal less willing to give Kreuger the benefit of the doubt. One event, in particular, should have warned me that there were shoals ahead. Late in the year 1931, I was invited to visit the gold mine at Boliden in

THE DIPLOMATIC CORRESPONDENT'S WORLD

THERE WAS no place for journalists in the respectable world of diplomacy of half a century ago. Before the First World War, they were not allowed inside the Foreign Office until the doorkeeper had first satisfied himself that there was a bit of news that could be fed to them. If senior officials had decided that there was nothing they wanted to say, the journalists waiting in the courtyard would be sent away and told to try again another day. In the early nineteen-twenties there came a change. The ordinary newspaper-reading public began to take an interest in the conduct of foreign policy; but since many Foreign Office people remained suspicious of the press and therefore uncooperative, journalists had to get their diplomatic news from other sources: from foreign capitals, perhaps, or from the representatives of foreign governments in London. This could mean that the British view was not adequately reflected in the columns of the daily press, even in those cases where British interests were directly involved; and that was something the politicians soon came to regard as unfortunate. Lord Curzon, the Foreign Secretary at the time, decided that something had to be done. He instructed his Assistant Private-Secretary to act as a sort of liaison officer between the press and the Foreign Office, and to make sure that His Lordship was given a good press while telling the journalists as little as possible. These liaison arrangements were gradually formalized and institutionalized in the News Department which came to handle all contacts with the press, British, Commonwealth and foreign, on behalf of the Foreign Secretary and his staff.

The News Department is at its best when Foreign Secretaries are allowed to do their work without constant interference by the Prime Minister of the day. It is paralysed when the head of the

Government becomes too publicity-conscious and too certain that he alone knows how foreign policy should be conducted. When Neville Chamberlain was at No. 10 Downing Street, and again when Anthony Eden was there, and during the early days of the Wilson Government, the channels of communication between the Foreign Office and the press were choked with publicity blurbs. But in spite of these occasional failures the system has worked reasonably well over a period of forty years or so.

But it seems to me that it is now on the point of breaking down. Relations between Foreign Secretaries and diplomatic correspondents are not as close as they had become over the years. There are, I think, two reasons for this. In the first place, relations between politicians and the public have been revolutionized by television. The politician gains no kudos out of a private talk with a handful of journalists; like Lord Curzon, he wants publicity. But he wants it in vast quantities, and only television can satisfy his insatiable appetite. His dearest wish is to be seen and heard on the television screen in disputations with 'television personalities'. When a Foreign Secretary arrives at London Airport after a long flight from Washington or Moscow, the first thing he looks for is the television camera: family, friends, senior officials with urgent messages—all are of secondary importance. Unshaved and unkempt, he insists upon being filmed; and he would feel cheated if he were not. No great harm is done so long as the politician who is being interviewed deals only with home affairs. But in foreign affairs, his statements and even his facial expression can have disastrous effects. Where the situation calls for the still small voice, the television camera tempts the star performer into boisterous gestures, into throwing boulders rather than fitting bits and pieces into a fine mosaic. A Foreign Secretary who comes back to London after quiet talks with political leaders in Washington or in Moscow, during the course of which he may have put over with success the British point of view on some problem or other, will undo all the good he has achieved if he responds to the camera's wicked invitation to tell an exciting story. If he boasts of having persuaded the Americans or the Russians to become more reasonable, about South-East Asia for instance, or about nuclear disarmament, a humiliating disavowal from one capital or another may follow within the hour. Yet if he says nothing at all in public, he feels that his 'public image' will suffer. So he may aim at a sort of half-way position and drop heavily between two stools. Moreover, he becomes so intent upon ingratiating himself with the television authorities, so busy chasing the television camera, that he has little time left for private talks with well-informed journalists who have spent much of their working lives in the field of foreign affairs. The give-and-take of these private chats provided what I believe was a valuable two-way traffic. Ernest Bevin and Anthony Eden were the masters of this particular technique and they talked with the greatest freedom on the problems that faced them. I do not know of any case where their confidences were betrayed, although I cannot formally assert that it never happened at any time. But all this belongs to a bygone age. I regret the change; but I dare not say that it is necessarily a change for the worse.

The second reason for the breakdown of the old machinery is that in the world of super-powers, the scope for British diplomacy is not as great as it was. Before the war, and, I suppose, up to the time of the Suez Crisis in 1956, when British influence in the world was still very strong, diplomatic news out of London was read with the greatest interest throughout the world. Even the sillier leading articles were studied with attention because British views then mattered. They helped to create political and diplomatic situations and they influenced the tone of the political debate in Europe. The Treaty of Locarno and the Munich Agreement, to mention but two milestones in diplomatic history, were the results of British initiatives or British manipulations. Now, with the decline of British power, what is said in London matters rather less than it did. Most of the news of diplomatic importance comes from Washington or Moscow or the United Nations. It seems to me also that people are not so interested as once they were in international affairs. In the nineteen-thirties there was an exciting public debate about the sanctions crisis, the Spanish Civil War, and the policy of appeasement. Foreign affairs were very much in the news. I do not think it is possible to say the same thing today. Perhaps General de Gaulle's grandiloquent negatives have produced a new isolationism. Why is it that France and Germany and Switzerland, with *Le Monde*, the *Frankfurter Allgemeine Zeitung* and the *Neue Zürcher Zeitung*, are able to maintain newspapers that devote far more space to the fundamentals of foreign affairs than British newspapers do? It is true that all these papers are often stodgy and long-winded and that they cannot be read with ease in buses or tubes. But is that the *only* reason? It is a question that I prefer to leave unanswered.

The world of the British diplomatic correspondent, then, is less spacious than it was, and less exciting. London is less important; British Foreign Secretaries no longer seem to be carrying the world upon their shoulders as Ernest Bevin did, and Anthony Eden. The great occasions are fewer and have less dramatic interest. This second factor does not necessarily reduce their importance, but it makes them difficult to report, and, even if adequately reported, hard to fit into the confines of our present newspapers and news bulletins on television and the radio. Moreover, Foreign Secretaries now report direct to the public. Their need for middlemen such as myself has greatly diminished. I, for my part, am glad to have worked under the old rules, in a field where the pioneers were W. N. Ewer of the old *Daily Herald* and Vernon Bartlett, best known for his work on the *News Chronicle*.

Northern Sweden which Kreuger had taken over. It is situated just south of the Arctic Circle, but it was easy enough to get there by the night train from Stockholm to Narvik in Northern Norway. Boliden did not look like a mining town; not at all the sort of Klondyke that the cinema had familiarized me with. It was more like a pleasant suburb. The mine itself was clean and bright. Great heaps of what they told me was arsenic lay stored in padlocked sheds around it; there was no market for the stuff, they said. It was a by-product of their mining operations and they were compelled by law to keep it under lock and key.

I spent a long time talking to the engineers, who all spoke with infectious enthusiasm of the job that they were doing. They told me how much ore they were extracting; and about the gold content of that ore. Between 17 and 18 grammes a ton, they said. On my way back to Stockholm I wrote my report for the paper. The Kreuger man who had travelled with me asked me to let him have a copy to show the Chief. And I was glad to give it to him, because there would then be a second check on my information, and an authoritative one. Within a very short time a message came back from Kreuger saying that the gold content of the ore was 20 grammes a ton, not between 17 and 18 as I had reported. Of course, I was told, the figure in my article was right. Mr. Kreuger did not doubt that it had been given to me by the mining engineers. But his mining engineers were cautious fellows, and tended to err on the conservative side. So I corrected the figure they had given to me.

I thought no more about all this until I learnt, in May 1932, that the Bank of Sweden had agreed to advance 40 million kronor (about £2 millions at the then rate of exchange) to the liquidators of the Kreuger enterprises against security of the shares in the Boliden Gold Mine. I then remembered how Kreuger had bumped up the gold content of the ore by some twelve per cent. I asked to see the Governor of the Bank on a matter of urgent importance and he received me without much delay. I told him my story and he was not amused. But he was good enough to say that he was grateful for my information; and when I re-visited Stockholm from time to time after my transfer to Paris, he always gave me a friendly reception. Incidentally, I have noticed that in the official handbooks published since 1932, the gold content of the Boliden ore is given as between 17 and 18 grammes per ton. So it seems that the engineers were right after all.

It is to the Kreuger crisis, then, that I owe my introduction to the world of international journalism, and in particular to that field of journalism that lies between finance and politics. My work for *The Financial Times* seemed to have impressed *The Times*, for in the summer of 1932 the paper invited me to become its Scandinavian correspondent. Its Foreign News Editor encouraged me to work on the sort of politico-financial journalism that developed naturally out of the Kreuger affair. The experience I then gained stood me in good stead when I was appointed a Paris correspondent of *The Times* in 1935, with a special responsibility for reporting French financial and economic affairs. It was to the Kreuger crisis, too, that I owe my friendship with Archie Clark Kerr, then British Minister in Stockholm; a friendship that took me to Moscow in 1943 as his personal assistant, not long after his appointment as Ambassador to the Soviet Union in succession to Stafford Cripps. Archie Clark Kerr, who died in 1949, is high on my list of heroes. The only man to whom I owe as great a debt is W. F. Casey, Editor of *The Times* for a few years before his untimely death. Clark Kerr was temperamental to a degree; highly sensitive; unorthodox; unusually perceptive; and by no means popular with all his colleagues, some of whom suspected him of holding heretical views on a variety of subjects. He was British Ambassador in Chungking before his appointment to Moscow. I remember meeting him in Piccadilly on the day his appointment to China was announced. He was tremendously elated. But he told me how surprised, and even shocked, he had been by Neville Chamberlain's conversation. 'The Prime Minister', he said, 'spoke of moving *his* ships and *his* troops in case of need, just as if he were a Royal Personage'. Clark Kerr came to have more influence with Chiang Kai-shek than anyone before him. In Moscow he left an abiding impression; and after more than twenty years, his name is still remembered. I wonder what Beriya thought when he heard that the British Ambassador had been giving swimming lessons to the leather-capped security guards who shadowed him wherever he went?

It was natural for me to begin my journalistic life in Scandinavia after a period of trial and error as a freelance. The languages were familiar to me. Both my parents were Norwegian. From my father I acquired the belief that the British Navy was the greatest power for good that the world had ever known; and that in so far as Divine Providence acted upon and within the world of power politics, it did so through the Royal Navy. From my father, too, I acquired a horror of financial excesses of all kinds. He was convinced that a man who asked his bank for an overdraft was little better than a crook. He refused to buy a house on mortgage because he believed that debts were an instrument of the devil. He would have found life in our present never-never world utterly unbearable. His was a farming family. He had no knowledge of the sea until his people migrated to the coast. His grandfather moved out of the Hallingdal district in Central Norway because he could no longer bear the prevailing drunkenness and brawling for which that part of Norway was notorious at the time. The whole family set out in the winter of 1831 to walk by easy stages to Hitra, an island some 28 miles long lying half-way between Kristiansund and Trondheim. The smaller children—the youngest was eight months—travelled by sledge. They arrived in April and immediately set about restoring the farm my great-grandfather had bought some time before. The farm was known as Barman, and was situated on the edge of the Barm fjord: in accordance with common usage, my great-grandfather adopted its name as his surname. My grandfather, who eventually took over the property, was the third son. He died in 1866 at the age of 45, when my father was only six years of age. His mother had died some years before, so he was left an orphan. He found it impossible to live a life of dependence upon relatives; and at the age of 14 he ran away to sea. To a Norwegian boy in the eighteen-seventies, life at sea meant life in sailing ships. Norwegian ship-owners were slower than others in turning to steam; and when foreign owners sold their sailing ships and bought steam vessels instead, the Norwegians took them over and made huge profits out of them. As long ago as 1870, Norway had a greater merchant fleet than any other country except Britain and the United States; but sail predominated. Something like 11 per cent of the world's tonnage of sailing ships was under Norwegian ownership, but only a little over one per cent of the steamship tonnage. So when my father went to sea the great boom was at its peak. He got his master's ticket in London in 1890. He was the first man to take a transatlantic liner through the Panama Canal—in 1915. He died in 1928.

From my mother, descended from a line of government

officials, merchants and Ministers of religion, I inherited the belief that size, bigness, was usually evil. When she quoted 'put not your trust in Princes' from the Book of Psalms, she spoke as if she meant it. She made me feel at home in the simple yet mysterious world of Hans Andersen which we read from the Danish, not in a Norwegian translation. Her heart was with the poor and the downtrodden. Heaven knows how many alcoholics she befriended in the later years of her life. She would do simple and rather absurd things, like brewing coffee early on a Christmas morning for taxi-drivers who had the misfortune to be on duty. She would carry the coffee-pot and some cups and bits of Christmas cake through the snow to the nearest cab-rank round the corner. She, also, had a horror of financial excesses, and above all, of ostentation. She listed simplicity among the greatest of virtues. Her reverential attitude to what the Prayer Book calls the bountiful liberality of God was due, I am sure, to the circumstances of her childhood. Her father's vicarage produced its own food, its own fuel, and all the clothes for a large family. The sheep grazing outside the windows provided the wool from which the thread was spun and the cloth was woven for the family's needs. Itinerant tailors came once or twice a year to make up the material into suits or dresses. In the late autumn, many of the cattle were slaughtered and the meat pickled against the leaner days of winter. In such a household, the great Christian festivals—Christmas with its abundance, and Easter with its promise of better days to come—were part of the stuff of life.

It was the Kreuger story that took me to Stockholm from Oslo at the end of 1931. The scale of the Match King's operations was increasing steadily, and it became almost impossible to follow them from a distance. One had to be on the spot. My Swedish friends made things easy for me. And when it became known that I was writing regularly for *The Financial Times*, people whom I had thought inaccessible became accessible to me. But the Stockholm of 1931 was not a very exciting place. The Swedish political scene was a distinctly parochial affair; you felt you were in a sort of backwater; and the mind was never fully stretched. In this respect I had done no more than move from one very pleasant backwater to another. And it had one great disadvantage. Stockholm is a town that turns its back upon the West: its people seemed to be more concerned with the affairs of the Baltic, with

Finland, and with the great bogey-man of Swedish history, Russia. Russo-phobia is, or was, very common. When I first heard people in Stockholm talking about Russia, I had the feeling that the withdrawal of Swedish forces from Finland in 1808 as the result of Russian pressure was something that had happened only a day or two ago. The Russian danger was always a safe subject for small talk in much the same way as the weather is in England. Quite naturally, therefore, many Swedes sympathized with the Germans during the First World War. They found no great merit in the Allied cause. Only the Social Democrats under Hjalmar Branting favoured the Western Powers although they, too, were agreed about the need for neutrality.

Another difficulty about life in Stockholm is that a sense of humour is not among the most conspicuous of Swedish virtues. People tend to be enormously impressed with the magnitude of their own achievements. They boast of them with all the pride and vanity of the self-made man. Before the war even a man's income tax return was made a matter for self-congratulation. If your declared income exceeded a certain level, then you were regarded as important enough to get your name into the newspapers. And year after year, with the opening of the income tax season, the newspapers would print long lists of people whose incomes were assessed at over £1,500 a year. I was told that there were people who actually declared a higher income than they earned in order to get their names into the papers. It has been said by a Swede of some distinction that what made Sweden such a tiresome country to live in was that her great men became so abominably great. Yet all Swedes are not equally pompous; those on the West coast, in their snug and friendly capital of Gothenburg, have a keener eye and a sharper ear for the ridiculous. They have a good deal in common with the people of the two other trading towns of the Scandinavian North—Copenhagen and Bergen. But even Gothenburg has—or had—its laborious form of address. The indirect form was compulsory in the years before the war, and you had to know a man's title, or his trade or his profession before you could say a word to him or to his wife. This made the small change of casual conversation extremely difficult. 'May I offer Mrs. the Female Colonel a drink?', with the reply, 'How very kind of you, Mr. the Wholesaler' is not the sort of small talk to set the world on fire. The practice in Victorian

England seems to have been almost the same, and even Mr. Pickwick lost some of his loquacity when he was introduced to Mrs. Colonel Wugsby and inveigled into playing whist with her. I did hear of one Swede who carved out a successful career for himself while lacking the essential prefix to his name: he was neither a Doctor, nor a Consul. This was Bjørn Prytz, who became the head of the Swedish Ball Bearings Company and eventually Swedish Ambassador in London. His hopes of promotion could hardly have been realized if he had called himself just Herr Prytz. So he acquired an air of mystery and distinction by using the English equivalent, Mister. Mister Bjørn Prytz. Just like that.

In this tepid and parochial environment, the death of Ivar Kreuger in 1932 was a cosmic event. The reputations of certain politicians and tycoons vanished overnight; and confidence in political and financial institutions was shaken. The depression deepened and unemployment rose; and in the background was the threat of more industrial violence. There had been a good deal of violence in the year 1931. In May there had been an outbreak of rioting at a woodpulp works in Central Sweden. Troops were called out to restore order after a clash between strikers and blacklegs and five people were killed. Demonstrations in many parts of Sweden were an inevitable consequence. On the day of the funeral—21 May—life in Stockholm was brought nearly to a standstill. All traffic was stopped while processions of various kinds marched through the town. Some unions called out their members for a twenty-four hour strike, notably the builders and the bakers. I can still recall the sinister sound of thousands of feet shuffling through the streets of an otherwise silent city. It needed no great effort of imagination on that day to see the Red Dawn climbing over the horizon. The rash of wild-cat strikes, a prominent feature of Swedish labour relations at the time, added to the prevailing uneasiness. The building industry, in particular, suffered from them. Almost every day there were advertisements in the Social Democratic newspapers in Stockholm announcing that this or that building-site had been blacklisted, and that neither men nor materials must be made available to it. You could not possibly miss those conspicious advertisements: each one was headed by the word 'Blockade' in heavy type and warned all concerned not to have any dealings with the site in question. The black-listing usually came into force when work on a building was at a critical stage: for instance, when the roof was on the point of going on. It was a skilful and well-planned piece of blackmail that usually succeeded. By 1938 all this anarchy had been brought under tough control and centralized discipline; and Sweden came to be regarded as a pioneer in the field of industrial relations.

It was against this background of industrial strife, wilting confidence and rising unemployment that the General Elections were fought in October 1932. The Social Democrats greatly increased their lead over the other parties, and something like 45 per cent of the seats in the Second Chamber fell to them. They formed a coalition government with the Farmers' Party and introduced drastic measures to deal with the depression and to restore confidence. No one, then, could have foreseen that they would remain in power for over thirty years; and that over this long period, apart from a short interregnum in 1934, the office of Prime Minister was to be held by only two men: Per Albin Hansson up to 1946; and then Tage Erlander.

Per Albin Hansson was a man of no great intellectual distinction but of considerable political acumen. He headed a brilliant team of Ministers; men with courage and integrity, qualities that were badly needed in a period of disillusion. Sandler at the Ministry for Foreign Affairs; Möller at the Ministry of the Interior; Wigforss at the Ministry of Finance: all lent distinction to their offices. They have been compared in quality to the men who held the main appointments in the British Liberal Administration of 1906. In the background were such gifted officials as Dag Hammarskiöld who at the astonishingly early age of 30 became Under-Secretary at the Ministry of Finance. Wigforss never left one in doubt about the debt he owed to the man who later became Secretary-General of the United Nations. At the Bank of Sweden, of which Hammarskiöld became Chairman of the board at the age of 31, they spoke of him with bated breath. And with these new men in office, the academic economists—people like Gunnar Myrdal and Bertil Ohlin, to name but two—suddenly became important political figures. They presented and defended their views in public, at public meetings and in newspaper articles. They were not content to remain sheltered in Ministerial antechambers, but were happy to risk their professional reputations on the hustings. Overnight, Stockholm became an exciting and stimulating place to be in. The air was sparkling with ideas. The debates in the Political Economy Club attracted capacity audiences. Visitors from abroad came to find out how Sweden was solving the problem of unemployment. Later, they came to study the new trends in labour relations and the organization of the welfare state. Soon the books began to appear about the Swedish experiment. The best, I suppose, was written by that distinguished American journalist, Marquis Childs. Its title aptly summed up the Swedish stance in those exciting years: *Sweden—The Middle Way*. It was published at a time when Britain and America appeared to have lost their bearings; when the Right, in the persons of Mussolini and Hitler, offered what appeared to be one solution; and the Left, in the shape of Communism, another.

Many of the Ministers in the Social Democratic administration of the late nineteen-thirties were easily accessible to journalists. Given the nature of my job, I saw more of the Foreign Minister, Rickard Sandler, than of the others. There was nothing spectacular about him: he was neither a thruster nor a go-getter. Behind his mild and pleasant manner, there were determination and integrity and a sense of purpose. He had a liberal cast of mind, like most of his colleagues in the Cabinet. During the dark days of the Russo–Finnish crisis in 1939, he was among the few who were ready to honour the promises and half-promises the Swedes had made to Finland in earlier years. Sandler felt there *was* a commitment, and did not hesitate to say so. He himself had done all he could to wean the Finns away from their German friendships, and to draw them closer to the three Northern Kingdoms. In the event, in spite of all the splendid dinner-parties devoted to Scandinavian unity, the Finns were left to fight alone; just as were the Danes in 1864, against Austria and Prussia, after a similar period of Scandinavian ebullience.

The Prime Minister of Sweden used much the same language about Finland in the autumn of 1939 as Neville Chamberlain did about Czechoslovakia in 1938. The Swedes, Hansson told his Socialist colleagues in Finland, were a complacent people who wanted to be left in peace. And a day or two later, another Swedish Minister explained to his Finnish friends that the people of Sweden would not understand it if their country were turned into a battlefield for the sake of Viborg. The sentiment brings to mind a headline in the Paris press in 1939: 'Mourir pour Dantzig?'. But Viborg stood for something more than Danzig. Its fortress was built in 1293 as a defence against the Slavs. It is one of the great symbolic place-names in Swedish history. It has the same sort of emotive appeal as Gibraltar; and to many Swedes the Minister's words sounded like a betrayal. Sandler himself felt badly let down and resigned from the Government. But his influence did not disappear with his resignation; and behind the scenes he helped to prevent things from getting a good deal worse than they might otherwise have been. His friendly relations with Madame Kollontay, the Soviet Minister in Stockholm, were of great importance since Madame Kollontay appeared to be about the only person in Russian service who was able to influence Stalin in any way. Unlike many other Soviet diplomatists she did not seclude herself in sulky isolation. I saw her fairly often in Stockholm, usually at parties and receptions given by Sandler. She was a woman of character and distinction. If there had been more people with her courage and ability in Moscow, Stalin might perhaps have been saved from his most costly mistakes.

Sandler came to Paris on an official visit in 1936, shortly after the assassination of King Alexander of Yugoslavia and Barthou, the French Foreign Minister. The crime led to a great tightening up of the French security services; and when I called upon the Swedish Foreign Minister at the Hôtel Crillon I had almost to fight my way past the guards posted in an around the Hôtel to guard his person. He took me out to a pleasant restaurant in Montmartre: *Aux Ducs de Bourgogne*, I think it was. When we left the Hôtel in the official car provided for him, we were preceded by two security police on motor cycles, followed by another two, and finally by a police car. This screeching cavalcade drove at great speed through the streets of Paris. Sandler found all this rather annoying; but I enjoyed it, since it was a novel experience for me. As soon as the dinner was over, Sandler insisted upon visiting a night-club he had got to know many years earlier when he was a student in Paris. Again, the cavalcade screamed its way through Paris, this time to Montparnasse, not far from the Sorbonne. Our destination turned out to be quiet and respectable, but what struck a rather bizarre note was that most of the girls in the establishment were Chinese. When we came to leave, Sandler was presented with several bills. They included six beers for the security guards. 'Tomorrow', he commented drily, 'my visit ceases to be official. There will be no guards, or perhaps just one. It will be cheaper and less noisy. And I shall be able to lead my own life again.'

CHAPTER 2

IT WAS in Stockholm that I had my headquarters in those years. And it was from Stockholm that I tried as best I could to follow the course of events in Norway and Denmark. *The Times* had its local men there, and they reported such day-to-day events as were worth reporting. But from time to time I took the night train to Oslo or to Copenhagen to collect material for some article I had to write or to gather background facts for the leader-writers in Printing House Square. In the summer of 1932 I got myself involved in the Greenland question—a question that drove nationalists in Denmark and Norway into near-apoplexy. It is hard now to recall the bitterness it caused, and the dangerous passions it unleashed. The dispute, which had its origins in the Middle Ages, concerned the sovereignty over this barren Arctic island. At a time when the political temperature in Europe was rising steadily, it seemed particularly sad that the relations between two such basically friendly countries as Denmark and Norway should be upset in any way. The Norwegian Government, which refused to recognize Danish sovereignty over the whole of Greenland, promulgated a decree in 1931 annexing parts of the east coast. Norwegian whalers and sealers were excluded from the west coast by the Danish State Trading Monopoly, and the Norwegians feared that the Danes were on the point of excluding them from the east also. Claims and counter-claims were referred to The Hague Court. And during the hearings, and in the intervals between them, relations between the two countries grew steadily worse.

I was approached by a Canadian friend who told me that King Haakon of Norway—a Dane by birth and a Norwegian by adoption and acclamation—was appalled by the turn of events, and was hoping for some miracle that would put an end to a dangerous but understandable quarrel. The King realized that it would be impossible for either the Norwegian or the Danish Government to make any move towards a compromise at the time. But he wondered (so my friend said) if a solution could be found in a Danish offer to Norway of a permanent leasehold in east Greenland in return for an unqualified Norwegian recognition of Danish sovereignty. I passed on all this information to the Foreign News Editor of *The Times*. And on 10 August 1932, a leading article appeared which recommended a solution very much on these lines. But it was not precisely the same recommendation as I had reported. The words 'a Norwegian recognition of Danish sovereignty' had become 'a definite statement that would allay all Danish fears'. Still, the meaning was clear enough. The article led to a violent uproar in the Danish and Norwegian press. Norwegian newspapers argued that *The Times* had fallen victim to Danish propaganda. Some Danish newspapers insisted that the article had been inspired by the Norwegians. So great was the heat that I thought it best to lie low for a while. I left it to the local correspondents to report the reactions. I slipped out of Stockholm in the hope of avoiding questions. But a member of the staff of the Danish Legation did manage to buttonhole me before I left and tried to find out what I knew. He wanted to know who had inspired the article. I was unfortunately unable to help him.

The Danish Foreign Minister at the time was Dr. Munch, one of the leaders of the Radical Party. As a private individual he was not without charm; as a public figure I thought he was as detestable as John Simon. In matters of national defence he represented the 'What's the good?' point of view, or the 'I couldn't care less' attitude. As I saw him, he symbolized all that was defeatist in the Europe of the time. But perhaps that was too harsh a judgment. Let me say instead that he was an idealist lost in the jungle of power politics. In dealing with Nazism, Munch thought it wisest to shut his eyes and ears to what was going on south of the border; and, on occasion, to abuse those who saw the things that he refused to see. His party was in fact an organized pacifist group exercising a powerful influence in Danish political life; and his views and those of his associates had so far prevailed that Denmark was almost defenceless when war broke out in 1939. In March 1932, the government of which he was a member reduced Army strength from three to two divisions. The annual intake of conscripts was cut from 8,500 to 7,500.

The arrival of Hitler at the Chancellery prompted some gloomy reflections in Denmark; but it did not lead to any stiffening of the national defences. Nor was this to be expected, in the light of the policy pursued by the British Government and in the way John Simon was able to clothe any betrayal in lofty moral verbiage. The Anglo-German Naval Agreement in 1935 came as a shock to those people in Denmark who wanted to goad their government into pursuing a firmer policy. As they saw it, the Agreement handed over the Baltic to Nazi Germany; and in a sense it tended to confirm Munch in his view that Denmark would be safer without guns than with them; with the proviso, of course, that her people refrained from criticizing or even commenting upon the crimes and brutalities of Nazi Germany. This sort of restraint, when applied to people with a liberal and humanitarian cast of mind, often has the strangest consequences. Inhibited by their leader from telling the truth about Nazism, the Radicals proved that their hearts were in the right place by attacking abuses that were remote, often very remote. That very radical newspaper, *Politiken*, superbly edited at the time, showed the way. It long maintained a cautious silence on the subject of Germany; but it did not fail, in the best traditions of Danish radicalism, to denounce the tyrannies of British imperialism in India. This interesting phenomenon led me to formulate a political theory which I believe has stood the test of time: namely, that the intensity of the heat generated in liberal and radical hearts by acts of tyranny varies directly with the cube of the distance between the observer and the event. The Swedish students burning the Stars and Stripes in Stockholm in protest against the war in Vietnam; the men and women demonstrating noisily outside South Africa House in London against the evils of apartheid, are all related to Munch and his Radicals. The abuses to be denounced are always so very far away; they are never on one's own doorstep.

Later in the year 1933, the Nazi pressure upon the so-called German minorities across the borders of Germany began to be felt in Denmark also. An appropriately-named minority leader, Pastor Peperkorn of South Jutland, spoke threateningly of moving the existing border north, to the line where it stood before the plebiscite. At the request of *The Times*, I went down to the border to see for myself. I talked to most of the local leaders; visited schools; and travelled for some distance along the border.

It seemed to me that life was becoming unpleasant for the people of South Jutland. It was not only the Danes who were unhappy. The moderately-minded Germans were beginning to be afraid to speak openly and felt much the same about the Nazi-organized agitation. They were happy in Denmark; they liked the freedom they had on terms of equality with their Danish-speaking fellow countrymen. I wrote one or two pieces about this which duly appeared in *The Times*.

They infuriated the Danish Foreign Minister who wanted to hear of no evil on his doorstep. At a private meeting of Danish editors and journalists in Copenhagen he referred angrily to my 'exaggerations and distortions'. Such writings, he said, could do only harm. There was nothing very much that I could do about it. Politicians of all nationalities find it hard to forgive journalists who make difficulties for them or who help to expose their follies or their lies. Munch was no exception. I should have preferred it if he had made his comment in public. I could then have argued my case in public. But I wrote a letter to the Ministry saying that I would not set foot in the place again until Munch had withdrawn his accusations. It was a silly thing to do and I do not suppose that either Munch or his officials cared very much. But it made things awkward and expensive for me in that whenever it was necessary for me to see a Ministry official, I had to invite him to lunch.

The World Conference of Churches held at Fanø, a pleasant seaside resort on the west coast of Denmark, was another event I was required to report for *The Times* in my Scandinavian period. There I met the Bishop of Chichester, Dr. George Bell, whose understanding and patience made an overwhelming impression upon me. The term Christian charity came to have a real and practical meaning for me when I saw how attentive he was, and how considerate, in dealing with the wild men of the so-called German Christian movement. Most of the proceedings were in private, including the proceedings of a Youth Conference which was being held at the same time, but from time to time there would be some public statement that would throw light on what was going on behind the scenes. I remember one elderly German cleric making a passionate speech in praise of Hitler. God had sent him to the German people, he cried, to save them from the bondage of despair. I do not know if George Bell had any influence upon such minds as these. But the Germans must have realized that he had not come to sit in judgment upon them. The American Churchmen at the Conference were more outspoken and less patient. I remember talking to one of them just after the Conference had broken up. He began by saying that he wanted to thank *The Times* for deciding to report the Conference. And then he went on: 'When I get back home, I'll tell my people that in Germany today you can only preach the Gospel through the key-hole'.

At this Conference I also got to know the German Pastor who was helping Norman Ebbutt, then *The Times* correspondent in Berlin, to report the facts about the Church dispute in Germany. He had travelled from Germany to Denmark by a roundabout route. He did not attend the Conference; that would have been too risky. Although we were in Denmark and therefore presumably in safety, he did not dare to leave, before dark, the little *pension* where he lived. So we used to meet in the late evening and take long walks well away from the Conference area in the hope that we should then not meet anyone who might recognize him. I told him what I knew about the day's proceedings. He usually knew a good deal more; and he knew the background and what was at stake. With his help, I was able to send reasonably adequate reports on events to London. It is astonishing to recall that one had to live and work in this sort of cloak-and-dagger atmosphere in the years before the war, in places far beyond Germany's borders.

My contacts with people and events in Finland were not as close as those with the rest of the Scandinavian north; but I did manage to pay one or two visits to that country before the outbreak of war. By great good fortune I was able to meet some of the more outstanding of Finnish personalities. Those Finns who reach the front rank in what is a very tough country are formidable personalities; and, as the winter war was to show, the people are exceedingly resilient. I have in mind, in particular, Risto Ryti, head of the Bank of Finland in the 'thirties, but later the country's President. I have in mind also Mr. Kekkonen, elected head of State in 1956, upon whom I called in the autumn of 1966 at his villa on the outskirts of Helsinki. I had gone to talk to him about some of the more important international problems, and notably East-West relations. He is an outstanding personality, by whatever standard he is judged. No one, I suppose, has succeeded in establishing better contacts with the Russians; notably with Mr. Krushchev. No one—apart from Marshal Tito—has a better knowledge of how their minds work. When I met him, on that lovely autumn afternoon, he told me something about his talks with Mr. Kosygin and about the impression that the Soviet Prime Minister had made upon him and also about the reasons behind certain Soviet attitudes towards the West. President Kekkonen did not use the same language about Western Germany as the Russians do; but he made it plain that he was no less alarmed than they about the growing German agitation for access to nuclear weapons in one form or another. It seems to me to be regrettable that there have been some British Ambassadors in Helsinki who have failed to get to know this extraordinary man. If Mr. Khrushchev found it possible to do business with President Kekkonen in a sauna, then perhaps the British Ambassador in Helsinki could do the same. We heard a great deal at one time about the importance of Mr. Nehru as a possible channel of communication between Russia and the West. I do not doubt that Mr. Kekkonen would be at least as helpful. It is true that when President Kekkonen first took office he was criticized by many Finns who would have preferred to see their government take a stronger anti-Communist line. But Mr. Kekkonen seems to have overcome most of these prejudices; he is now recognized as a great national figure; and if his speeches on foreign affairs occasionally take the Finnish Cabinet by surprise, they are none the worse for that.

Risto Ryti was a man of totally different type. He was reserved and rather shy where Mr. Kekkonen is expansive and boisterous. He was an intellectual, with an olive complexion that gave him an almost Levantine look. Mr. Kekkonen is a ruddy-faced out-of-doors man with the stamina of a birch tree. He loves politics. I doubt if Ryti did: I am sure he was more at home among the discreet silences of Central Banking than in navigating through the petty intrigues of the Chamber. He was an Anglophile, as so many Central Bankers are, with the possible exception of the French. Ryti became Prime Minister of Finland during the winter war, and President in 1940. He was among those held responsible for linking his country with Germany's war against the Soviet Union in 1941, so he went to jail as a war criminal in 1946. He was released some years later owing to ill health, and when he died in 1956 he was given a State funeral. President Kekkonen, who attended it, and who had opposed Ryti's policies for many years, said at the time that 'Whatever he did, he did it to serve his country'.

It is impossible to understand the motives that inspired Ryti, and wholly unreasonable to condemn him, without knowing something about the state of Finland in the 'thirties. The first point to be made is that the country had not yet recovered from the ferocious civil war in 1919 and 1920, in which the most terrible atrocities were committed by Reds and Whites alike. It left a legacy of bitterness and hate in many parts of Northern Europe. I have myself met skilled men in Sweden and Norway unable to get work in their own trade and in their own country many years after the civil war because they had fought as volunteers on the 'wrong' side. They were not anti-Reds; they fought in order to prevent a seepage of Slav power into Scandinavia. In the 'thirties Finland was still a divided country, with fears of a Communist take-over ever present in many people's minds. When I was in Finland in 1966, I visited a churchyard on the outskirts of Helsinki together with some Finnish friends and saw a tombstone that marked a civil war date. I asked, with some diffidence, if the civil war had now been forgotten. Yes, they said, it had. 'We think it has; but the wounds can be re-opened if you really try.'

There was, then, an uneasy sort of conspiratorial atmosphere in the country at the time. On the extreme Left, there was the egregious Kuusinen filling Stalin's mind with masses of misinformation. On the Right, there were mysterious rumblings—I was never able to get my teeth into the story—about Finnish extremist plans to join up with the Germans and the Japanese against the Soviet Union. The most dangerous ingredient of all was the obtuse folly of Soviet policy under Stalin. His many mistakes are self-evident now: his Chinese policy, for instance, which crashed in ruins; in appeasing the Germans he went even further than Laval, Bonnet and Chamberlain; and he completely mistook the temper of the Americans in 1945. He was so sure that the American economic system was bound to collapse and so give Communism its chance. Towards Finland, Soviet policy was inept beyond belief. I have already recorded how the Swedes failed to help the Finns in 1939/40. After the winter war had ended, the Swedes renewed their attempts to keep Finland among the neutrals. Stockholm, at the time, knew what the Germans were planning in Finland. Swedish experts had broken the German cypher at an early stage in the war, and were well informed about German troop movements in the north. They made strong efforts to persuade the Finns to dissociate themselves from all German initiatives. Eventually, the suggestion came up that Sweden and Finland would do well to sign some form of neutrality treaty. If this had been done, the Finns might not have fallen into German hands in the way they did. But Stalin would not hear of any arrangement between Stockholm and Helsinki. And so the Finnish leaders concluded they had no alternative to some association with the Germans.

President Ryti based his policy on the assumption that Germany would win the war. So did a great many other respectable people. And if Ryti concluded that whatever the outcome of the war, both Germany and Russia would emerge from it greatly weakened, he was arguing on much the same lines as President Benes of Czechoslovakia. Both men came to believe that the emasculation of the rapacious wolves in Moscow and in Berlin would make life easier for the smaller nations that were being terrorized, now by one, now by the other, and often by both.

While the Finns were too hard pressed to draw a sharp distinction between Germans and Nazis, the Swedes had no difficulty in doing so. I have already recorded how pro-German they were in the First World War, and how their sympathies were for many years upon the German side. French policy after the signature of the Treaty of Versailles shocked and disgusted them; they were horrified by French actions in the Ruhr and the Rhineland, angered by the evident French determination to torpedo the Hoover moratorium, and dismayed by French unwillingness to cooperate in the efforts that were being made at the time to solve the international monetary crisis. Some of my Swedish friends felt so strongly about all this that they carried out a kind of unofficial sanctions policy. They refused to buy or to drink French wine—to note only one example—and invariably served German instead. There are very similar anti-French feelings in the air these days; due, this time, to the foreign policy of General de Gaulle. Responsibility for the revival of nationalism in Germany is laid upon his shoulders; and if there is a breakdown in the world's monetary system, the French will certainly be blamed for it. Another development that is fanning the embers of Francophobia in the north is the attempt to blackmail the middle-ranking diplomatic representatives of the smaller powers when in contact with the French. They are warned, cautiously, of course, and almost inaudibly, that if they oppose the French in this matter or in that they will fail to get French *agrément* for a posting in Paris (when the time comes), or for appointment to any international job that requires French support.

In pre-war Sweden, once the Nazis had taken over, friendship for Germany disappeared, except among a handful of crackpots, mainly in southern Sweden. Why were the Swedes so certain so soon that Nazism was evil? Looking back upon that extraordinary period, I can see many reasons for it. With an active and purposeful Social Democracy in the ascendant, as it was from 1932 onwards, the prevailing political wind in Sweden was pro-Western, although it was laden with distinctly anti-Russian scents at times. The Swedish Lutheran Church was another important factor in holding Swedish opinion steady. Its leaders had very close contacts with German Lutherans; and they knew at a very early stage the sort of mischief that the Nazis were plotting. As long ago as 1934 there was published in Stockholm a well-documented account of the German religious crisis by the well-known theologian, Professor Anders Nygren of Lund University. 'At Easter time,' he wrote, 'the sermons are about the Resurrection; but not so much the Resurrection of Christ, as the Resurrection of the German spirit. They speak of the Christian miracle: what they have in mind is the miracle that has taken place in present-day Germany. They speak of being born again, and they think of national regeneration. To celebrate the victory at the polls, there was held a service of thanksgiving, with Bishop Hossenfelder, leader of the German Christians, preaching a sermon with the text: "Thanks be to God which giveth *us* the victory".' The contacts between Swedish churchmen and their friends and colleagues in Germany were close and constant; and some Swedish pastors knew far more about what was going on in the Third Reich than many politicians or diplomatists. Where it could be done without risk, they passed on such information as they had to responsible people in the Swedish press. This was among the reasons why Swedish newspapers were so well informed about the turn of events in Germany.

Most senior officials, too, were bitterly hostile to Nazism, although not to Germany. Erik Boheman, Permanent Head of the Swedish Foreign Office during the war, has described in his autobiography how Swedish experts broke the German diplomatic cypher, and were able to warn the British Government with great accuracy of the German plans to attack the Soviet Union. Boheman recalls that Stafford Cripps, then British Ambassador in Moscow, passed through Stockholm early in 1941 on his way home to report. The British Minister, Victor Mallett, invited Cripps and Boheman to dine with him; and Boheman notes that they had a most interesting talk. Cripps, he says, developed the argument, with the greatest emphasis, that the Germans would not attack the Soviet Union. The main purpose of the menacing stance adopted by the Germans was to wring more concessions out of the Russians, mainly on the question of supply. Cripps was in no doubt that Stalin was ready to make almost any concession to buy off a German attack. And Cripps told Boheman that he was now on his way to London to report to the Cabinet in this sense.

Boheman knew that Cripps was wrong, because his experts had broken the German cypher and were therefore well-informed about German intentions. The Germans, Boheman explained to Cripps, had made up their minds to attack the Soviet Union, no matter how many concessions the Russians made. He added, 'I do not believe any kind of negotiation will get under way before the attack is launched. It will come suddenly, in one vast operation along the whole length of the front, in accordance with German practice. Without in any way giving away my sources, I told Cripps that I was absolutely certain that I was right, and that the attack was timed for some day between June 20 and June 25.' So Cripps was able to warn the War Cabinet some days before the event about the German invasion of the Soviet Union. Boheman adds that in due course he received a letter from Cripps, in his own handwriting, warmly thanking him for the information given to him at the time.

It is hard to imagine senior Swedish officials behaving in this way during the First World War; and harder still to believe that they would have been bold enough to speak in public of what they had done to help the Western allies, if they could have brought themselves to do anything at all. Of course, public opinion was

#1 Wed 11 Mar 1998 01:32PM Item(s
) checked out to McMahon, Daithi Ea
rman.

TITLE
BARCODE DUEDATE

Diplomatic correspondent.
31888007037840 13 Apr 1998

The hundred days to Hitler / by Rog
er 31888004907847 13 Apr 1998

The spirit and structure of German
fas 31888005203493 13 Apr 1998

Inside the Third Reich: memoirs, Tr
ans 31888007131353 13 Apr 1998

The Third Reich; a study published
und 31888005335550 13 Apr 1998

[illegible] 13 Apr 1998 01:30PM Item[illegible]
checked out to [illegible]
[illegible]

TITLE
BARCODE DUE DATE

Diplomacy [illegible] establishment
[illegible] 13 Apr 1998

The hundred days Napoleon [illegible]
er [illegible] 13 Apr 1998

The equality and structure of [illegible]
[illegible] 13 Apr 1998

[illegible] Third Reich memoirs [illegible]
[illegible] 13 Apr 1998

The Third Reich: a study published
[illegible] 13 Apr 1998

on their side in the 'thirties; there was the Church; there were the trade unions; the academic world; and the Swedish press. The part played by the responsible Swedish press was altogether admirable; its record is at least as good as, if not better than, that of any other country in the world. What was in a way unusual was that it was the newspapers read by what *The Times* once called the top people that led the way in denouncing the evils of Nazism. They were getting at the very readers who out of fear or hatred for the Reds might conceivably have formed the hard core of Nazism in Sweden.

Among other journalists who stood firm against all kinds of Nazi pressure were Otto Järte and Gustaf Stridsberg, both of *Svenska Dagbladet*, a high-Tory paper published in Stockholm. In the First World War, Järte had wanted Sweden to join in on Germany's side. He thought that victory would give his country the leadership of the Nordic peoples, a semi-protectorate over Finland, and the assurance that Norway and Denmark would plod obediently in Sweden's footsteps. I cannot conceive of any plan more calculated to infuriate Norwegians and Danes and Finns. Gustaf Stridsberg, too, was on the German side in those years. I remember his telling me, in 1933, that he had been on the British Government's black-list for many years and that Clark Kerr was the first British Minister ever to invite him to a meal at the British Legation. His attitude, and Järte's, and that of other Swedes changed completely after Hitler came in. I recall talking to Järte one evening, very early in the 'thirties, after his return from a holiday in Germany. He had seen Hitler and had heard him speak at a political meeting. A look of distaste came over his face. 'He is unclean,' he said, with a shiver of disgust. 'Everything about him is wrong, his clothes, his moustache, his voice, the look in his eye.'

Gustaf Stridsberg was one of the most extraordinary characters I have ever met. He was a hunchback, very slow in his movements, who always wore a sort of *redingote*, and looked rather like a seedy pastor in an Ibsen play. He had never been to school: his mother had taught him to read, to love books, and languages and history. I went up to his flat after working hours from time to time, and was fascinated by his conversation and his intimate knowledge of the world of politics. He used to sit in a rocking chair and talk with a sort of grunt, in a harsh and gritty voice. He could read English and German and French and Italian—and no doubt other languages—with the greatest of ease; but he could only just speak them. Apart from regular summer holidays in one of the Baltic States, he never went abroad. But he could discuss British politics as if he had known Palmerston personally and Disraeli and Gladstone and Asquith and Lloyd George. He had read a good deal of Thackeray in old copies of *Punch*. He could not bear H. G. Wells—a commonplace mind, he said. He agreed strongly with those who had protested against the sensationalism of *The Times* when the paper decided to put headlines over its leading articles. And he was enraged by the introduction of a picture-page. His favourite Sunday reading when I first knew him was the large edition of the Oxford English Dictionary. He was a sort of living history book to me. And his technical skill as a journalist was phenomenal. He used to come into his untidy office early in the afternoon, an office littered with books and magazines and newspapers and dust, remain silent for ten minutes or so, write a single sentence on a bit of paper, and ring the bell for a secretary. When the girl came in he would dictate a leading article to the conclusion of the sentence he had written down. Unlike most journalists, who work *from* an opening sentence, Stridsberg worked *to* the final one.

Clark Kerr was immensely impressed by him, and was determined to get him to pay a visit to England. Stridsberg seemed interested; he knew all about the places that we suggested he should see. A grand tour was worked out, with the help of all sorts of willing people in London and elsewhere: a visit to the House of Lords; tea with a member of the Athenaeum; a day at Oxford; that sort of thing. But when it came to the point, Stridsberg would not hear of it. 'No,' he said, 'I cannot do it. Everything is very clear in my mind now: but I am afraid my ideas will be distorted if I see these things in the flesh.'

This Swedish high-Tory, instinctively pro-German, was not only anti-Nazi. He was against all kinds of dictatorship, all kinds of anti-democratic rule. And his influence in *Svenska Dagbladet* in all those critical years was almost unquestioned. He became furious when innocent Swedes came back from Italy full of enthusiasm because the trains were running on time, because order had been restored, because strikes were illegal. He took a firm line against the Fascist movement in Finland, the so-called Lappo movement, in spite of his romantic attachment to the cause of Finnish independence. Like his colleague, Otto Järte, he had met Göring during one of his visits to Sweden. They were interested in the man; and for a time, perhaps, even fascinated by him. But not for long. They came down heavily on the other side. The decision to oppose a right-wing dictatorship was not an easy one to take for a right-wing journalist in Sweden in the late 'twenties and the early 'thirties when trade union tyranny, as I have already related, was at its worst. The fact that Stridsberg and Järte took it, in spite of their social prejudices and convictions, is a tribute to them and to the high standard of Swedish journalism.

Stridsberg, I like to believe, played some part in helping Anthony Eden to understand the significance of what was happening in Germany. He had been invited to lunch at the British Legation to meet Eden, who, as Minister for League of Nations Affairs, was on a short visit to Sweden. Stridsberg began by being rather stiff and formal; he was unable to take a very active part in the conversation since his spoken English was very halting, and, at times, barely intelligible. Gradually, he thawed. And then he brought out the fact that Antonina Vallentin's biography of Heine, in an English translation, had just been published by Gollancz. He had the book with him. Slowly and awkwardly he told us that the author had quoted one of Heine's sayings that seemed to him to be highly relevant to the existing international situation. The piece was then read:

'It is the greatest merit of Christianity to have assuaged the joy of the German in brutal bellicosity, but it has not been able to eradicate that joy completely; and when, one day, the Cross of Christ is broken, the savagery of the old warriors, the wild Berserker wrath, will break forth anew in all its barbaric fury of which our Nordic poets tell in song and saga. Even today the talisman of Christianity has begun to rot, and the day will come when its power will pitiably collapse. Then will the old stone gods arise from the accumulated rubbish of the past, and rub the dust of ages from their eyes. Thor will leap forth, brandishing his mighty hammer, to break the Gothic Cathedrals. Neighbours! When that day comes, and when you hear the hurly-burly and the rattle of arms, take good care, Frenchmen, and do not interfere with those affairs which we are settling among ourselves. If you interfere, you will have cause for repentance. Do not sneer at one who foretells the same revolution in the world of action which has been accomplished in the world of thought. Thought precedes action as surely as lightning precedes thunder. German thunder is admittedly German: it is not very agile, and it rumbles a bit slowly: but it will come one day, and, when you hear an explosion such as has never yet occurred in the history of the world, then you will know that it is German thunder.'

Eden's comment, so far as I can recall it, was 'My God!' It seemed to me that the prophesy had shocked him.

My friendship with Gustaf Stridsberg came under severe strain at times. Not through any fault of mine, but because of the editorial policy of *The Times*. *Svenska Dagbladet* had its London offices in Printing House Square, and its London correspondent had access to all the material coming into *The Times* on the eve of publication. By midnight, therefore, Stridsberg would know all about the contents of the next day's paper; and he would also have the text of the main leading articles. If he felt particularly enraged by some new folly, he would telephone to me and speak sharply about the loss of nerve in London, about the blindness of the Editor, about the lack of perception and will in high places. There was no obvious reply that I could make; I am not, perhaps, in a good debating mood at one o'clock in the morning. All that I could do was to go on reporting as best I could on the trend of opinion in Sweden and in Scandinavia generally; and, in particular, about the effects of British policy and British statements, official and unofficial, upon public opinion. W. F. Casey, then Assistant Editor with a special responsibility for the paper's foreign news policy, was an inexhaustible source of encouragement to me at the time; and to many others on the staff. I could never forget the remark he made to me at a very early stage in our acquaintance. 'A good foreign correspondent,' he said, 'is judged by his ability to get news into the paper that conflicts with editorial policy.'

The correspondents who achieved the highest standards in this matter were the stars of the anti-appeasement gang, Norman Ebbutt in Berlin and Thomas Cadett in Paris. Many attempts were made by the Nazis to destroy them and their reputations, sometimes with the connivance of British officials. If Neville Henderson had behaved more like a British Ambassador in Berlin and less like a Nazi public relations officer, Norman Ebbutt might not have been expelled from Germany. I do not believe that

Dawson would have tamely acquiesced in the expulsion if Henderson had lodged a strong protest. In these matters, *The Times* was usually on the right side, even if it did not necessarily approve the correspondent's work. A minor incident in my own life comes to mind. Some time in the middle 'thirties, I was told by the Foreign News Editor that some of my reports from Scandinavia were much resented by officials at the German Embassy in London. Over dinner one evening, one of these officials took it upon himself to congratulate the Editor of *The Times* on his good fortune in having such a well-informed correspondent in Northern Europe. Then he added, with a meaningful sigh: 'It is a pity that he drinks so much.'

I must explain that if one had decided to become a heavy drinker in pre-war Sweden, one had to be prepared to do a great deal of spade-work first. You could not buy beer except at the chemist's. You could buy neither wine nor spirits unless you had a special identity card, known as a *Motbok*. With your card, you could buy all the wine you wanted; and up to two bottles of spirits a month. If you failed to pay your income tax, your card was withdrawn. I can even remember a case where a man had his card taken away because he was not paying his tailor's bill. If you went to a café or a restaurant you could have spirits only with a cooked meal: a plain sandwich would not do. The quantity was carefully measured; with a smaller ration for women than for men. I had a colleague who kept a dog for the sole purpose of making it possible for him to have a whisky and soda in a restaurant of an evening. For the dog, he would order the cheapest cooked dish on the menu; for himself, a whisky and soda. If he wanted another drink, he would have to go to another restaurant and repeat the performance. His pet seemed overweight to me, which is hardly surprising. Occasionally, my friend would lend his dog to a colleague. It would come home in very poor shape after a late night in the company of alien masters. If you could not lay your hands on a dog, you would have to borrow some foreigner's passport. A foreigner making a short stay in Sweden—too short to justify giving him a *motbok*—could always get a bottle of spirits by producing his passport to the man behind the counter in the State Monopoly Shop. Many a foreigner who arrived in Sweden in those days was puzzled by the extraordinarily warm welcome accorded to him by comparative strangers. It was his passport they were after, of course. The formula was simple: one foreigner = one passport = one bottle of whisky. Norway and Finland, like Sweden, have also toyed with various liquor regulations from time to time. These rest on the assumption that while sex is the great evil of the Latins, drink is the curse of the Northerners and must therefore be regulated. Denmark, on the other hand, is more open-minded about these matters. The trade in drink in that country is a private enterprise affair; bars are open at almost all times; and people suffering from certain ailments—diabetes, for instance—are able to buy one or two bottles of duty-free spirits a month.

Perhaps the German Embassy did not know all the facts when they tried to plant their story on *The Times*. Fortunately for me, it had no effect. And I have no doubt that other stories were told about me, and about my colleagues, in the hope of destroying our reputations.

CHAPTER 3

STOCKHOLM IN the nineteen-twenties was one of the cheapest capitals in Western Europe. It had the atmosphere of a small town; which indeed it was. For two or three of the summer months, the place was almost deserted at weekends. Families were parked out in cottages and bungalows on the islands in the archipelago so soon as the school holidays began, and fathers joined them every Friday for a long weekend, travelling in what came to be known as the Papa-Boats. You could get a good lunch at the Grand Hotel—the equivalent of the Savoy Hotel in London—for as little as 1*s.* 9*d.* It was all very quiet and peaceful in those days before the invention of juvenile delinquency.

The Times in the 'thirties had a very high reputation among editors and journalists, not just in Sweden as I have already noted, but upon the Continent in general. Its leading articles were carefully scanned for indications of Government policy; rather in the way that people used to study *Pravda* in the hope of throwing light upon Stalin's intentions. And when *The Times* showed feebleness and indecision, it tended to affect the attitudes of journalists and editors, managers and proprietors, of newspapers in those countries that normally looked to Britain for leadership. Mostly managers and proprietors, perhaps, since they are always looking over their shoulders at circulation figures and advertising revenue. In Sweden, the leading newspapers stood firm in spite of *The Times*. Its policy made them angry, but it did not cause them to abandon their principles. In Denmark the going was rougher. The country was much nearer to Germany than Sweden was, that was one factor. Another was that Denmark was virtually defenceless. A third, was the political nihilism of the Foreign Minister and other Radicals. And then there is what one might perhaps call the characteristic national attitude of the Danish people. 'Whatever you do, don't slam the door.' So when *The*

Times provided them with an example of how not to slam doors, many Danes tended to take the easy way out. There was an intellectual dishonesty about the political debate, about newspaper comment on international questions that can only be compared with the moral equivocations in which Neville Chamberlain and Horace Wilson and Neville Henderson and others appeared to flourish.

Nazi influence in Denmark was pervasive and insidious in the last two years before the war. I do not criticize the attitude of such Danish men and women as were defeatist. After all, what hope was there for Denmark in the Europe of the time—except the hope of escaping by the pretence that no danger existed? The British Government, it seemed to many Danes, had made it plain that there was nothing they could do. Every day added to the long record of British and French retreats and equivocations in the face of Nazi demands and the Nazis played very skilfully upon the general feeling of uncertainty and hopelessness. I was told that they had rigged up a camera on the first floor room in one of the buildings opposite the British Minister's official residence, and that all visitors were photographed for the record. When the day of reckoning came, so it was understood, it would be easy to separate the sheep from the goats. I never got to know if this story was true or not. But it was given wide circulation. I know that some people believed it to be true; and to that extent it had a deterrent effect.

If a Danish Conservative leader had a thankless task before the war, his Swedish and Norwegian colleagues had a seemingly hopeless one. The Norwegian Labour Party had been in office since 1935, and there was no hope of dislodging it. This was among the reasons for the growth of the National Unity Party in Norway (Nasjonal Samling) under Quisling. Another reason was that the Labour Party had got itself an extremely radical reputation in the 'twenties; it did not leave the Communist International until 1923; and even when it did finally break away, it kept its revolutionary principles intact. It remained committed to carrying the class war to the conclusion of a Socialist society through the dictatorship of the proletariat. The economic and financial catastrophes of the middle 'twenties kept several trade unions on a very extreme course, and so added to the general uneasiness and uncertainty. Some of the noblest poetry of those unhappy years had a sharp class-conscious edge, with strong revolutionary rumblings.

In the general elections of 1927, the Norwegian Labour Party, reunited after its split over membership of the Comintern, became the largest single party in the country, although it was a minority once the opposition spoke with a united voice. In spite of its revolutionary reputation and its programme, King Haakon invited its leader to form a government, which it did on 27 January 1928. It did not last very long. Among the reasons for its short life was that its leaders found it necessary to re-state the Party's revolutionary aims in the programme submitted to the Storting. 'Honesty,' it was said at the time, 'triumphed over expediency.' Only a great many people used the word 'stupidity' instead of 'honesty'. As was only to be expected, the financial community panicked. A motion of no confidence was passed by a united opposition in the Storting. Unemployment continued to rise, bankruptcies to increase. And the men who succeeded the Labour government continued the then so fashionable deflationary policies.

Against this background, therefore, there was a good deal of wild talk about the dangers of Communism at the time, and in the years immediately thereafter. This gave Quisling his opportunity; not that his party, even when apparently constitutional, ever received more than an insignificant fraction of the total vote. In the background, too, there was the romantic illusion about the noble qualities of Nordic man, worm-eaten now by ineffective Parliamentary institutions which tended to divide a nation rather than unite it. Belief in the virtues of Nordic man is part of the folklore of Northern Europe; and a reference to it in an after-dinner speech is always good for a cheer. With it, there goes a suspicious attitude to the South and the Mediterranean influences. I have seen some quite rational people in Oslo work themselves into a passion of rage over the neo-classical architecture of the old University Building there. 'How damn silly those columns look,' they would shout, 'with snow between them.'

In the Quisling movement, then, there were many crackpots and misfits, but also a very small number of honest and well-meaning men. After all, they reflected, Quisling had been Fridtjof Nansen's principal assistant in his great relief work in the Soviet Union. He therefore knew all that there was to know about

Bolshevism. But once Quisling's supporters understood that he and his movement were linked with Germany, the good elements among them withdrew. The result was that the party fell into the hands, exclusively, of extremists, lunatics, and even criminal elements. Eventually they and their German masters came up against something unexpectedly hard: Norwegian patriotism. National feeling in Norway is tied to the soil, to the landscape, to the fjords, the sea, the mountains, even the glaciers, rather than to historic memories, ancient buildings, institutions or persons. As the historian Gathorne Hardy has pointed out, there is only one class in Norway that is fully Norse in the real meaning of the term, and that is the class of the farmers. The rural population survived centuries of foreign domination, he observed, until in the nineteenth century it came once more into its own as the heart and kernel of Norwegian democracy. So the deepest patriotism is linked with the land; and the very thought of a proud conqueror striding through a Norwegian forest or trampling upon a Norwegian mountain is intolerable. It stirs up ancestral memories and ancestral passions. The resistance movement was therefore spontaneous and inevitable and there was no need to organize it from outside, although organization added greatly to its effectiveness. The name of Quisling became synonymous with treason.

While the evils of party politics often came under attack in those years by people who would not have dreamt of associating with the Quisling movement in any way, I never found anyone in the Scandinavian North prepared to argue seriously that the country's politicians were corrupt or bought. It was all very different in Belgium where stories about corrupt politicians were the small change of political life. There was a widespread and deeply-held suspicion that every politician had his price. Scandal-mongering about the banks and the country's financial and industrial institutions was a commonplace. I gather that it still is. All this was part of the stock-in-trade of the Rexist movement under the leadership of Degrelle. Its terminology was largely derived from the Action Française group in France. The linguistic quarrel contributed some inflammatory items to its programme. The victory of the Front Populaire in the French general elections in 1936 also played its part. One of the first acts of the government that took office in Paris under Léon Blum was to legalize *congés payés* thereby making annual holidays on full pay available for the first time to the bulk of the French working class. Some of these holiday-makers cruised round Flanders in motor coaches, shouting Socialist and Communist slogans, waving the clenched fist, and generally behaving like sansculottes. Unfortunately, they found themselves among Roman Catholics in Flanders; most of them respectable and conventional, some with strong Conservative inclinations. The Flemings were not amused: the rowdyism confirmed the awfulness of the French; and strengthened the suspicion that Parliamentary institutions were not, perhaps, a Good Thing.

And finally there was the Monarchy, or rather the Monarch himself. So long as Queen Astrid was alive, King Leopold steered a safe and constitutional course. So far as one is entitled to judge these things by external evidence, her influence over the King, that is to say her influence for good, was considerable. No one in those early years ever accused King Leopold of putting a foot wrong. But with the death of the Queen, some element of commonsense in the Palace seemed to vanish. And commonsense was what was most needed in those critical years, when the King's every action was under constant scrutiny. When he spoke Flemish, he was criticized in Brussels and in the Walloon part of the country. When he spoke French he lost popularity in Flanders—although the Flemish Roman Catholics on the whole were loyal to the Monarchy. Some people spoke of him as if he were under the influence of high finance. Others whispered that the international aspects of the Rexist movement attracted him: notably the old plan to carve a state to be called Dietschland out of Belgium, parts of French Flanders, the Roman Catholic parts of The Netherlands, and Luxembourg. I have no doubt that some such bit of Nazi bait was dangled before the Rexists at some time or other. There is not the slightest evidence to suggest that the King was in sympathy with any of this lunacy. I mention it here because it illustrates how chaotic the political situation was in Belgium in those pre-war years, and how essential it was to steer a tactful middle course if disaster was to be avoided.

King Leopold's international reputation—as distinct from his domestic political standing—came under fire after a Cabinet meeting in October 1936. At it, he made a speech saying in effect that after the remilitarization of the Rhineland, Belgium could no longer consider herself bound by existing military undertakings.

She would have to seek a neutrality status similar to that of The Netherlands or even Switzerland. Both the British and French Governments reacted sharply to this unexpected announcement, and their Ambassadors were instructed to ask for an urgent explanation. The British Ambassador in Brussels at that time was Sir Esmond Ovey; and I went to see him when feelings on both sides of the Straits were still running high. On the whole, I thought that Ovey was far more sympathetic to the Belgian point of view than the Foreign Office was. And I believe that when he made his representations in Brussels, he spoke soothing words on his own behalf, rather than strong Foreign Office words as he had been instructed to do. Whatever the Belgian Foreign Minister or King Leopold said about the remilitarization of the Rhineland, and the violation of the Treaty of Locarno, there was no doubt in my mind that the new policy was inspired by Flemish hostility to France, which had become stronger than ever after the Front Populaire elections. In the circumstances of the time, national unity could be preserved only by cutting off some of Belgium's links with Paris.

The neutrality declaration did not help to solve the crisis although it may have mitigated some of its rigours. The Rexists continued their noisy agitation in and out of Parliament. There were occasional riots and disturbances, and while the situation did not at any time get out of hand, things were sometimes unpleasant. I myself was caught in a disagreeable Rexist riot sometime in 1936. Fortunately, I was well prepared for the occcasion. An experienced colleague had advised me never to go out of doors during the rioting season in Belgium or France without a bowler hat and an umbrella. These two implements, he said, were accepted by the police as evidence of respectability and good faith. (My friend Thomas Cadett, who was meticulous about the use of bowler hats and umbrellas in cases of emergency, once made the mistake in Paris of going without them during an Algérie-Française riot after the war. He had no hat and wore a tweed jacket. He was promptly arrested and pushed into a black maria.) In Brussels, I greeted the Rexists in style. I had bought myself a bowler hat at Locks and carried a splendidly-rolled umbrella. I mixed with the Rexists who stood about in the Place de la Brouckère, shouting slogans and waving banners. They were determined, it seemed, to make their way to the Rue de la Loi, the Whitehall of Brussels, which is out of bounds to all organized demonstrations. There were a lot of police about, some on foot, some mounted, and also some tough-looking units of the gendarmerie. When the Rexists began to move I found myself walking just behind the marchers. Suddenly I became conscious of a sea of faces. Faces are things you do not want to see when you are supposed to be walking behind a crowd on the move: they mean that for one reason or another the marchers have turned round and are coming towards you. The reason here was that the mounted police had decided to charge. I saw them bashing away at such heads and shoulders as were within their reach. There was no point in trying to run away, so I stood my ground with my heart beating. I clutched my umbrella and pointed to my bowler hat; the men swerved and I was left standing alone in the middle of the square, with bits of paper and torn banners and a hat or two around me.

In many of these crises, M. Spaak was usually involved in one way or another. He had been Belgium's Foreign Minister for so many years that he came in time to be regarded as a permanency. His is an interesting personality. He began his political career as a window-smashing Radical. After 1940 he became a Pillar of Society, and adopted a sort of Churchillian pose, with jutting jaw and determined glare. But I suspect that his air of dogged tenacity marks weakness rather than strength. The part he played in King Leopold's neutrality declaration does not provoke my admiration. The King made his declaration in the course of a speech to the Cabinet. The Ministers asked for the text to be published, with the consequence that the King became personally associated with and responsible for the new policy. It was later explained that the Cabinet had had domestic political considerations in mind when deciding upon publication; and it was admitted at the time that the possible international repercussions had been lost sight of. But a man of Spaak's experience could not possibly have overlooked them, or disregarded them: the Declaration dealt with topics that he had been discussing with the French Government only a few days before. In the course of those discussions, the international status of Belgium had come up; but the form of words used by the Belgian Ambassador in Paris, and in London, had not given rise to any anxiety. The King's speech injected a new element into the situation; and it seemed that what was now at stake was not only the immediate difficulty created by the re-militarization of the Rhineland, but Belgium's responsibilities to the League of Nations and her status in what remained of the Western security system. Spaak seems to have devoted as much of his time to explaining away the King's speech as in re-defining foreign policy in the light of the speech.

This seems the right place to say a word or two about Spaak's period of office as Secretary-General of the North Atlantic Treaty Organization. He was appointed in 1957 to succeed Lord Ismay, after a great many comings and going and intrigues. At the last minute a 'stop Spaak' movement got under way, and the name of Sir Ian Jacob was put forward. But it was too late; and Spaak became Secretary-General. I thought at the time that the appointment of a Belgian, no matter how eminent, to the top job in NATO was a serious mistake. The French are not disposed to take advice from Belgians, General de Gaulle least of all. *Les braves Belges* are country cousins, no more; and their views are not regarded as particularly valuable unless they coincide with those that suit Paris. The only appointment that would have made sense then was that of Mr. Lester Pearson, one of the founders of the North Atlantic Alliance, and then leader of the Opposition in Canada. The Canadians are in the enviable position of being able to speak home truths to all comers, to British and French and Americans alike, without causing lasting offence, and with some hopes of being listened to. No one but a Canadian could have prevented the split in NATO from widening. A Belgian was powerless. In another way, too, Spaak's appointment was unfortunate. It put a stop to all attempts by the Secretary-General of NATO to mediate in the Cyprus dispute. I remember asking a Greek official if they intended to ask Spaak for help. 'Great heavens, no,' he said. 'We would turn to Ismay without any hesitation. But Spaak is too much of an imperialist.'

As an exercise in public relations, the appointment of Spaak was a failure. Ismay, his predecessor, was one of the greatest public relations artists I have ever met. He conducted a press conference as Malcolm Sargent conducted an orchestra. He could bluff or wheedle or charm his way out of any situation. He gave absolutely nothing away, yet left everybody feeling happy and important and well-informed. He used to put on a splendid act of being an international civil servant, and of having lost all his objectionable British prejudices and characteristics. There was one occasion where he had kept a large number of journalists waiting for something like half an hour. He came on the platform from a side door, his face beaming, all prepared to sing his old song 'The Man without a Care in the World'. He fiddled a bit with the microphone, and with bits of paper on his desk, which I am sure were all blank. 'I am very sorry,' he said, 'very sorry to be late. It's all the fault of those British. They held me up with their talk.' And with that, he got down to business; except for the fact that there was no business to get down to. He just chatted amiably for some fifteen or twenty minutes, and then withdrew with a smile and a wave of the hand, rather like a nice uncle who had come to see how the nephews at school were getting on, but who was not going to be trapped into giving them supper afterwards.

Spaak tried so hard to please. He was so anxious to be helpful. He would come straight to the Conference from his office after mastering his brief; sometimes he would even appear in carpet-slippers. Then he would make a speech, the sort of speech a French politician might make on laying a foundation stone somewhere, in strict obedience to the rules that govern elocution as taught in French secondary schools. Then he would say: 'Questions, please'. A forced smile would follow; there would be much waving of the hands; then an answer, sometimes a sharp answer. But his words did not carry conviction. He annoyed many of those present, especially my American colleagues. One of them got up to remind Spaak that he had travelled a long way at vast expense to his paper to attend this press Conference. He had listened carefully to all the questions. He did not think any of them had been answered. What did M. Spaak intend to do about it? Spaak was ruffled and annoyed. When the proceedings mercifully ended, we all came away unhappy and ill-at-ease. What was so regrettable was that Spaak had tried hard to be helpful, and no doubt thought that he had been helpful. His magisterial manner was against him. In private conversation, he is an altogether different person: jovial, informal and communicative. His vision has always extended far beyond the Belgian horizon and without him the European idea would not have got very far. Not that that ever made him popular in Paris. There were people there who tended to write him off with a sneer. '*L'Europe verbale*,' they often called him.

Nor could Van Zeeland be described as a tower of strength in the critical pre-war period in Belgian history. He was Prime Minister at the time of the Neutrality Declaration; and he also pushed the King forward as the man responsible for it. The fact that he was closely associated with some of the most powerful financial interests in Belgium was a source of political weakness rather than of strength. His is the sort of personality that flickers like a candle and vanishes when the winds of political crisis blow. One says of him, as one says of so many of the governments in office in Europe in the 'thirties, that they were small men faced with problems far too great for them.

There were exceptions, of course. The then Prime Minister of The Netherlands, Dr. Colijn, was one. He and Queen Wilhelmina formed a strange sort of political tandem that carried the country past some awkward corners. He played the part of Disraeli to Wilhelmina's Victoria; and if the Court and the men surrounding the Prime Minister were thought to be rather stuffy, they helped to maintain certain standards that might perhaps be described as good and old fashioned. Colijn was a Calvinist of the old school. He had seen service in the Dutch East Indies as a young man, and there were traces of it in his manner. He had a Bible on a lectern standing in his room and next to it a box of cigars. He was the moving spirit behind the agreement—the so-called Oslo Convention—between The Netherlands, Belgium, the three Scandinavian Kingdoms and Finland to try to save something from the wreckage of international trade after the collapse of currencies and the rash of trade barriers that were springing up as a sort of aftermath to the Ottawa Agreements. There had been contacts going back to the year 1930 when these countries had agreed not to raise customs duties against each other without previous consultation. Early in 1937 Dr. Colijn proposed that the governments involved should meet to consider further steps aimed at liberalizing international trade. When I interviewed him for *The Times*, Dr. Colijn told me that 'the small nations have the enormous advantage of having no political axe to grind. They only want to secure a little more prosperity and nothing else. It seems to me that those of us who still believe in the value of democracy have so much in common that it ought to be easy for us to widen our cultural, financial, economic and political contacts and relations so as mutually to strengthen and safeguard our common heritage.

That way lies the salvation of all we hold dear.' This is rather what the small nations in the European Free Trade Association are saying today. They have no wish but to secure a little more prosperity.

In all these countries I found I could tap much useful information about developments in Nazi Germany, information that did not seem so easily accessible in Paris where I had my headquarters. I found a greater willingness to face facts and to consider the situation as it was—rather than as the politicians in London and Paris hoped it would turn out to be—among Central Bankers and Ministers of religion than among most other sections of the community. The Central Bankers seemed to be exceptionally well-informed. If I was able to be of some use to *The Times* in those days, it was largely because of the information that came my way through the Central Banks. It goes without saying that I was not in touch with the Bank of England because that was the responsibility of the City Editor, and not of a foreign correspondent. And in any case, from what I heard at the time, Montagu Norman was too much of a mystic to have clear ideas about what went on in the heart of the Continent. Berlin was never a port of call: I travelled through Berlin fairly often, but usually my route by rail to Scandinavia lay through Hamburg. One had always on these occasions to take great care not to carry any compromising newspapers, periodicals or books on crossing the German border at Osnabruck. One day late in 1936 I suddenly remembered with a shock, just before the customs people and the passport officers came to the compartment, that I had a copy of *The New Statesman* in my suitcase, as well as a working-model of a Hitler moustache that I had bought at a wig-maker's place in London. I supposed I would get away with *The New Statesman*, but the Hitler moustache was another matter altogether. I managed to set fire to it in an ashtray, and when the customs people came into my smoke-filled compartment they no doubt concluded that I had been smoking a villainous cigar. Fortunately, there were traces of cigar-ash in the tray as well as of the remnants of a moustache. *The New Statesman* they took in with a glance, but said not a word. When I got to Hamburg, I found that I had just missed my connection to Copenhagen. It meant spending twelve hours waiting for the next train, and I had only two or three marks in my pocket after paying for my taxi. But I was determined not to change any of my sterling into marks. 'My pounds would help to finance the Nazis,' I thought, and I spent the whole day without another meal. In the afternoon, I went to a newsreel cinema to keep warm. I stayed there so long as I dared and then walked to the station where I had left my luggage. The young toughs I saw on my way, so bumptious, so idle, so very uniformed brought me face to face with a world that had obviously reversed all the moral values I had been brought up on. Long passages from Hans Andersen's tale of the Snow Queen passed through my mind, from that dreadful world of icy hearts where all that is good is contemptible and all that is evil is clothed in righteousness and generosity.

CHAPTER 4

I STILL WONDER at my good fortune in being sent to Paris in the 'thirties. To a journalist it was one of the most exciting political centres in the world, and I would not have changed places with anyone. French politicians, whether in office or out of it, were accessible and usually willing to talk freely, and they did not take offence even when they were called to the telephone by one of us in the middle of the night. The key to many international developments was to be found in Paris; and the French attitude was often of crucial importance. The evolution of British foreign policy under Neville Chamberlain could sometimes be observed with greater clarity from Paris than in London. The one thing to be avoided at all costs, I soon discovered, was to become emotionally involved in the day's events, in all the bad news that was so plentiful at the time. I tried hard to maintain the detached look of an observer who is more interested in the technical skill, or absence of skill, of the actors on the stage than in the play itself. Once you did get involved, you found it hard to go to sleep. I have tried to observe this rule ever since those Paris days; but I have not always succeeded. It was hard not to become obsessed by the political and social tensions of the time which were far greater in Paris than in London. Just before the Munich meeting, the air became almost unbearable; and the regular testing of the air-raid warning system which began at about that time did not help to relieve it. I slipped over to London for a day or two; and I was relieved to find how calm people were, and how they were able to go about their business without much apparent concern for the future. I was not alone in observing this contrast between the two cities, but I am unable to draw a moral from it.

So long as one could contract out of this feeling of what I can only call excited despair, the Paris of the mid-'thirties, unlike the

Paris of the late 'sixties, was a pleasant and attractive place to live in. People still had time; there was no need to rush off into the countryside over the weekend in search of relaxation and peace since it was still to be had in Paris. You could still sit at some *terrasse* or other for hours on end, at the cost of a cup of coffee or a glass of beer and watch the procession of cranks, foreigners and *habitués*. The Parisians were still reasonably good-tempered and not excessively ill-mannered. They had not yet been perverted by the motor car and corrupted by the modern religion of growth. Now, almost everyone has his own car, and Paris has become a city of bullies; it tingles with a rage that is not always suppressed. The women, and especially the smart and prosperous women you see round the Faubourg St. Honoré, are hard-faced and thrusting, with sharp metallic voices. The young have no great desire to linger over a good meal as their fathers and grandfathers used to do. They are always on the move, spending their money not on good food, but on gadgets and on rushing about the countryside in cars or on scooters. The quiet restaurant with its unpretentious air, at which you were given a good meal at a reasonable price, provided you were willing to wait for it, is gradually going out of business. There will be nothing, soon, between the raucous eating places that serve cold snacks and hot music, and the luxurious establishments whose finances are based on expense accounts. Many of the restaurants I was able to include in a guide-book to Paris that I compiled some years before the war have gone out of business, or have been transformed into something very different and often unattractive.

Perhaps the religion of growth has done even more harm to France than the motor car. It has given a new edge to what is the worst of French national characteristics, the sin of avarice. It is untrue to say, as some English puritans have long been saying, that France is the country of pornography and adultery. (Did we not catch even Ernest Bevin on one occasion dismissing the French novel with a suggestive chuckle?) The French were, and I think still are, a great deal more conventional in these matters than people in this country; and in any case, they regard sex as something normal. The semi-pornographic periodicals on sale at many kiosks in Paris before the war were not bought by Frenchmen, but by British tourists, or Germans, or Scandinavians. What was especially noticeable was that the magazines with sadistic or masochistic overtones were usually bought by Northerners, by representatives of what the Nazis called the master race. The chief vice of the French, then—in so far as it is possible to generalize about national vices and virtues—is avarice. I do not suppose there is any country in Western Europe that has a worse record than France for crimes of violence committed for what turns out to be a pittance. The pattern of French industrial relations in the 'thirties confirmed me in my belief that many French hearts were as cold as tombstones and that the term Christian charity has very little meaning for them. Very soon after my arrival in Paris, Thomas Cadett and I gave lunch to a great French industrialist. We were discussing the prevailing labour unrest in France and its effects upon the French economy. As our guest was finishing off another oyster, he said casually: 'France will not be prosperous or orderly again so long as the working classes are sleek and well-fed.'

At the other end of the social scale, there was the young man who used to cut my hair in a small barber's shop near the Opéra. He had voted for Socialism and Progress in the Front Populaire elections in 1936 and against 'reaction and speculation'. One day he told me with great satisfaction that he had a bar of gold tucked away in a safe place in his house, and that he was saving up to buy another. This was at a time when the left-wing press was indignantly denouncing the capitalists for speculating against the franc, and for endangering the national welfare by buying gold and foreign currencies. Soon after the end of the war in 1945 people of all classes were again salting their savings away in a form that could not be traced by tax inspectors: in Swiss or American banks, or in foreign bank-notes under the bed. I knew several people who, in 1947, decided to dispose of all their property and possessions in France, including real estate, and to emigrate to North Africa where they felt confident that a tough colonial administration would protect their property against Communism and social reform. I do not find it hard to believe that when the government of France was at the end of its economic tether in 1947/48 and was saved from disaster by Marshall Aid, French citizens had more gold and foreign currencies hidden away at home and abroad than the total amount of Aid allocated to their government. The State has often been bankrupt in France; the rich have stayed rich.

For eighteen years after the First World War, until the explosion of 1936, the so-called capitalist system bore more heavily upon the workers of France than upon those of any other country in Western Europe, except perhaps Germany. The attempts of radical or leftish governments to break out of the stranglehold of high finance were invariably checked by the Bank of France and the powerful financial and industrial groups that controlled it—the members of the 200 families as they were polemically described at the time. The trade unions led a precarious existence; they had few members; and most employers refused to deal with their officials. Reform governments were often driven from office by financial pressure of various kinds; and financial pressure was easy to apply because the French money market was a very rudimentary affair. British governments turn to the market when their cash resources need to be replenished. French governments had to go to the Bank of France. If the Bank did not approve of the government's policy, credits might be refused. If the government persisted in its demand, facts surrounding its application would be leaked to the press and to right-wing critics. And when the story of financial stringency was broken to the public, even radicals found it impossible to remain unmoved. The French electorate could always be made to swing right with the cry that its savings were in danger. Until the Front Populaire came in, most French solutions (in so far as there were any) were right-wing solutions, acceptable to safe bourgeois minds regardless of age, sex, income level or social background. That meant deflation and government by decree. Unfortunately for the Left, Vincent Auriol, the Minister of Finance under Léon Blum, was nothing like bold enough. My own description of him in *The Times* was, I think, eminently fair. I said he was a sheep in wolf's clothing.

The last pre-war government to govern by financial decree on any substantial scale was the government of Pierre Laval in 1935. In order 'to save the franc' as the phrase went, he promulgated a series of measures cutting wages, pensions, rent and prices. Cutting wages and salaries was easy enough at a time when the trade unions were virtually powerless. But the decree on prices was not very effective: at least it was very hard to see any evidence of it by those of us who went out shopping. On the day the decrees were to be published, a crowd of journalists gathered at the Quai d'Orsay waiting for news. We had to go there because Laval was

Foreign Minister as well as Prime Minister and he used the Ministry as his headquarters. Some of us had been sitting on the steps of the Ministry for some hours before we were invited in; and it was fairly late in the evening by the time Laval was able to receive us. He began reading his texts as soon as we had got into the room. Suddenly the light went out, and Laval had to stop. With equal suddenness it came on again, and he was able to continue. Again it went off; and again he had to stop. He was becoming edgy and bad-tempered; his dark complexion made him look like a villain in a Hollywood film. When the light came on again, Laval noticed what had been happening. One of the journalists had been leaning heavily against his desk, and had pushed the plug connecting the electric lamp half-way out of its socket. Laval waved his hand at him. The man took no notice; and again the light went out. With an oath, Laval threw all his papers into the air, and left the room. We did not see him again on that occasion.

Laval's government lasted for some six months and became increasingly unpopular, with the Left as well as with the Right. The government of Sarraut which succeeded him did no better. And in the spring came the great swing towards the Communist Party which led in June to the formation of the Front Populaire government under Léon Blum. His assumption of office coincided with a great wave of strikes, unorganized, not controlled by the trade unions, yet perfectly disciplined. This mass demonstration of discontent frightened the employers and the bankers; it frightened every Frenchman with a bourgeois attitude to life and to savings. What seemed so sinister to them was that the strikers stayed in the factories instead of going off fishing. The analogy of the Bolshevik take-over of factories and workshops in Russia in 1917 and 1918 immediately sprang to mind, and the employing class as a whole lost its nerve. Its leaders paled into silence and forgot all the bold words they had used in the past about the need for order and discipline. And while they lost faith in the country's existing institutions, because they suddenly realized they could no longer manipulate them to serve their own interests, they acquired instead a sense of grievance, as we were to learn in the appeasement years that followed. Their support for the policy of surrender was one ingredient in the class war. They were too rich to be brave, so they took refuge instead in prejudices, above all in class prejudices. And if in 1936, they gave tacit and grudging support to the policy of social reform, for almost any concession that would get the men out of the factories and back to work, there was also the unspoken determination to break working-class resistance at the first opportunity.

The Spanish Civil War and Stalin's pact with Hitler which eventually led the Communist Party to sabotage the war effort provided the *bien-pensants* with excellent arguments for repressing articulate left-wing and working-class organizations. It was this class of frightened but rancorous bourgeois that was most hostile to General de Gaulle in 1940. When he got back to Paris in 1944 it was widely feared that he would give orders for a massive purge of the Right and that he would rid the country of all those who had put the security of their possessions above the interests of the nation. But de Gaulle seems to have accommodated himself without difficulty to the habits and beliefs of the *bien-pensants*. M. Pompidou, his Prime Minister for many years, who was a partner in the House of Rothschild, is undoubtedly one of them; but the record of the Rothschilds in the appeasement years, unlike that of some other merchant bankers, is excellent. The House did all within its power to stiffen the backbone of French political leaders in 1938 and 1939.

The strikers won three major concessions: paid holidays; higher pay; and compulsory collective bargaining. The effects of the first two were felt almost at once. With paid holidays, ordinary wage earners were able to enjoy a holiday some distance away from home for the first time in their working lives; and the South of France, also for the first time, established itself as a summer holiday place. Higher wages led to an immediate increase in the demand for better quality foodstuffs, and above all for the better cuts of beef. So the price of beefsteak and good joints rose sharply, and passed beyond the means of a section of the middle-class whose housewives were forced back upon the cheaper cuts and whose households therefore had to make do with *ragoûts* and stewed meats of all kinds. The housewife now had to spend rather more time in the kitchen than before; but since cooking is a middle-class vocation in France this was no great hardship. In so far as all this made for fresh grievances among respectable middle-class people, they counted against the Front Populaire government. The opposition slogan might well have been 'Communism and *ragoûts* go together'.

What was so tragic about the Front Populaire period was not that it angered the middle-classes and terrified the rich. It was that the cause of social reform in France was sacrificed to the national interests of Russia. Stalin did not want to see a weakened France in the face of the mounting Nazi danger, so the strikes were called off as soon as the most pressing needs of working men and working women had been met. The essential structural reforms were not carried out, and within a few months the Front Populaire had broken up. In the early nineteen-fifties, French national interests were again trampled underfoot by Russia, this time because the Russians wanted to weaken France and to use the French working class as the basis for an attack on the Western security system. In May 1952 there were scenes of mob violence in Paris on the occasion of General Ridgway's arrival to succeed General Eisenhower at SHAPE. The French police behaved with their accustomed brutality and several priests were beaten up for taking part in the demonstrations. All this served Russian interests, in that the efforts of the French Communist Party were diverted into the international field, in deference to Russian security needs, and away from pressing domestic problems. The snivelling sycophancy of French Communist leaders towards Stalin and his friends made the creation of a powerful Radical movement in France impossible. If their attitude had been different, a radical Labour Party might possibly have emerged in France after 1945, especially in the light of developments in Britain. The government of Clement Attlee, unlike the government of Harold Wilson, enjoyed immense prestige on the Continent, at least until 1949, and greatly encouraged left-wing movements in many countries. It could also be argued, I think, that Marshall Aid was almost as great a disaster for France as Stalinism. It made structural reforms unnecessary. Without Marshall Aid, the rich tax evaders would have been forced to devote some of their money, which they had in plenty, to national purposes. With Marshall Aid, there was no need to trouble them.

In 1936 a great deal was made of the heavy Communist vote in the Front Populaire elections. It showed, some people said, that France was basically unreliable. Others said it proved that the class war in France was a far more serious affair than had been suspected. Something more was involved in that vote than working-class determination to curb the powers of the employers and of the governments whose policies they dictated. Foreign policy was also an issue. There were unusual Frenchmen, vigorously anti-Communist, who had voted Communist because they disapproved of the foreign policies of all the respectable political parties. In 1936 the Soviet Union appeared to be more active in resisting the dictatorships than most other countries; and the French Communist Party, obsequious as usual, toed the Russian line with breathless alacrity. The anti-dictatorship part of the programme undoubtedly attracted some abnormal votes. One case was personally known to me: a private banker who might be expected to vote anti-Radical, and certainly anti-Communist, whatever the circumstances, and who voted 'for Moscow' in disgust. I must add that he was not a Jew, since this could have explained his vote as a vote against Nazism. In this respect, then, Stalin had succeeded, for a while, in making Communism respectable in France. I suspect that General de Gaulle thirty years later performed much the same miracle. If the Communist vote remains high, that is not because there are more Communists there than in other countries. It is because the party's programme now provides the only alternative to domestic policies that have become distasteful to many people. It is a protest vote, not a vote for any particular party. Moreover, if a pro-Russian foreign policy has become desirable the Communists are clearly better equipped to pursue it than other political parties.

I was kept moving between Paris and London for a while before settling down in France. The Foreign News Editor wanted me to do a stint in Printing House Square because he thought it important I should know something about the rules of the office before finally going abroad as a fully-fledged foreign correspondent. For a short time, I acted as a very junior foreign sub-editor; and not a successful one. Then, also for a short while, as assistant to the Foreign News Editor. This was little more than a bottle-washing job. Finally, and for a longer period, I worked as a leader-writer. After having done odd jobs in almost every editorial department of *The Times*, I am bound to say that leader-writing is the easiest of them all. But I was terrified at first. I had always thought of *Times* leader-writers as a college of potent, grave and reverend signiors working out acceptable policies after many hours of meditation and deliberation. It was with much diffidence, then, that I attended the afternoon editorial conference over which Geoffrey Dawson, the Editor, presided. He used to sit with his elbows on the table, occasionally pulling back to make a point, while blowing clouds of cigarette smoke at the ceiling. He did not seem to be listening as the Home News Editor outlined the various news items that would be appearing in next day's paper. He withdrew even further into remoteness when Ralph Deakin, the Foreign News Editor, catalogued his items. There was one occasion when Deakin got himself involved in outlining a rather complicated development taking place in a distant country. In the middle of his exposition, Dawson turned to Peter Fleming, who attended these editorial conferences from time to time, and said, 'How are the Moors, Peter?' This puzzled me. It was not until much later that it dawned upon me that the Editor's mind had been far away from the conference table. He had been thinking of shooting rather than editing. As an incidental by-product, he had also put the Foreign News Editor in his place together with his fatuous foreign news.

The occasion when I was first asked to do the main leader—the 'first leader'—stands out as a landmark in my life. Something between 750 and 800 words was wanted; and I was not quite sure how to set about it. I consulted a knowledgeable friend who said, 'If you don't want to commit yourself, look up the old cuttings and just do a paraphrase. You won't be far wrong if you do it that way.' I was grateful for the advice but it was not relevant on this particular occasion since I had been asked to compose a leader on yet another political crisis in France. And while French political crises before the war had many points in common, they did not always have the same origins. But I got to work. After a while the door to my little room opened and the Editor became visible. It was his custom, in the late afternoon, to look in upon the leader-writers working in their rabbit-hutches to find out how they were getting on. I thought I ought to say something. 'I propose to say . . .', I began. He interrupted me. 'I don't care what you say,' he said, 'I want my leader by seven o'clock. I've got an early dinner engagement.' And then he disappeared. In spite of this apparently casual attitude, the Editor took great pains over the final product; and if he thought you were not in tune with the spirit of the paper, you would not find yourself writing leaders for very long. Nevertheless, his attitude depressed me at the time. I felt very deflated. It was not easy to get rid of the conviction that political leading articles should be written only after the most elaborate discussions over which the Editor himself would preside; and that the end-product would be a sort of collective view. I must add that there were serious-minded people on the staff who took a frivolous and light-hearted view of the place of the leading article in daily journalism. 'Our leaders,' they said, 'are intended for the Foreign Office and for foreigners. Without them the members of the diplomatic corps in London would be virtually idle. Think of the mischief they would be up to if they had no homework to do.'

And it was precisely because the diplomatic corps in London and Foreign Ministries abroad spent so much time reading and interpreting the leading articles in *The Times* that they occasionally had such a disproportionate effect. It is hard to recall now the explosion caused by the leading article that appeared on 7 September 1938 and which once again advocated the partition of Czechoslovakia. This article had been lying about in the office for some time. It had been ordered by Barrington-Ward, the Assistant Editor, who was in charge in Dawson's absence, and left in some pigeon-hole for use on a later day. When the Editor got back to Printing House Square he found himself short of leaders and began to rummage among the moth-balls. There he found a leader on the Czechoslovak crisis which he thought might be suitable. After all, the Runciman Mission was still in Prague so its subject matter was still topical. He gave it a casual glance and passed it for publication. When it got into the night editorial room, Casey was horrified. In the meantime the Editor himself had had second thoughts and asked Casey for his views. According to the Official History of *The Times*, Casey said he did not like it much. He told me himself that he had been shocked and dismayed. Dawson made one or two alterations; but this only made matters worse. And at this point my recollection of what Casey told me is in conflict with what appears in the Official History. When the article came back into the night editor's room, Casey saw at once that the final section only made matters worse. He tried to convince Dawson of it; but unfortunately Dawson did not get the point; and so the leader was finally passed for press and duly appeared in the paper. The effects were disastrous, as Casey knew they would be. It was widely assumed that the article had been officially inspired; an assumption that was not shaken by

Foreign Office denials. The fact that it expressed a personal view was just not believed. The same view had been given currency in *The Times* on several occasions earlier in the year; it had also been advocated by certain left-wing journals, notably *The New Statesman*. But it was, I repeat, a personal view; distorted on this occasion by the Editor in a mood of petulance. Coming when it did, very few diplomatists were prepared to believe that it owed nothing to Foreign Office inspiration.

And personal views, I eventually discovered, counted for a great deal in the matter of leader-writing. A year or two after I had been transferred to Paris, Barrington-Ward came through to me on the telephone to say that he was running short of leading articles, and asking me if I had any useful ideas. I was in a considerable state of excitement at the time because of the speculation that was going on in the foreign exchange markets of the world. I was beginning to understand how these speculative transactions might influence the foreign policies of the British and French Governments. The French franc had been devalued yet again in September 1936, and London and Washington had agreed with Paris to set up Exchange Equalization Funds 'so as to avoid so far as possible any disturbances of the basis of international exchanges resulting from' this devaluation. The creation of the Funds could not prevent gambling but it could help to check it and possibly to make it unprofitable. Nevertheless, the markets were at times in the grip of a speculative fever that cost the Central Banks a great deal of their reserves. So when Barrington-Ward asked me to produce a first leader, I thought the opportunity to discuss currency speculation too good to miss. I outlined my ideas to him and he told me to go ahead; and in due course my piece was telephoned to Printing House Square. I realized, of course, that in denouncing speculation I might well be accused of harbouring dangerous thoughts; but I was confident that if I produced the right quotations as stiffening for my arguments there would be no great difficulty, and no painful consequences. When giving expression to unorthodox views, you were usually safe if you used little bits from past statements by the Pope or the Archbishop of Canterbury or the Governor of the Bank of England or Stanley Baldwin or Lionel Curtis or Walter Bagehot, or someone equally respectable, alive or dead. They were among the Gods in the Mythology of Printing House Square and if you quoted them with a touch of reverence, a charge of heresy would not easily stick. My article was published on 24 September 1937, and I must confess that I still regard it as a sound piece of work. If I now quote one or two passages from it, it is to demonstrate that it was possible in those days to get unpalatable views into print, and that the staff of *The Times* was not so hamstrung as many critics have since made out:

'Many who are today converting their francs into other currencies are undoubtedly acting in good faith, in the belief that thus only can they safeguard their own interests. But they overlook that by so doing they are playing into the hands of gamblers and speculators, "those clever men" as Pope Pius XI called them in his Encyclical *Quadragesimo Anno* "who do not hesitate to arouse the worst instincts . . . in order to make use of them for the furtherance of their own interests". Of all forms of gambling none is more anti-social than gambling in a currency. Speculation in foreign exchange, it has been said, is like gambling in the life-blood of the nation. . . . Commerce and finance have to rid themselves of what Bagehot called "the dirty crowd of little men" who follow in the wake of enterprise and who seek to turn wars and rumours of war to their advantage. Government action, perhaps international action, might be required ultimately to cope with the notorious evil of holding companies and speculative syndicates domiciled in some of the petty States on the continent. . . . A halt to gambling will be a contribution to political steadiness in France. . . . A "Nyon Arrangement" against financial piracy would be effective against what is becoming a threat to all institutions that free people hold dear.'

The publication of this leader led to a minor uproar. Many people in the City disliked it. I was told that the City's principal representative on the Board of Directors, Robert (later Lord) Brand, was far from amused. Abroad, the customary misunderstandings followed and also the usual attempts to show that occult forces were at work in Printing House Square. A weekly periodical in Paris quoted my article in full under the headline 'Young Conservatives in Revolt'. Its argument was that the young men in the Party had gone into action against the Old Gang. When I told Ernest Rowe-Dutton, the financial Attaché at the British Embassy in Paris, that I had written the piece he shook his head. Things had come to a pretty pass, he said, when *The Times* found it possible to denounce the workings of a free market in a free economy. 'In any case,' he added, 'speculation invariably cancels out. If people speculate on the forward exchange market by selling what they have not got, they have got to buy it back sooner or later. So everything comes right in the end.' I was not impressed with this orthodox argument, and I never have been. Ruthless operations on the foreign exchange markets of the world, backed by skilful and unscrupulous propaganda, stand a good chance of influencing policy, and have undoubtedly done so in the past. They changed the course of British policy in 1956 during the Suez crisis. I was very glad that I had had this opportunity to speak out. It was an experience I thoroughly enjoyed.

At least one door on *The Times* was shut to me as a result of my unorthodox ideas. Early in 1937, the Manager told me that I was being considered for an appointment to the City Office, with the possibility—he put it no higher than that—that I might one day take over the City Editorship. I was warned that I should be asked to meet the people directly concerned with such an appointment, including Brand. The day came; I went to lunch; and I was asked a number of questions which I believe I answered with decorum and discretion. I explained that I thought British financial journalism lacked one feature that I regarded as important and useful. It did not deal to any extent, I said, with the no-man's-land lying between politics and finance; a field that was adequately covered only by the *Neue Zürcher Zeitung*. If I were given the opportunity, I added, I would try to develop it. I thought things were going rather well, and in my mind's eye I could already see myself revolutionizing the City pages. The next day I went off to my tailor and ordered what in those days was regarded as the essential uniform for a City job: a black coat and waistcoat and striped trousers to match. Alas, I never had occasion to wear this splendid outfit. I still have it, and it is as good as new. The bowler hat I had acquired on an earlier occasion was bartered some time later against a bottle of gin.

CHAPTER 5

THE GENERAL assumption that there was such a thing as a 'Printing House Square' view does not bear examination. *The Times* was a house divided against itself. There were those who by conviction were completely on the Editor's side, people like Barrington-Ward and A. L. Kennedy. There were others, W. F. Casey, D. D. Braham (one of the principal leader-writers) and Iverach MacDonald (then Diplomatic Correspondent) who held diametrically opposite views on the question of the government's appeasement policy, and who did their best to get them into the paper in spite of Dawson. MacDonald was so upset at times that he could be heard muttering to himself words of Old Testament vengeance as he came out of the office. The anti-appeasement group deplored the blindness and imperial self-righteousness that were responsible for Dawson's attitude to European affairs. A glance at some of the leading articles of the time shows that there was a constant tug-of-war in the office. A particularly striking example of it is to be found in the pieces written about the June 1934 purges in Germany. The first comments after that bloody weekend were not unfavourable to the Nazi case; they showed what Hitler would have called 'comprehension'. But the next day the paper took a much tougher line. 'So far as the methods of Government and respect for human life and human freedom are concerned,' it said, 'Germany has ceased for the time being to be a modern European country. She has reverted to medieval conditions.' This was strong meat in the prevailing circumstances. People in Western Europe who followed these things breathed more easily; they thought that the paper's editorial views were stiffening. But nothing had changed. The article was written by Braham and he had no lasting influence on policy which continued its zig-zag course. He was a shy and stubborn man of generosity and integrity who found it hard to live in a moral twilight in which evil was allowed to flourish so painlessly. In the ordinary way, he was responsible for leading articles on American affairs and other innocuous subjects.

The Official History of *The Times* makes out that all would have been very different if only the paper had had a Foreign Editor. I do not believe the presence of even a superman would have made the slightest difference. Moses and the prophets were there; but Dawson would not hear them. He was too sure of his political judgment, too much at home in the world of power to brook any kind of interference even if expert. The Official History says bluntly that neither Dawson nor Barrington-Ward liked 'viewy' men. This is but another way of saying that they did not like men whose views differed from theirs. And those who now argue that the foreign policy of *The Times* would have been different if only Dawson had appointed a Foreign Editor are committed to the consequential view that Dawson would have been prepared to accept an anti-appeasement line on the advice of an expert, at the cost of cutting himself off from that environment in which he knew he could play the part of statesman. This strikes me as inconceivable. Dawson can hardly have forgotten that one of his predecessors had been denied entry to the Foreign Office because a leading article for which he was regarded as responsible had expressed views on the Middle East that were unacceptable to the official mind. It was not that Dawson was anti-European. He considered that the maintenance of the imperial connection must be the most important aim of British foreign policy; and with it, the maintenance of the link with the United States in so far as it was required for the preservation of the Empire.

I am more than ever convinced that Dawson's basic fault was not so much that he held certain views on foreign policy, but that he thought of himself as a statesman rather than as a journalist. The two are incompatible. The first Lord Rothermere thought he was being very statesmanlike when he instructed us to take our hats off to France at the time of the occupation of the Ruhr; but his campaign did not increase the stature of the *Daily Mail* as a newspaper. Nor did Lord Beaverbrook's Empire Free Trade campaign add to the lustre of the *Daily Express* or deepen its influence with its readers. Dawson's pursuit of appeasement as a consistent policy, often through the suppression of news that militated against that policy, violated what must remain the basic principle of good journalism. It therefore diminished the reputation of *The Times* at a time when its influence was sorely needed. I do not find it unreasonable for a politician to ask that a certain piece of information calculated to distress or inflame public opinion be suppressed or conjured away at a time when he is engaged in some delicate negotiation. But a journalist cannot and should not see things in the same light: it is his job to bring the facts into the open, except in those circumstances where he knows that publication would lead to public mischief.

There was one occasion in which I was involved, when the views of the journalist and the statesman came into sharp conflict. I had been recalled to London from Paris to help report the proceedings of the Imperial Conference in 1937. I had not then done much reporting work in London, so I was counting upon getting a good deal of help from the office in the way of introductions. In the event, I got no help at all: I had to find my own way and to nose out my own sources. I was very lucky in that I made friends with a senior member of one of the delegations who was willing to give me a full account, day by day, of the proceedings, on the understanding that I could make discreet use of what he told me, but without in any way involving him or his delegation. This worked well, and I was able to keep *The Times* reasonably well-informed. Then, one morning, the Editor sent for me. 'You seem to be getting all the facts from the Conference,' he began. 'It embarrasses me. I don't quite know what to do. You see, I get a full account every evening in the strictest confidence from the people at No. 10. When they see your stuff in the paper the next morning, they obviously think that I have been leaking. I don't like it.' I was able to assure him that my source was perfectly orthodox. He allowed me to continue as before. But it was a near thing. This was the sort of pressure that he was always under. Members of the Cabinet, the Prime Minister himself, would give him all the facts and rely upon him to keep them out of the paper if they came to him from another source. Sometimes he gave way. We were all under this sort of pressure in the office; and when the Editor himself gave way, there was nothing we could do.

In his determination to keep out of *The Times* any news about Nazism that might conflict with the general policy of appeasement, or that might enlighten readers about the true nature of the

Hitler movement and thus make them critical of the government's policy, Dawson was fully supported by Barrington-Ward. This determination involved rather more than cutting out the nasty bits about concentration camps or Norman Ebbutt's circumstantial reports of the Church conflict. It led also to the toning down of criticisms of foreign governments, of foreign Ministers, who were pursuing appeasement policies. In Paris we found that we had to be very circumspect in handling the speeches and activities of Georges Bonnet, the Foreign Minister, who was the high priest of French appeasement in 1938 and 1939. In all this, Barrington-Ward was as rigorous as Dawson ever was. But he was more difficult to deal with: where Dawson had all the normal man's healthy laziness and might thus from time to time let things slip, Barrington-Ward was extremely hardworking and did not miss anything; where Dawson would take a man-of-the-world view of things, Barrington-Ward was conscientious to a degree; where Dawson was at times slapdash, as in the matter of the leading article on the Sudetenland, Barrington-Ward was infuriatingly painstaking. In slightly different circumstances he might have been a Nonconformist Doctor of Divinity with pacifist leanings. His pacifism was rooted in his experiences in the First World War. His bravery earned him both the DSO and the MC; but he could not forget the horror of it all, and was willing to pay almost any price to save the coming generation from the fate that had overtaken him.

The effect of his views on editorial policy was more damaging than Dawson's because they were more deeply felt, and were the product of great moral strivings. At times of crisis, he was highly emotional. On the evening when it was announced that the Nazis had moved into Austria, Barrington-Ward came into the night-editor's room, and paced up and down while clutching his brow. 'We must remain calm,' he said, 'we must remain calm.' So far as I could see, everybody in the room *was* calm, very calm. None of us was excited; we were all depressed and disheartened by this further piece of bad news. But Barrington-Ward was deeply stirred. I never knew whether it was because of the magnitude of the crisis, or because his policy of appeasement was so obviously falling into ruins. He had a more tender conscience than Dawson; and, as regards foreign policy, he was more firmly committed to a narrow set of principles. When he came to writing a leading article, his views would find expression in a sort of nagging do-good-ism that infuriated the foreign reader.

For Dawson as a craftsman I came to have the greatest respect, and I am very glad that I was allowed to spend some months working in Printing House Square while he was in control. He worked at great speed, and his expertise never failed to astonish me. On the days when he was editing, he made up the principal newspage himself—the bill page as it was called. He wrote all the main headlines, and decided how the various items of news were to be arranged. If some reporter was slow in producing his copy, as I was at times, Dawson would send for him, and ask him to give an oral summary of what he was going to write. Then and there, without a moment's hesitation, the headlines would be written. His best leading articles were outstanding. I suppose his denunciation of the Hoare–Laval plan, published under the heading of 'A Corridor for Camels', was one of the most effective leaders he ever wrote. This was anti-appeasement stuff of the most vigorous kind. It certainly took Samuel Hoare by surprise: when he discussed the position with his officials who hurried to Dover to meet him on his return from France to break the bad news to him, he could not understand what all the fuss was about. He thought he had pulled off a great diplomatic coup with his plan. Unlike Hoare, Dawson saw in it an ultimate threat to the Suez Canal and to the imperial connection. Not until it was too late did he detect the greater threat to British interests and British security in Nazi policy.

Dawson pursued his appeasement policy not because he was pro-Nazi but because, as I have already observed, he cared above all else for the imperial connection which helped to maintain the illusion that Britain was a great power. As he saw it, Europe was a tiresome sideshow; and its sordid politics must not be allowed to intrude upon the stage of imperial affairs. Hugh Gaitskell's ideas, thirty years later, ran on much the same lines, although he expressed them rather differently. His famous Brighton speech in October 1962 was in the best imperial tradition, romantic and nostalgic. If we go into Europe, he said, it 'is the end of a thousand years of history. It does mean the end of the Commonwealth. How can one seriously suppose that if the mother country, the centre of the Commonwealth, is a province of Europe it could continue to exist as the mother country of a series of independent nations?' If Dawson and his friends could have heard Harold Wilson say that he was not going to be corralled in Europe—a statement he made before his conversion to the European idea, that is to say before the financial crisis of 1966 and the disastrous Commonwealth Conference in the same year—they could scarcely have refrained from saying that he was one of them.

There is nothing new about this debate on the relative merits of Europe as against the Commonwealth and vice versa. It has gone on in different forms, and in different circumstances, ever since the end of the First World War. What is new is the attitude of some members of the Labour Party towards the ideal of European unity. It is rather like Stalin's. In 1928, when Stalin denounced Briand's plan for a United States of Europe he suggested instead a Federation of Soviet Republics, that is to say an association of like-minded States enjoying the same type of government. Some Labour politicians have very much the same idea; only they want a Federation of Social Democracies, not a Union of Soviets or of Christian Democracies.

The obvious weakness of the Chamberlain–Dawson policy lay in its failure to realize that British prosperity and British security were balanced on a knife-edge, with little room for error. One of the major differences between Britain and America, as Professor Galbraith has pointed out, is that America's wealth provides her government with an immense latitude for mistakes. After all, they can so often be papered over with dollar bills. Government management in Britain, he writes, 'has to be far more precise than it is with us. An average Congress occupying the House of Commons and functioning in accustomed fashion would, on numerous recent occasions, have brought about a fairly prompt liquidation of what remains of the British Empire.' That is why it seems to me to be essential to encourage political debate in Britain instead of stifling it, because only by debate and reasoned argument can a national policy be evolved that takes all the relevant circumstances into account. The policy that was pursued in the 'thirties had not been debated to any extent because so much of the essential information was withheld from the public. When unpleasant facts did come too near the surface, Chamberlain and his friends did their best to cover them up. Even those who knew some of the facts, and who disagreed with the government's policy, preferred to remain loyal to the Party and the government, even at the cost of the national interest, rather than to destroy them by openly attacking Chamberlain. In this respect there is not much difference in kind between them and those Germans who supported Hitler, and those Russians who supported Stalin. They too were reluctant to break away, often out of a misconceived idea of loyalty. Those members of Parliament who by their silences and their votes helped to perpetuate the Chamberlain policy were inspired by some of the same motives.

But party loyalty was not the only factor that contributed to the catastrophe of 1939. There was an almost general loss of nerve; the fear that another war would lead to a universal breakdown that would destroy almost everything that made civilized life possible. There was also the fear that the major beneficiary of such a breakdown would be Stalinism. We are inclined to forget that the Russians in those days were talking in much the same way as the Chinese do today. Paul Reynaud, in his autobiography, recalls that when the French Minister of War in the Laval Cabinet asked the Soviet Ambassador in Paris if the thought of war did not frighten him, the reply was 'Why should it frighten us? *Soviet* Russia came out of the last war. *Soviet* Europe will emerge from the next.' On earlier pages in this book, I have tried to describe the feelings that prevailed throughout Western Europe in the 'thirties; and now, looking back, it seems to me that the failure of nerve was no greater in London than in other capitals. There were people who even wanted Neville Chamberlain to have the Nobel Peace Prize; a not very surprising wish in the light of Stanley Baldwin's moan that the 'bomber would always get through' and Colonel Lindbergh's fearful tales of Nazi air superiority.

Moscow, as Stafford Cripps eventually reported, would have paid almost any price for peace, in spite of the boasts of the Soviet Ambassador in Paris. Among Stalin's first acts, after appointing himself head of the Soviet Government in May 1941, was to establish diplomatic relations with the pro-Nazi government of Iraq, and to ask the Belgian, Norwegian and Yugoslav Governments to wind up their Embassies in Moscow because their Governments had ceased to exist. Molotov himself defended the Nazi–Soviet pact in these terms: 'The art of politics in the sphere of foreign relations does not consist in increasing the number of one's enemies for one's country. On the contrary, the art of politics in this sphere is to reduce the number of such enemies and to make the enemies of yesterday into neighbours maintaining peaceable relations with one another.' Nazi–Soviet friendship lasted for some two years, and the Russians made all sorts of concessions in the hope of keeping Hitler quiet. But eventually they, too, were overwhelmed. When the Soviet Foreign Minister received the Ambassador representing a minor power shortly after the Nazi invasion, his nerve had gone. 'Just imagine,' he moaned, 'just imagine. They did not even give us an ultimatum.' Stalin in some of his more boisterous moods did not hesitate to taunt Molotov with being chicken-hearted. 'And where were you,' he asked, 'when the Nazis invaded? Hiding under the table.' The people who said at the time that the Russians would not fight were right. What they did not allow for was that the Germans would force them to fight. The spirit of the time is best summed up, I think, in the title of one of Professor Namier's books: *Europe in Decay*. Nor was much comfort to be derived from the United States. The Neutrality Act of May 1937 was not calculated to encourage the resisters.

There is, I believe, something profoundly significant about the efforts made in Britain and France after the First World War to sublimate the feelings of hatred and grief created by those fearful casualties in the trenches of Flanders. In the political field, they finally found expression in the policy of appeasement. In emotional and religious terms, we had the Unknown Warrior, canonized, so to speak, in his Tomb in Westminster Abbey. In France, he was laid to rest under the Arc de Triomphe. And when the Unknown Warrior was held up to ridicule or contempt as a Paris audience believed in the play *Le Tombeau sous l'Arc de Triomphe* in February 1924 there was such a commotion that the actors could hardly make themselves heard. 'A large section of the audience,' *The Times* observed, 'loudly protested against what they regarded as the anti-militarist tendency of the play, and it was some time before quiet could be restored and the performance continued.' In Germany, as Georges Bernanos has pointed out, the Unknown Warrior remained among the living in the person of Hitler. The Western leaders could not believe that this victim of trench warfare had survived. In the presence of this vicious and rancorous remnant from the past, their nerve failed them.

With this general loss of nerve, there went also the feeling that a great many things reported from Germany just could not be true; and that Hitler's more bombastic statements were just bits of hyperbole of much the same kind as any politician may find useful during an election campaign. The purges, the concentration camps, the persecution of the Jews, even if they did happen, were isolated events to which one should not pay too much attention. After all, governments had to establish themselves in their own way; and by common consent there was a great deal of spring-cleaning to be done in Germany. This attitude goes, I suppose, with the reluctance of modern man to believe in the reality of sin, in the fact of human wickedness. If you assume that a devil is only a frustrated angel with some unfortunate complexes, then it becomes possible to deal with a man such as Hitler in the belief that a concession here and a concession there will serve to turn him into a responsible member of the community of nations. It was on this assumption that Chamberlain's policy rested. But before we again denounce him for his folly in trusting Hitler in the matter of Czechoslovakia and the Sudetenland, it is perhaps worth noting that Churchill showed just as much confidence in Stalin over Poland. In February 1945, after Stalin had got his way over the Eastern boundary, Churchill told the House of Commons that he knew of no government which stood to its obligations, 'even in its own despite, more solidly than the Russian Soviet Government'. He went on to say, 'I decline absolutely to embark here upon a discussion about Russian good faith'. I offer no criticism of Churchill in supporting Stalin's claim to what was Polish territory in 1939 and in paying tribute to his honesty. He was in an impossible position, and he was fully entitled to plead 'raison d'état'.

When the Germans began to crack on the Eastern front there arose the fear in London and Washington that the Red Army would halt its victory march upon the Curzon Line. It was suspected for a time that when the Russians had got to the new frontier upon which Stalin was determined, they would take no further part in the war. It was therefore essential to keep the Russian dictator in a cooperative frame of mind, and to pander to his views. One does not therefore lightly say that Churchill made the same mistake about Stalin and his promises as Chamberlain made about Hitler. But the fact remains that he did. Like Chamberlain, he assumed that he was dealing with the Head of a

Government, who was rational and whose words could be relied upon. But had they, have we, any right to assume that the leaders of great nations must of necessity be rational? Those of us who defend the policy of the mutual deterrent make just that assumption. We take it for granted that no madman will again force his way into power in Moscow, and that no psychopath will ever be elected to the White House.

The responsibility of the Czechoslovak leaders for the events of 1938 and 1939 is not often mentioned. We have heard over and over again of British guilt and French guilt in forcing the Munich Agreement upon Benes and his government. There are also Germans who want to pin the blame for the Second World War upon the Western Powers. If only the British had stood firm in 1934 or 1935 or 1936, they say, and called Hitler's bluff, for bluff it was, then everything would have turned out differently. But the story begins in Prague. The duty to resist Nazi encroachment fell in the first instance upon the Government of Czechoslovakia, although the equivocal attitude of the Polish Government was an encouragement to irresolution. Benes could have declined the surrender terms that were eventually imposed upon him. This might have led to the outbreak of the Second World War in 1938 instead of in 1939: the risks to Britain and France might have been correspondingly greater, although Churchill has insisted that they would have been less. But Benes, like Chamberlain, was not prepared to take responsibility for such a war. While the analogy is not wholly valid, it is nevertheless tempting to compare the Czechoslovak record in 1938 with that of the Belgians in 1914. King Albert stood firm, although he knew that the Belgian army was ill-prepared to meet the German attack. I remember as a boy hearing from the Belgian soldiers who were quartered upon us in our home on the outskirts of Antwerp, that in the engagement at Liège, some men had had nothing better to fight with than imitation rifles. This may well have been a piece of hyperbole, bred out of defeat and despair, but it illustrates the fears that prevailed at the time and also the feeling that German might and German military equipment were no match for a small country. King Albert must have been well aware of his country's inferiority when, with his Cabinet, he decided to stand firm. The German ultimatum asking for the right of passage through Belgium was presented in Brussels on the evening of 2 August 1914. The

Cabinet rejected it; and on 3 August King Albert sent a telegram to King George making 'a supreme appeal to the diplomatic intervention of Your Majesty's Government to safeguard the integrity of Belgium'. The King was asking for diplomatic intervention, not military support.

CHAPTER 6

IF THE virtue of appeasement eventually turned into the vice of surrender, there was nothing specifically British or French about this transformation. Or even Russian, for that matter, although Stalin was the greatest appeaser of them all. Most of the countries that were overrun in 1940, with the exception of Yugoslavia and Greece, went from appeasement to surrender in much the same way. In this sense, most of the governments of Europe were Chamberlain governments, and all had the same flaw. If the British Government had a greater responsibility than any other, it was, as Harold Nicolson reminded the House of Commons at the time of Munich, because they had a special tradition, a good reputation among the smaller States of Western Europe. They were trusted by them, and they looked to London for leadership. The British Government failed to provide it. All over Europe, the mood was defeatist: Neville Chamberlain reflected that mood. He personified the spirit of the time.

The Times, then, was in tune with the current mood—or at least Dawson and Barrington-Ward were. Casey, the third man in the foreign policy triangle, was not. I find it hard to write of him with restraint. He stood for all that was best on the paper; he was a consistent influence for good; he had as strong a conscience as Barrington-Ward but he did not flaunt it. It did not lead him into enunciating general principles, but rather into encouraging others to work out principles that lay well within the possible, the morally possible. If his father had had a peerage, he might well have had some influence upon Dawson; but Casey was just a generous, perceptive and warm-hearted Irishman. He had tried to establish himself as a barrister in Dublin, but he failed to make enough money to make ends meet. 'One year,' he used to say, 'one brief, one guinea.' So he went into journalism in London. I remember his asking me once if there were any men of distinction or importance in my family. I reflected for a second or two.

'Oh yes,' I said, 'I have an uncle who is a Bishop.' 'That's fine,' he answered. 'You'll be all right on *The Times*.' It would not have helped me if I had gone on to explain that my uncle was at the time the Bishop of Trondheim. Dawson, I suspect, collected the Christian names of peers in much the same way as a Red Indian used to collect scalps. There were occasions of a morning when he found time to gossip with junior members of the staff. He sent for me one day just before lunch and began talking of his experiences of the previous day. 'I was having a word with Edward,' he began, 'about that Czech business.' I must have looked puzzled, because he suddenly stopped. 'You know him, of course?' he asked. I was silent. 'Lord Halifax,' he said impatiently. He went on: 'I was on my way to the Travellers' and I had stopped at the Athenaeum for a wash.'

Casey had worked in every editorial department of *The Times* and knew more about the paper and its ways than most of the others on the staff. He was always accessible to the younger men in the office; always prepared to listen, always prepared to help, but never offering advice to the unreceptive. He was the only man within the editorial hierarchy who appeared to know that human relations mattered, and acted on that knowledge. He could not have done what Dawson did when Norman Ebbutt came up the corridor just outside the Editor's office while on a short visit to London. 'Oh Ebbutt,' Dawson said, 'when are you going back?' Ebbutt, who had only just arrived, was hoping to tell people in the office about the latest developments in Berlin. It goes without saying that Casey would have given him an attentive hearing. He took the trouble to write personal letters to those of us who spent most of our time abroad, and who were therefore out of touch with the cross-currents in the office. He used to write at some length, praising you for some good work that you had done, or telling you candidly that you had made an ass of yourself. He was too kind-hearted to quarrel with anybody. If he thought a man was obnoxious he just avoided him so far as he could. In moments of despair he used to refer to *The Times* office as 'that bloody bureau'. His dislike of the paper's appeasement policy had a physical effect upon him. At the end of a bad working day his face would be flushed, his glance remote, and his voice listless. He would cheer up a little when told that he would be driven home in the Editor's car, in the company of an Irish colleague.

On one occasion they were driven through the streets of London singing Irish songs with an anti-English flavour. Next day he was in a better mood.

Casey had a well-developed sixth sense which no journalist with editorial responsibilities can afford to be without. He often asked me to join him for dinner in a pub in Fleet Street where we used to gossip for an hour or so. When he got back to his desk at about nine o'clock, he would find it covered in galley-proofs: the contents of next morning's papers in the raw. Sometimes he would say: 'Oh, there's nothing here. Nothing worth looking at. I am sure it's all right.' And he would sweep the lot into an enormous waste-paper basket. He was usually right: there *was* nothing wrong: no crumbs for the libel-specialists; no word calculated to raise the blood pressure in Downing Street or the Foreign Office. At other times, he would settle down at once to some serious proof-reading. Under his glance, the errors and misunderstandings became as obvious as beetles in a neglected basement. You could almost see them crawling out of the proofs. Once again, Casey was right. I can think of only one other person who has the same astonishing sense developed to the same degree, namely Sir Campbell Stuart. When Lord Northcliffe put in Stuart over the heads of senior people on the *Daily Mail* to become its Managing Editor, it led to a great deal of bad feeling in the office. And I have been told by one of the men who was then on the staff, that traps were laid in the hope of exposing Stuart's ignorance and innocence. But Stuart never put a foot wrong. He was without detailed editorial experience, but he always knew where the landmines were to be found.

⋆

Those who believe in the conspiratorial theory of history will not find much evidence for it in Printing House Square or in the Foreign Office. It has no relevance to the appeasement years. Looking back upon them now, it seems to me that the main characteristic of British foreign policy at the time was that it was haphazard, casual and unplanned, like so many of the leading articles in *The Times*. It did not seem to occur to those responsible for policy or for public statements that what the British Government did or said had effects all over the world; and that when Neville Chamberlain and Horace Wilson and Geoffrey Dawson thought they were being realistic, our friends abroad thought they were short-sighted and stupid. When Samuel Hoare spoke of giving Italy and other countries access to essential raw materials during the great League of Nations debate in 1935, he held the imagination of all Britain's friends in the world, and particularly of her friends in the smaller nations of Europe. When John Simon produced his tortuous and intellectually dishonest defence of some particularly shabby act by the British Government, and sought to dress it up in the cloak of moral rectitude, he nauseated and antagonized our best friends. A speech by Simon had about the same effect as a lost battle.

Yet his utterances were often haphazard affairs, like the actions and statements of the Government as a whole. Even the appointment of Neville Henderson to the Embassy in Berlin was fortuitous. Many people assumed at the time that his was a carefully hand-picked appointment, and that Neville Chamberlain himself had had a hand in it. But Henderson owed his appointment to an accident. He was in the good books of the Foreign Office because he had accepted without argument an appointment to the Embassy at Buenos Aires, unlike one of his colleagues to whom it had first been offered. When the Berlin post fell vacant, it was thought proper to reward Henderson for his cooperative attitude. His views on Germany and the German problem were not generally known, and when he aired them to a friend in the office, he was advised in his own interest not to lecture Vansittart in the same terms. He remained discreet, at least in so far as Anglo-German relations were concerned, when he saw the Permanent Under-Secretary of State. Vansittart, therefore, did not know what Henderson's views were until his telegrams from Berlin began to come in. They delighted Neville Chamberlain and, later, Horace Wilson. Both took a personal and direct interest in them and by the time Vansittart realized what he was up against, it was too late for him to take action. Neville Henderson had become securely entrenched in the Prime Minister's favour, although most of his colleagues greatly disliked him. There is also the interesting case of Eric Phipps. In Berlin, he was tough and uncompromising. In Paris, he seemed to lose hope. No one could have foreseen that. His reports can hardly have failed to strengthen the views in No. 10 that the French were not to be relied upon.

The inter-relation between French and British policies in this period remains puzzling and confusing, even at this distance of time. I found it then, as I find it now, impossible to distinguish between cause and effect. In London, there was the view that the French were weak, vacillating, unreliable, and too much under the influence of Moscow-dictated Communism, and that no responsible British Government could commit itself to a French line, no matter what it was, without cast-iron assurances that the line would hold. In Paris, on the other hand, it was felt that the British were far too detached, altogether too platonic in their European attitude, too superior towards the benighted and unruly Continentals, and therefore quite incapable of acting in the true interests of Europe. Hitler summed up the prevailing Continental view of British policy in August 1939 when he told his generals that Britain was not taking her commitments to Poland seriously. If she had taken them seriously, he explained, she would not be quarrelling with the Poles over the terms of a miserable credit of £8 millions while investing £500 millions in China. There was also a widespread belief on the Continent that Paris was wholly under the influence of London in this period. Colonel Beck, then Polish Foreign Minister, records in his autobiography that from the end of 1937 up to the outbreak of war, it could be observed that the French Government, even in day-to-day matters, subordinated its foreign policy to the Foreign Office, excepting only in those cases where Soviet Communism made its influence felt externally or internally. It would be nearer the truth to say that the weaknesses and hesitations in London and Paris were mutually contagious, and that each capital blamed the other for its own failings. What is certain is that there were British politicians and officials who did what they could to undermine the French will to resist on those occasions when it seemed as if a more robust policy might be taking shape in Paris.

No doubt Vansittart would have replaced some of the more obvious misfits in the diplomatic service if he had had a free hand. But he had not got it: the Prime Minister and Horace Wilson were taking a strong personal interest in all appointments, and there was little that the Permanent Under-Secretary could do. Increasingly, therefore, an Ambassador's position came to be dependent upon Chamberlain and his entourage. I know of one middle-ranking official who was told in 1938 that his prospects were bleak because of his anti-appeasement views. He reported the facts to Vansittart. 'Nonsense,' he said. 'Horace Wilson hasn't got that kind of influence here.' Before the week was out my friend had been moved to a not particularly attractive post abroad. The Foreign Office in the late 'thirties had become demoralized by the pressure of irrelevant outsiders, and by the prejudices of intolerant politicians.

The reforms that came into effect after the war were designed, in part, to buttress the independence of the Foreign Office and its officials. Under the new regulations, the Treasury cannot interfere as it did in the years before the war. But of course there can be no real protection against the vagaries of a Prime Minister. There was one occasion in Moscow when something went very wrong between the Prime Minister and Clark Kerr—a most extraordinary event, since usually they were on the best of terms. It was a development for which I was in some small degree responsible. I had become more and more impressed by the success with which the Russians appeared to be grabbing left-wing opinion in occupied Europe. British and American broadcasts to Europe, after all, were full of panegyrics to the glorious Red Army. I concluded that this was going to make it increasingly difficult for British foreign policy to pull its weight. So I drafted a minute in which I pointed to the dangers of this development, and observed that Yugoslavia seemed to me to be a text-book case. I expressed no views about the Tito–Mihailovic quarrel; but I emphasized that out of regard for the Yugoslav Royal Family we appeared to be handing over to the Russians a victory in the propaganda war, in spite of all that the Government were doing to help Tito. Clark Kerr thought that my arguments were not unreasonable and, after making some necessary amendments, telegraphed my minute to London over his own signature. The reaction was immediate: there was a stern reproof which, judging by its language, must have been drafted, in part at least, by the Prime Minister himself. Most of it was irrelevant since it described what the Government were doing to help Tito, of which we were all aware, and ignored all the propaganda points that I had tried to make. It was all very tiresome. As a result of this affair, I became unpopular for a while with senior members of the Embassy staff. Another effect was that it soured the Ambassador's relations with Whitehall. Up to that time, he had been very highly thought of. He got his way in most things, all the way from an RAF aircraft for special journeys down to minor matters relating to his own comfort. After his telegram, he was treated as an ordinary mortal, at least for some weeks. His requests met with mysterious delays. Clearly, he was no longer a Hero in that part of Whitehall that mattered to him.

Churchill had other ways of making his displeasure felt, ways that could possibly have dissuaded an Ambassador from expressing a frank opinion that ran contrary to the Prime Minister's own. On one or two occasions in Moscow, he withdrew into a sulk when offered unpalatable advice and insisted upon getting Averell Harriman, the American Ambassador, to come round to talk with him. He would then flaunt their friendship and remind Clark Kerr of the great respect he had for the American's judgment. 'Averell and I have discussed this problem,' he would say. Then he would look at Clark Kerr and ask in a distant sort of voice: 'And what do *you* think, Mr. Ambassador?', carefully avoiding the use of the Christian name. Clark Kerr told me once that when the Prime Minister was in a difficult and contrary mood, there was only one way out. 'I talk to him about his mother,' he said. 'I take him by the arm and we go for a walk in the garden, and I talk to him about his mother. Then his mind and his mood become more receptive.' No regulations can protect the diplomatic service from the sort of Ministerial and departmental pressure I have described. Nor can they prevent Ministers from going their own way, regardless of Ambassadors. Anthony Eden's behaviour over the Suez crisis is proof enough of that.

CHAPTER 7

MY UP-TO-DATE knowledge of the workings of Printing House Square stood me in good stead when I was finally moved to France. The Paris Office of *The Times* in those days was run on curiously anachronistic lines. H. G. Daniels was still there when I arrived; he was the former Berlin correspondent from whom Norman Ebbutt had taken over. He was an aloof figure and I did not see very much of him. He sat in a secluded office of his own, well away from his juniors, and kept regular office hours which none of the others did. In the outer office there were, at one time or another, David Scott, who succeeded Daniels as Chief Correspondent, Thomas Cadett, Darsie Gillie, and Aubrey Jones, who became head of the Prices and Incomes Board under Harold Wilson. *The Times* eventually decided that Thomas Cadett was a better reporter of diplomatic news than David Scott was, and they hived off to him this part of the Paris Correspondent's job. They also decided that I should take over the financial and economic reporting from Paris, apart from the news that normally went into the City pages of the paper, for which they had made separate arrangements. These restrictions left Scott with the descriptive reporting and with responsibility for recording the French political scene, although most of it at the time was governed by economic and financial news and therefore fell to me. Scott was without doubt one of the best descriptive writers of his day; and whenever that sort of job came his way—the destruction of the R101 springs to mind in this connection—the result was superb. It seemed to us that these arrangements were not altogether fair to him. After all, he was the Chief Correspondent and the most important jobs, the policy jobs, so to speak, should have been left to him. Scott did not take kindly to them either; after a while he resigned and went to the *News Chronicle*. Although he did very well for a while, I am sure that he was wrong to leave. What he failed to realize was that the style of reporting at which he excelled needed a great deal of space and that only *The Times* could provide it. The *News Chronicle* was too cramped to accommodate his work with any comfort.

Darsie Gillie, who knew more about the French political scene than most other foreign correspondents in Paris, came to *The Times* after the absorption of the *Morning Post* by the *Daily Telegraph*. Before that, he had been the *Morning Post*'s correspondent in Warsaw. There, too, he had become a recognized authority on the local scene. He did not stay very long with *The Times*; and after his war-time spell as head of the French section of the BBC, he went to the *Guardian*, whose Paris correspondent he remained for some twenty years. His nonconformist spirit still haunts the corridors of the BBC, and so do the legends of his great battles with authority. The *Guardian*, under its brilliant Editor, Wadsworth, adapted itself to Gillie's ways, not the other way round. Gillie was not successful in adjusting himself to the ways of *The Times*, with its fixed routines and its rigid time-tables. In matters of this kind, Gillie was an anarchist. On the *Guardian* he could select the topics that interested him most and leave the rest of the news to Reuter's and the other news agencies. This arrangement worked to everybody's advantage, because it was soon discovered that what interested Gillie also interested the paper's readers. The *Guardian* did not ask him to supply a complete news service from France, as we had to do on *The Times* where the rules were strict. If, on occasion, *The Times* printed a report from France that had come, not from us, but from a news agency, we regarded it as a disaster. There would be a sharp reminder from the Foreign News Editor if we failed more than once or twice to supply the news that had come in during the evening or the night from other sources.

We never regarded Aubrey Jones as a permanent resident in the world of journalism. He wanted to gain experience in a foreign country, and I am sure he learned many useful things in Paris, and particularly the need to avoid purple passages in bread-and-butter journalism. He had a weakness in those days for esoteric adjectives. He wrote one piece in which he recorded his impressions of Paris at dawn, and described the milk cans he had seen as 'astonished'. For days we quoted this passage at him; and Thomas Cadett even sang it to a tune of his own composition.

I do not believe that Aubrey Jones enjoyed himself in our company. I am sure that the office was too noisy a place for a man of his temperament. And I am sure also that he did not approve of the practical jokes we played. He was far too serious-minded for that. I suppose that if I were pressed to explain all this schoolboy behaviour, I might rationalize and say the reason was that we were angered and frustrated by the editorial policy of *The Times*, and by the way—but this came later—our criticisms of Bonnet, the Foreign Minister, were doctored by the Editor. I am afraid this laboured explanation would not be true. It was just one of those things.

Alexander Werth, who was the Paris correspondent of the *Manchester Guardian* (as it was then) in the years before the war, was another skilful reporter and knowledgeable observer of the French political scene. He had many useful contacts among the politicians of the Left, something that stood him in very good stead in the Front Populaire era. His books on France were exceptionally well-informed, but I thought at the time that his black characters were far too black. The *Guardian* no doubt encouraged him in this, for the paper's enthusiasm for the Front Populaire appeared to be unbounded. What Werth did succeed in doing, to an extent that few others did, was to bring the French story to life and to make it exciting and worth reading.

Many explanations have been offered for the French débâcle in 1940. Some have said there was treason on the Right. Others have argued that there was betrayal on the Left. There was blindness everywhere and complacency in high places, not least in the leadership of the army. Yet that does not altogether explain why France was defeated more completely than any other country among the Allied and Associated powers. It is true that the Danes put up even less resistance to the advancing German armies than the French did; but Danish morale was not broken to the extent that French was. So the question of the French collapse remains. One reason, perhaps, is that the French are a nation of sceptics. The national religion is the religion of doubt; a persistent determination to look for mercenary or contemptible motives in every action no matter how noble. Many of us became very conscious of this in the 'thirties. There was no faith: no faith in God, or in France, or in man. No one believed that men in public life could be honest. As Chesterton might have said, their scepticism had cast them out of life. They lived in a grey world of suspicion in which nothing was worth fighting for. When the challenge came in 1939 and 1940 there was no faith to meet it. The Poles did not collapse into inertia, nor did the Serbs; although from any rational point of view, their position, unlike the French, was without hope.

De Gaulle's achievement has been to lift the people of France out of the morass of doubt and despair, at least for a time. But the old spirit of scepticism and disbelief has not been eradicated; and one notices its presence among young people in particular. It comes out sharply when you discuss with them such questions as the war in Vietnam. They express their views in a mixture of Gaullist and Marxist terms, using a sophisticated vocabulary, with no independent thought behind it. They say they are convinced that the main reason, perhaps the only reason, for the American presence in Vietnam is that the Americans are in quest of loot, in search of profits and dividends. There are great commercial concessions to be had in South-East Asia, I have been told; and there are vast profits to be made by getting and keeping a foothold there. They look upon me as a badly-informed romantic when I try to argue that the great tragedy of American foreign policy is that it is so well-meaning and often so altruistic. I cannot make them believe that the Americans are a crusading people always trying to do good, and wanting to impose order and happiness upon the world, even if it may mean the use of force on occasion to achieve the sort of perfection that American idealism aspires to. As George Kennan wrote in 1954, when discussing the foreign policy of the United States Government: 'We saw ourselves moving benevolently, helpfully, among the waiting peoples of the world, our experience now finally recognized as relevant to a wider sphere of humanity, our virtues no longer just the virtues of the American frontier, but the virtues of the world at large.' The Americans, in short, are members of the sort of philanthropic society that is described in Gogol's *Dead Souls*: 'A society with the very broad aim of bringing enduring happiness to the whole of mankind from the banks of the Thames as far as Kamchatka.'

This belief that altruism is just another word for self-interest lies at the root of many of the deepest Franco-American misunderstandings. It was responsible, too, for many Anglo-French differences before the war. Never were French doubts of British motives more acute than at the time of the Italo-Abyssinian war. Our friends and acquaintances in Paris could not believe that intelligent people in Britain had other than commercial motives in mind when demanding sanctions. In their eyes, the call for them was humbug. The thought that one or two Ministers might actually have been honest when they spoke of the rule of law did not occur to them. It seemed much more plausible that British politicians were defending their shareholding interests, and their investments generally. Throughout the whole of that period and then again during the Spanish Civil War the atmosphere in Paris was distinctly unpleasant. Among the well-to-do, there was a current of opinion that was strongly anti-British, and in the more prosperous parts of Paris one was often conscious of it. What aroused the bitterest feelings was the belief that the British Government, for commercial reasons, were determined to check political movements in Italy, in Germany and in Spain that were keeping Communism at bay.

One Saturday evening during the height of the Abyssinian crisis we went to a cinema to see the latest newsreels from the war. The camera-man had shot some very good scenes showing the Emperor of Abyssinia; and after all the cheers with which the audience had greeted pictures of Mussolini, my friends and I thought we should clap our hands discreetly in order to show where our sympathies lay. We were booed and hissed by the audience; and the atmosphere became so unpleasant that we came away. It was during the Abyssinian crisis, too, that the prosperous people of Paris went through a novel and, for them, an unnerving experience. A group of well-dressed people might gather outside come café or other shouting *Vive l'Italie* or something like that. The police would ask them to move on. If they did not, the *flics* would move in sharply, swinging their heavy cloaks before them, and cutting a swathe through the crowd. It is all very well for the poor to be pushed around by the police but for prosperous citizens to be manhandled is an altogether different story. The women, in particular, were not accustomed to being treated with lack of respect by common men in uniform. They did what they could to prove that they were good and law-abiding citizens; they even shouted *Vive la police* in a voice they no doubt hoped sounded convincing. But it did not do them any good. They, too, were swished out of the way with the rest.

The West-enders of Paris had perhaps good reason to be fearful of Communism. Possibly, too, past sins had given them a guilty conscience. In some villages, *curés* had appeared on the same platform as Communist speakers during the election campaign that led to the Front Populaire victory at the polls. If, as is argued on an earlier page, the Communists had been less subservient to Moscow (or alternatively, if Stalin had been a little more perceptive) and less willing to say that white was black when Stalin told them to say it, they might have exercised a dominant influence on French politics. Something that has long puzzled me about the French is that in matters of religious faith there has always been a slight edginess in the relations between their Church and the Vatican. There has always been a whiff of heresy in the air; but within the secular religion of Communism, orthodoxy has been impeccable. Thorez and his men have been abject in their obedience. It is one of the puzzles of French history, of the French character.

If the Communists in France were subservient, the Socialists were spineless. Their leader, Léon Blum, lacked the ruthlessness that was so essential in the late 'thirties. As a man who could bring ideas to life and who could inspire others, he was superb. As a man of action, he was a failure. His difficulties and dilemmas were of the same order as those that faced our own Labour Party at the time. His supporters wanted a coherent foreign policy; they wanted their country to stand up to the dictators, above all to Mussolini for whom they had a great contempt, as indeed many Frenchmen had at the time. When discussing Laval's agreement with Mussolini on the Abyssinian question with a senior French official some months after the end of the Italo-Abyssinian war, I was told that no one could understand why British people had got so worked up about it. 'It's all very simple,' my informant said. 'You give the Italians all they ask for until a war breaks out. Then you take it all back.' Those who supported the Front Populaire did not want to pay for arms. They wanted social welfare in the first place, and they got it. This meant that the price for standing firm could not be paid. At the root of this attitude lay the assumption, implicit or explicit, that France had ceased to be a great power and could no longer undertake the same responsibilities as in the past. We had a very hot discussion on this topic one day with the Assistant Secretary-General of the French Trade Union Confederation, Belin. He argued fiercely against a strong foreign policy. He insisted that France had to accept the fact that she had now become a smaller power, unable to exercise much influence in the world. She could not, he said, give effective support to her friends in Eastern Europe. She would have to make her position quite clear, without equivocation. All that France would be able to do in the future would be to defend her own territory, metropolitan France. There was no trace of cynicism in all this; Belin was speaking from the heart, with passionate conviction. He was honest and did not disguise his views behind a commonplace set of clichés about peace and honour and the rights of self-determination and the injustices of the Treaty of Versailles.

Arguments of this kind, especially when coming from a non-Communist trade union source, were grist to the Nazi mill. The Germans used them effectively in Eastern Europe; and eventually they began treating the French with open contempt. How far they dared to go became apparent during the official visit that Ribbentrop paid to Paris at the end of 1938. He stayed at the Hôtel Crillon on the Place de la Concorde, and large sections of this great square had to be cordoned off to ensure his safety. On the roof of the hotel there stood policemen armed with rifles: their threatening figures could be seen clearly outlined against the autumn sky. Large parts of the West-end of Paris seemed to have been occupied by security forces in the Nazi interest. The crowning indignity was the invitation of a number of distinguished public figures to a banquet for which the menu included *Jambon de Prague*, as Thomas Cadett reported at the time. The invitations were sent out in German, instead of in French as they should have been in accordance with correct diplomatic usage; and several were returned to the German Embassy with the request for a translation. German, the writers explained, was a language they did not understand. Ribbentrop had come to Paris as a conqueror, flaunting his diplomatic triumphs. It was not until this humiliating visit that the ordinary Frenchman understood what had happened to the Europe he thought he knew. People turned their eyes away when you mentioned his name to them; the comments of taxi-drivers and concierges were unprintable.

They had been given a preview of the catastrophe of 1940.

From the year 1937 onwards we all lived in a world of confusion and doubt. Every familiar point in the political landscape seemed to be shifting position. Those of us who worked in *The Times* office felt that Printing House Square was constantly letting us down by contradicting in its leaders almost every point that we tried to make in the news columns. Some of us looked for other jobs in the hope of finding something that was not too uncongenial, and I myself applied for a job with the BBC but failed to get it. From time to time, visitors came in to commiserate with us, or, alternatively, to insist that we were misguided in criticizing Dawson's editorial policy. Among these latter was Margot Asquith. She turned up in the office once or twice a year and occupied for hours on end the only comfortable chair we had. Her conversation was always topical and absorbing. The account she gave us one day of a call she had paid on Mussolini was hilarious. It ran on something like these lines: 'I was punctual for my appointment. I always am. But he kept me hanging about. And I don't like waiting. So I made a lot of noise as near as I could to the door of what I took to be his room. Eventually, he came out to greet me. There was a smile on his face. I noticed that he was wearing breeches and riding-boots. I told him that I didn't like men who rode indoors. The remark passed over his head. Then he invited me to sit down on some sort of couch or settle at the far end of the room. "May I sit next to you?" he asked. "No, Your Excellency," I replied. "I can't talk to men sideways." So he moved away.

'After a while he began to talk about a party I had attended at the British Embassy the evening before. "You said something that was not very nice," he complained. "You said that three British capital ships would be able to blow the whole Italian navy out of the water." I had quite forgotten what I did say,' Margot Asquith added, 'but I was not going to let him get away with that. "You seem to have got part of the story right, Your Excellency," I said. "But I think you should instruct your agents to be more accurate. I said that two capital ships could do the job." There was not very much more to be said after that, but he invited me to come again.'

We lunched with her occasionally at the Ritz where she was a fairly conspicuous figure, partly, I think, because she often drank a glass of beer—or what appeared to be beer—through a noisy straw. It was by no means easy to carry on any kind of conversation with her. She might begin by putting a question to you, and when you were launched upon an answer, her eyes and her mind would wander. 'Look at that extraordinary woman over there,' she would say. 'Look now, at once, or you may miss her.' We used to come away exhausted from these encounters. But her conversation, her stories of battles with important people were always worth listening to, and only a fool would have interrupted the flow of her words. Her conversation moved back and forth across a great expanse of time, as if the passage of days and weeks and years had lost its meaning for her. Yesterday, today and tomorrow were as one.

She had been asked, she once told us, to speak to King George V about the bad effect of his bullying methods upon his children. A lot of names had been put forward for this unenviable job; and ultimately it had fallen to her to do it. Not only was she the Prime Minister's consort; she was also Margot. 'I remember it all very clearly,' she began. 'I walked out upon the terrace with him after luncheon. It was at Windsor. I am sure of that. And I began very carefully. I told him how very wrong it was to keep the Prince of Wales at arm's length; and how his disciplinary methods were bound to have a bad effect upon Prince Albert. The King was not pleased. He told me, in polite language, to mind my own business.' And then there was her caustic comment on the resignation of Anthony Eden in 1938. We had a long discussion with her about the whole political background, and about the events that precipitated Eden's action. She was not impressed. 'When we were Prime Minister,' she said primly, 'young men never resigned.' She did not again refer to him.

To those of us who had doubts about Neville Chamberlain's foreign policy, Eden stood as a symbol of the only possible alternative. Anti-appeasers throughout Europe also regarded him as a symbol, and they looked upon his resignation as a final confirmation of all their fears. I wrote a long and despairing letter about this to a friend in the Labour Party who suggested that he would take me along to see the Leader of the Opposition when next I was in London. It would be useful, he thought, if I could tell Attlee just what I had written in my letter. I came back to

London within a week or two, and got in touch with my friend, who took me along to Attlee's room in the House of Commons. I told my story to him; I said I thought that the disappearance of Anthony Eden could not fail to impair the credibility of British foreign policy unless the decision had already been taken to surrender everything; and that every waverer in Europe would now be convinced that surrender was inevitable. I cannot recall that Attlee made any reply to what I said; although he may have muttered yes once or twice. All that I do remember is that he said thank you and that I withdrew with my tail between my legs. He made me feel as if I had strayed into a field from which all trespassers were barred; and that if I would only mind my own business he would have more time to mind his.

Another regular visitor to *The Times* office in Paris was Margot Asquith's daughter, Princess Elizabeth Bibesco. She greatly admired Léon Blum, and I suspect she thought we were not giving him enough of a boost in the columns of *The Times*. So she wrote a very eulogistic article which duly appeared under the title: 'Léon Blum—The "Aristocrate" of the Left. By a Friend.' A rather silly headline, I thought at the time. I do not think it did the Socialist leader any good. Praise for left-wing leaders from persons of prominence in Britain was not highly regarded by the respectable part of Paris. This was partly because they assumed that the British were still pursuing the old Palmerstonian policy of encouraging revolution abroad while pursuing a conservative policy at home; and partly because the Left had not yet been absorbed into respectable society. It was reluctantly accepted that the British Ambassador might be under the professional obligation to meet left-wing politicians but he would have been found guilty of an unpardonable solecism if he had invited anyone to the left of Herriot to a social function to which respectable French people had also been invited. I do not therefore believe that Elizabeth Bibesco's well-meant praise of Blum did him, or his Government, any good at all. I myself wrote a piece in defence of some of the financial measures carried out by his Government. When it was quoted in the Senate, Caillaux treated it with noisy contempt.

Elizabeth Bibesco and her husband took us to dinner one evening at the Rumanian Pavilion in that sinister Paris Exhibition of 1937. I call it sinister because it symbolized and illustrated both the tense international situation and the prevailing chaos in France. Only the German, Russian and Italian pavilions were ready on the opening day. Some of the others, so far as I can remember, were never finished. And everybody blamed the Front Populaire Government for this: the long holidays with pay, and the shortened working week had made it impossible to complete the Exhibition, just as they were making it impossible to produce the armaments required to give substance to French foreign policy. The German and Russian pavilions were in full order, and glowered at each other in mute hostility. They occupied more space than any of the other national pavilions and, in particular, far more than the British. In the circumstances of the time, the British pavilion was a pathetic affair. Its main display was of horses and cricket-bats and tennis rackets, or rather photographs of these symbols of a prosperous peace. No doubt the person responsible for the exhibits had set out to demonstrate that Britain was not only a country of decent sportsmen, but also of honest peacemongers. Its effect was lamentable.

The inner ring of politicians in Paris, as in London, were at cross-purposes and arguing bitterly among themselves, but without much conviction, about the sort of policy that would best suit the circumstances of the time. Most French journalists, or rather most French newspaper proprietors, were on the appeasement side. But there were some stalwart exceptions, such as Pertinax of the *Echo de Paris* and the erratic Geneviève Tabouis of *L'Oeuvre*. La Tabouis, incidentally, was as difficult to pin down in a conversation as Margot Asquith. Her monologues were amusing and often brilliant, but they were monologues. Some years after the war, she wrote to Harold Nicolson to announce that she was coming over to London and that she wanted to see him on a matter of urgent importance. Nicolson telephoned me to say that he had invited La Tabouis to lunch and asked me to join the party. I accepted with enthusiasm, in the hope of listening to some good talk. But it was a monologue. Geneviève Tabouis talked all the time. Nicolson hardly got a word in. He gave us a good lunch but I am sure that La Tabouis was not conscious of it. She was too absorbed in her own chatter. She just talked of this and that and not very coherently. And when it was all over and she had gone, Nicolson turned to me and said: 'I wonder what she wanted?' I do not think he was ever told.

Her stamina and staying-power would put many young men to shame. She was among the three or four journalists who had the strength and the patience to wait outside the *Palais des Nations* in Geneva in the summer of 1954 to pick up the latest news about the Indo-Chinese armistice talks. It was a very chilly summer night, with a suspicion of drizzle in the air, and the news did not come out until dawn. But La Tabouis was not put off. She remained on duty with a handful of others. A long working day did not affect her spirits; she was always tingling with energy.

The confusion in matters of foreign policy was even more complete in Paris at the time than in London. Ministers were openly at loggerheads. Georges Bonnet, the Foreign Minister, was barely on speaking terms with Paul Reynaud, the Minister of Justice and later Minister of Finance, or with Georges Mandel, the tough Minister of Communications. Mandel had the magic of leadership in him, and I believe that the record in 1938 and 1939 and 1940 would have been very different if he had had the necessary authority. But unfortunately for France he was a Jew; and given the prejudices of the time he would never have been given the necessary powers. The leadership of the anti-appeasement group in politics therefore fell to Paul Reynaud. We used to go and see him regularly to find out what was happening. He was very frank with us and made no effort to hide his opinions of his colleagues, and least of all his opinion of Bonnet for whom he had a great contempt. On one occasion that is still very fresh in my mind, he asked me to slip out by the back door of his Ministry so as not to be seen. He suspected that one of his junior officials, perhaps even one of the *huissiers*, had been given the job of reporting on his visitors to Bonnet who wanted to prevent at almost any cost the leakage of foreign policy information to the press. We used to see Bonnet from time to time, but I cannot recall ever having had a discussion with him. He may well have been a charming and well-meaning man in private life, but Bonnet the politician we found detestable.

I became convinced that financial interests in both Paris and London played a dubious part on the foreign exchange market at various crucial stages in the appeasement policies of the French and British Governments. Whatever the explanation, there was the extraordinary fact that when the French Cabinet showed signs of firmness in relation to the Nazis, there would be a wave of selling of francs. The same curious movements took place in sterling. I am familiar with all the arguments in favour of a free market economy, and with the theory that fluctuations iron themselves out over a period of time; but they can do a lot of political damage before they are ironed out. The heavy sales of francs and sterling that took place at intervals in 1937 and 1938 went far beyond normal market movements. I had got to know a senior official at the Bank of France shortly after my arrival in Paris. He knew a great deal about the operations of the Exchange Equalization Fund; and when he realized that I could be trusted not to rush into print with what he told me or try to use it for speculative purposes, he found it possible to tell me what was actually happening; to give me the names of the banks through which the sales came; and the actual volume of business done by them. He was a man of character and integrity who hated the tricks and intrigues with which the foreign policy of France was being conducted at the time. He thought that the policy of appeasement, or rather the dishonesty with which it was being presented, would almost certainly lead his country to disaster.

One afternoon when I went to see him, he was very unhappy. He told me that they had had a black day. There had been a great pressure to sell sterling. It had come near to demoralizing the market. And he explained that something like one half of the total world sales of sterling had come through one London bank. It is, of course, quite possible that by some strange coincidence on that particular day most people who were selling their pounds had decided to pass their orders through the same bank. But it is easier to believe, and seems rather more probable to me, that the bank in question had been urging its contacts and correspondents throughout the world to sell sterling. The bank wanted to make sure, my friend argued, that the policy of appeasement was maintained. Everything that I have since learnt confirms me in the view that these exchange operations, when backed by well-planned propaganda, preferably oral so as to make it more difficult to trace, and designed to spread doubt and suspicion, can and do have the effect of influencing the acts of governments.

I have no doubt at all that some of the weakness of the pound under the Wilson Government has been due to French political selling. When Patrick Gordon Walker and Douglas Jay went to that dreadful meeting of the European Free Trade

Association in Geneva in November 1964, they were driven in self-defence into painting the short-term prospects for the British economy in gloomy colours; and this provided ample raw material for those who at the time were running a propaganda campaign against the pound. And I am sure that French interests played a considerable part in the selling operation. On Monday, 23 November, it will be recalled, the bank rate was raised to the crisis level of seven per cent. On the preceding Friday evening I had been told by a French friend that sterling was having a very sticky time, and that the visible reserves of the Bank of England were virtually exhausted. 'Why,' he said, 'don't your people come to Paris? We could have given them the money; enough money to hold on.' It is by no means inconceivable that French interests hoped at the time to divert the British financial connection from New York to Paris and the Continent generally; or, at the very least, to make London dependent upon Paris rather than upon New York. I still do not know whether the suggestion made to me late on that Friday evening, and the facts that were to be revealed to the public three days later, were just a coincidence.

It is a valid criticism of Mr. Wilson's Government to say that it was taken by surprise in the late autumn of 1964 by the events that took place soon after it came into office. Anyone with any knowledge of the mental processes of the financial community must know that it is bound to be apprehensive when a government of the Left takes office. The bankers and financiers were frightened when the Front Populaire took over in France in 1936; they went into hysterics when the first Labour Government took office in Norway in 1928; they suffered from sleepless nights when the Social Democrats took over the Government of Sweden in 1935, although they were soon reassured. If there was no great sterling panic in 1945 when the Labour Government was returned with a large majority, that was because there were so many financial controls as to make it very difficult for currency speculators to put their funds out of danger. But it is perhaps worth recalling that the American loan to Britain, so painfully negotiated by Keynes, was exhausted within a few months. A contributory factor, perhaps, was the advice given by one London banker to his American counterpart not to advance any more funds to the British Government until it had got the country's finances into better shape.

There was certainly never any doubt in my mind that the appeasement forces were backed by powerful financial interests. The people involved were not pro-Nazi or pro-German; they were just frightened. They were convinced that war would lead to the collapse of Europe into anarchy and Communism. They operated at all levels; on the foreign exchange market; on the stock exchange; in diplomacy; in politics; through the press. If it is true that the public as a whole shared their views and that the current of opinion was in favour of 'understanding Germany', it is also true that these financial interests helped to mould public opinion. Otherwise there would not have been those cheers outside No. 10 Downing Street when Chamberlain came back from Munich with the claim that he had brought back peace in our time. Nor is it irrelevant to remember that if French Cabinet Ministers had to lie in order to get their way, the British Government had a far easier was out. All *its* members had to say was that they could do nothing without consulting the Commonwealth. And the Commonwealth would then be encouraged or persuaded to express views that coincided with the prevailing winds in London. If someone like John Simon was then put up to give a moral twist to bad advice, the British case appeared to be watertight, at least as seen from the auditorium. From the wings, it looked rather different.

Whatever we may think of some French politicians and their dishonesty in the appeasement years, it is important not to forget that they were aided and abetted by certain British politicians and officials in what they did. When Chamberlain made his second broadcast in that strange interlude that ended with Munich, he gave some of us the impression that he was preparing the public for bad news. On 27 September, after returning from Godesberg, his voice strained, he described Hitler's attitude as unreasonable. 'I would not hesitate to pay even a third visit to Germany if I thought it would do any good. But at this moment I can see nothing further that I can usefully do in the way of mediation. . . . I am myself a man of peace to the depths of my soul . . . but if I were convinced that any nation had made up its mind to dominate the world by fear of its force, I should feel that it must be resisted.' It sounded like a warning to the British public as well as to Hitler, and a reassurance to the French that there was a point beyond which the British Government would not go. Within minutes of the end of the broadcast, a senior British official telephoned to Reynaud to ask him if he had heard it. He then tried to convince Reynaud that Chamberlain was on the point of climbing down; and that the thing to look for was the hidden meaning behind some of the obscurities of language. The intention was clearly to cast doubt on Chamberlain's firmness and so to keep French Ministers in a malleable frame of mind. But Reynaud was not moved by this message. He was still too tough; and he remained a powerful force in French politics until his mistress destroyed his will to resist.

In 1938 and 1939 he took a very robust view of the intrigues and plots that were current in Paris. He came to lunch with us one day to meet Vansittart who, by that time, had been put on the shelf as Chief Diplomatic Adviser to the Government. Reynaud came in with a broad grin and a flourish. 'Gentlemen,' he said, 'may I introduce myself? *Voici le buveur de sang*.' It was as a blood-thirsty warmonger that he was habitually described in the right-wing gutter-press of the time. He went on to tell us how he was doing his utmost to thwart the efforts of those who were working for bigger and better appeasement. 'I did agree with my colleagues that we should send Marshal Pétain as special Ambassador to Spain,' he said. 'That will certainly please the Right. He will be smothered in decorations and horse-feathers. That should keep them quiet for a while. Good luck to him.' And he raised his glass.

When Reynaud was transferred from the Ministry of Justice to the Ministry of Finance, he made it clear that he was going to deal severely with income tax evaders. He was going to force the well-to-do to pay taxes, not in accordance with the figures shown in their tax returns, but on the evidence of their visible expenditure. He told me that he had appointed a number of inspectors who had been making discreet inquiries into the sort of expenditure that rich people in the West-end of Paris were incurring. If they could establish that a man had a Rolls-Royce and a yacht and was keeping a couple of *midinettes* while his tax return showed that he was earning a miserable £1,000 a year, the Ministry would take action. They would assess him for, say, £10,000 and leave it to the victim to prove that he was making nothing like as much. Reynaud added that they had already had several interesting cases on their books but they had had no protests worth the term.

Their absence proved, he thought, that the arbitrary assessment was not high enough; and he would do better in future. His policies did not, of course, endear him to the rich. They felt themselves very much on the same side as the gangsters of the extreme Right who denounced him as a dangerous war-monger.

Most income tax returns in France are works of fiction; and all Ministers of Finance who try to inject some element of truth into them become excessively unpopular. One rather under-sized Minister in the middle 'thirties became the butt of the cartoonists under the caption 'Public Enemy No. 0.5'. The authorities were always on the look-out for a simple method of getting people with sizeable incomes to make a reasonable contribution to the national exchequer. In the case of foreign journalists living in Paris this led to some strange anomalies. I myself was allowed to choose between sending in a normal return, or accepting an assessment made for me by the inspectors. I chose the latter method when I discovered how the thing was worked. I was first asked what rent I was paying: the figure the inspector wanted was the net rent, exclusive of central heating, water rates, *concierge* charges and so on. He multiplied this figure by five and told me that the product would be regarded as my gross income. He then noted that since I was a journalist, he could allow me a deduction of 30 per cent from my gross income for professional expenses. So the figures worked out at something like these: rent, £100; gross income, £500; expenses, £150; taxable income, £350. I accepted my assessment without argument but also without visible enthusiasm.

While Reynaud thought he was beginning to succeed in bringing the rich to heel, his policies were not very effective in keeping prices down. I wrote a piece in the paper at the time and concluded that life in Paris was becoming increasingly expensive. Gaston Palewski, Reynaud's *Chef de Cabinet*, sent for me and told me that the Minister was most upset by my comments and that I was not being helpful—the usual complaint made by politicians when press comment goes against them. A fortnight later, Palewski again asked me to call on him. 'I want to talk to you about the cost of living,' he began as soon as I came into his office. 'I managed to get away for a few days last week. I went into the country. And I did find that lots of things had gone up and had become very expensive. I am sorry to say that you were quite right in what you reported.' And then he looked at the button-hole in the lapel of my jacket. He fingered it absent-mindedly. 'There's nothing there,' he said. 'It would look nice with a small ribbon, wouldn't it?' But the decoration was never offered. I was to meet Palewski again, shortly after the fall of France. We were having lunch at the same club and I caught sight of him hurrying through the lobby. I took him by the arm and asked him how things were. 'Alas,' he said. 'I am a poor refugee.' I told him that it would be very pleasant if we could meet over a meal, and asked him where he was staying. 'With the Rothschilds,' he replied mournfully.

In the late spring of 1939 I was asked to call on Sir Campbell Stuart who had just arrived in Paris and was staying at the Hôtel Crillon. It was a warm, bright day, and Paris was at its best; the *terrasses* were crowded with people enjoying their apéritifs and coffees. When I arrived at the Crillon, the Hall Porter told me that Stuart was not feeling well, and that he was in bed. But he undertook to ask if he would be prepared to see me. I was told to go up. When I opened the door, I found that I had stepped into an over-heated dark-room. After the brightness outside it took a minute or two to get used to the unexpected gloom. I then saw that the blinds had been pulled down to keep out the sun; and that the windows had been shut to keep out the draught. Stuart was lying on his bed, on top of the bed-clothes, wrapped in an immense dressing-gown. I could just see the gent's full-length heavy wool underpants running into his socks. His bedside table was decorated with medicine glasses and tumblers of various sizes and medicine bottles. He had got some sort of cold, and he believed that his life teetered on the threshold of death. But he managed to give me a smile from the edge of the grave; and to speak a few words, in a husky Canadian voice, about the imminence of war. He told me that because of his experience in the First World War, the Prime Minister had asked him to take on the running of an enemy propaganda department, whose foundations were now being laid, in case the worst happened. Would I care to join him? All the details would have to be settled in due course: things like my release from *The Times*, my specific duties, my salary. I said yes without any hesitation; I was flattered by his invitation. Stuart waved an emaciated hand at me. Thank you, he sighed softly. I tip-toed out of the room, leaving the invalid to nurse his illness in gloomy solitude. I was told later that if war did break out, I should be sent for; that I should have to leave Paris at short notice, and to report to Electra House on the Victoria Embankment so soon as I arrived. It was not until after the war had broken out that I was told what my final destination was to be.

PART TWO

POLITICAL WARFARE: WOBURN; ALGIERS; CAIRO

CHAPTER 8

I WAS DRIVEN off to a secret destination almost as soon as I got back to London. I reported for duty with a few belongings at Electra House on the Victoria Embankment on the morning after my arrival from Paris. There I found a small group of people waiting, and three or four cars drawn up to take us away. We did not know our address until we arrived at Woburn Park, although we had our suspicions when we drove through Luton. The Riding School attached to the Abbey had been partitioned off into rabbit-hutches to form offices, while in the Abbey itself the old Duke was still in residence. He did not take kindly to this invasion by a mixed bag of journalists, advertising executives, novelists and Foreign Office officials. But, as he confided to a friend, it might have been a good deal worse; if he had refused to accommodate all those dreadful temporary civil servants, he might instead have been afflicted with evacuee children from the East End of London. It was not until his death in 1940 that we moved into the main building. Much of it had been converted into offices for us, although such museum pieces as the bedroom in which Queen Victoria had once spent a night were left untouched. The place was so enormous and had so many large windows that the men responsible for ensuring that the black-out was fool-proof began their work at around two in the afternoon during the winter.

The trouble with Woburn Park in September 1939 was that it was full of deer, ferocious deer, some said. Many of us were afraid of them. There was one awful morning when two of my colleagues who had done Home Guard duty, came in looking wet, dishevelled and distraught. They had spent the whole of the night crouching in a ditch, sheltering from deer that had become fiercely bellicose in the rutting season. My colleagues went about with sticks after that. There is also the story, possibly apocryphal, that Campbell

Stuart, shortly after his arrival, asked the Duke's agent for a chart showing the precise location of each and every deer in the Park so that he might manoeuvre with safety during an after-lunch walk. He lived half a mile away from the Abbey and its riding school in a place called Paris House. This was a strange timber building that had been on exhibition in Paris in 1889 and which had greatly impressed the then Duke of Bedford. He bought it as it stood, had it dismantled and transported to Woburn. The Duchess used to lend it to friends and distant relatives. I spent many pleasant evenings there; the house was comfortable and easily heated.

All of us in the Enemy Propaganda Department, known as Department E. H., (derived from Electra House), were put up in different houses in the neighbourhood of Woburn, some in Bedfordshire, others in Buckinghamshire. I myself was exceptionally fortunate. I had been allocated a room in a house in the village of Eversholt which turned out to be the home of the Duke's chief agent, Colonel Gordon. There were four or five of us living there, and we must have been an abominable nuisance to the Colonel and his wife, since we could not help but wreck their peaceful and well-ordered domestic existence. But they remained patient, kind and cheerful in circumstances that must have been very trying for them. Rex Leeper was there for a short time until he moved into another house in the neighbourhood, a house that formed the headquarters of the Political Intelligence Department of the Foreign Office. Valentine Williams, the author of the Club Foot novels, was also there, until he and I moved into another house in the village of Woburn itself. Dallas Brooks, later Governor of Victoria, stayed with the Gordons during his weekend visits to Woburn. He was Stuart's military adviser. All of us were under strict instructions not to communicate our address to any outsider, or to tell anybody what we were supposed to be doing. We were not allowed to post letters from any local pillar-box. They all had to be sent up to London for posting there. We led a quiet and bucolic life, except when our work moved up to London for a couple of days each week. But we got our full share of excitement when the news broke in June 1941 of the arrival of Hess in Scotland. Some people in London apparently believed that we had got him hidden away somewhere in Woburn Abbey. Journalists turned up at the *Bedford Arms* where some of us used to go for a drink of an evening, in the hope of picking up a useful scrap of information. We were unable to help them; we knew no more than they did.

In addition to those I have already mentioned, Stuart's propaganda department included F. A. Voigt, Ralph Murray, later British Ambassador to Greece, Richard Crossman, and, for a short time, Vernon Bartlett. We worked closely with Leeper's Political Intelligence Department which included Christopher Warner, later British Ambassador to Belgium, Gathorne-Hardy, the historian, and Brigadier Skaife. Skaife was one of the few who had correctly understood what he had seen at the military display in Russia in 1936, when Military Attaché in Moscow. He was not among those who believed that the Germans would march to a quick victory against Moscow. The fact that he was right did not add to his popularity among service people.

Not long after joining the Enemy Propaganda Department, I was told to call on George Bell, the Bishop of Chichester, and find out if he was willing to help us in our work. We all knew of the efforts he made over the years to maintain some sort of contact with the better elements in Germany; Richard Crossman and I had both seen him in action at the Church Conference in Fanø in the year 1934. Crossman had accompanied Bell as a sort of political adviser; and I had gone to Fanø, as related on an earlier page, to report the proceedings for *The Times*. I was driven down from Woburn to Chichester and found the Bishop to be a very receptive listener. I explained to him what we were doing and what we hoped to do. I asked him if he would consider the possibility of working with us in some advisory capacity. It seemed to me that he was interested, and as he talked I became more convinced than ever that his mere presence would have a balancing and moderating effect upon the work of the Department. My hopes were high as I returned to Woburn Abbey.

A little later we heard that the then Archbishop of Canterbury did not think it appropriate for George Bell to associate himself with this particular aspect of the war effort. This was a great disappointment to us. If he had taken a hand in our propaganda, our appeal to the so-called good Germans might have been rather stronger than it was. The events of 1944 might have taken a different and more effective turn. On the other hand, given the Government's policy of unconditional surrender, and its attitude to the Stockholm Conference in 1942, it was perhaps just as well that George Bell did not get involved with us. He would almost certainly have collided head-on with the Prime Minister; and his association with our work would undoubtedly have made the Russians even more suspicious of British good faith than they were.

Shortly afterwards, and again under instructions, I got into touch with Nora Waln, an American Quaker, then resident in this country, whose moving book on Germany, under the title *Reaching for the Stars*, had recently been published. 'Whenever I am gripped by despair,' she had written, 'or roused by angry passions by anything the Germans do, I think of the nicer Germans. When rough and brutal voices shout, I can listen undaunted, because I have heard better German voices. In an age when some Germans are testing out the might of threat and fear as weapons of State, and must batter ruthlessly before they can learn that they have chosen powerless weapons, it is encouraging to remember other Germans who conquer successfully all who come near them.' Nora Waln was thinking not only of the German poets and musicians to whom we owe so much, but of the many ordinary decent folk she had met in Germany during her stay there. She was speaking the same language as George Bell. But she was not to be persuaded to join us. She thought it best to remain aloof. I am glad for her sake that she did. It is impossible to keep your hands clean when engaged in political warfare.

A third mission that fell to me about the same time involved long and very detailed negotiations with Stephen King-Hall. By some curious coincidence he became a nuisance to Stuart at about the same time as the Ministry of Information were considering the possibility of sending some high-powered person on a tour of Latin America. King-Hall had been criticizing, vigorously at times, the work of Stuart's Department; and his activities were causing growing irritation. A solution flashed into our minds. 'The very man for the South American tour,' Stuart said. 'A truly excellent suggestion. Who made it?' So I was asked to get into touch with King-Hall and to persuade him to undertake the job. He was exceedingly suspicious, and he asked me all sorts of questions. I thought at one time that I had succeeded in persuading him to accept the offer when he suddenly exclaimed: 'I know. Campbell wants to get me out of the country.' The suggestion horrified me; and I told him so. We promised to meet again a few days later, to give King-Hall further time for reflection. When I saw him he said: 'All right. I'll take it on.' I reported the good news to the office. Before the arrangements for his tour could be completed it was announced that King-Hall had been adopted as a National Labour candidate for Ormskirk. So the deal was off.

Others have told the story of Department E. H. and of the many changes it suffered as the war went on; of SOE (Special Operations Executive) under Hugh Dalton; of that unhappy triumvirate consisting of Anthony Eden, Brendan Bracken and Hugh Dalton which was supposed to symbolize the fruitful co-operation between the Foreign Office, the Ministry of Information and the Ministry of Economic Warfare, but which turned out to be a bickering shop generating an immense amount of ill-feeling; and how finally the whole propaganda set-up was rationalized in the Political Warfare Executive under Robert Bruce-Lockhart. There is not much that I can add to the official and unofficial accounts that have been published since the end of the war. Moreover, the Department went though its major expansion process and attained its greatest influence after I had taken up my job in Moscow, so my knowledge does not extend to this period.

We started off in a very minor key. Neville Chamberlain did not object to our producing leaflets to be dropped by the RAF so long as they were inoffensive, that is to say so long as they were not dropped in such heavy bundles that Germans would actually be killed by them. Naturally enough, the RAF did not think highly of this form of warfare. So we tended to concentrate upon getting ourselves organized against the day when our services and our knowledge and experience would be urgently required. There was not very much we could say to the enemy in those early days. After Poland had been crushed, we drifted into the period of the phoney war. There was a certain spurious activity when Russia attacked Finland. People spoke with a knowing look of doing something to help the Finns, by bombing the Caucasian oil fields, for instance. Konni Zilliacus came to see me shortly after the beginning of the winter war and pleaded to be allowed to broadcast to Finland. He said he was sure that if he could be allowed to talk to the Finns in their own language, the war would soon be over. He failed to convince anybody of the wisdom of this course, and so the unconverted Finns fought on. When France fell and the rest of Europe was overrun, the difficulties facing the Department became overwhelming: there was plenty of news, of course, but it was all bad for us and good for the enemy. It was not the sort of raw material out of which effective propaganda could be made. Those directly responsible for output, particularly in the BBC, were determined to report things as they were and not to disguise or distort disagreeable facts.

By that time the original plans for the Enemy Propaganda Department had had to be recast. Everything became much more complicated; our story now had to be told in many different languages, and not just in German. It was essential to ensure that it was the same story regardless of language, since major discrepancies could have been fatal to the established reputation of the BBC, with which Department E. H. had become more closely identified as the war went on. The need to coordinate all open propaganda in the form of leaflets and news-sheets dropped by the RAF and of broadcasts by the BBC, led inevitably to friction. This became more acute after the various *émigré* Governments had settled down in London and were beginning to play their part in policy-making.

Whitehall was sharply divided on this subject. One group of officials considered that most of the Governments concerned were tarred with the same brush as the Chamberlain Government. They argued that if Chamberlain was a guilty man, so were these Governments; and if Chamberlain had been blind, so had they. There was no reason to treat these *émigré* Cabinet Ministers as if they were men with vision who had discovered the truth in the early 'thirties and had never faltered. They should not, therefore, be given full access to British propaganda facilities, and in particular to the BBC since this would merely enable them to rehabilitate themselves—or to try to rehabilitate themselves—among their own people with the help of British resources. What would the British people have thought if Britain had been overrun in 1940 and Neville Chamberlain had been broadcasting words of encouragement and defiance from across the Atlantic? I myself agreed emphatically with this point of view. It was not shared by Ivone Kirkpatrick, the senior Foreign Office official responsible for these policy matters. He considered that the *émigré* Governments should be given their head, and, in so far as it could be squared with British security, that they should be allowed one or more fixed periods every day in which to broadcast to their own people in their own way. Kirkpatrick's view prevailed. The result was that while the news bulletins of the BBC in all their different languages remained a BBC responsibility, some of the comments and talks were inspired by the *émigré* Governments who often supplied their own staffs for this purpose, responsible not to the BBC or to anyone in Whitehall, but to their respective Governments. The Propaganda Department issued regular directives to the BBC on how the news should be presented, that is to say on the points that might usefully be emphasized. But I very much doubt if Noel Newsome, the able and tough-minded head of the news services, paid very much attention to them. Looking back now, when tempers have cooled, I think he was right. But at the time I did not. I was as critical of him as most of my colleagues were.

Where the British Government did keep complete control was over the editorial content of the leaflets that eventually came to be dropped on a very substantial scale over enemy-occupied territory; and also over the underground or black propaganda carried out by its secret radio stations. Some Governments, and particularly the Norwegian Government, greatly resented this: they thought it most improper that a foreign Government in alliance with them should be speaking to their people over their heads. The Norwegian Foreign Minister, Trygve Lie, offered to pay the cost of the leaflets dropped over Norway by the RAF and to pay for the aircraft doing the job; but his suggestion was rejected. The offer was made to me in the first instance. I reported the facts without delay to Hugh Gaitskell, at that time Dalton's Private Secretary. But the matter was not pursued at the time. Lie also objected to some of the broadcasts carried by our secret radio station with its output beamed to Norway. He thought it concentrated too much on King Haakon, and too little on the Government. Our instructions were to recall that the King had become, more than ever, a unifying figure in Norway and that most of the politicians, although worthy, were of nothing like the same importance to people living under Nazi occupation. Neither Lie nor any other Foreign Minister had been officially informed of the existence of these secret radio stations; and the facts came to his knowledge through an indiscretion by one of the senior executives in SOE.

Lie took action in support of his Government's views, directed in the first instance at myself. He assumed that I had complete authority in these matters; and he complained strongly to me and later to Eden. I was told later that in making representations to Eden he had conceded that while I might well be the greatest living authority on Swedish and Danish affairs, I knew very little about Norway, and the sooner these matters were turned over to the Norwegian Government's experts the better. He failed to see that I had no responsibility for policy, and that my job was only to see that policy was carried out. We finally invited the Norwegian Defence Minister, Oscar Torp, down to Woburn for a peace conference. We found it necessary to deal with him rather than with Lie because underground or black propaganda was linked to operations in enemy-occupied Norway, and these fell within the competence of the Minister of Defence. Torp, who later became Prime Minister, was an attractive personality with a genuine working-class background. He had a dry sense of humour that endeared him to many people and made him a pleasant companion. He was not, I discovered, particularly devoted to Lie and this made it all the easier to come to a satisfactory arrangement with him. He came accompanied by the Norwegian Press Counsellor, Herman Lehmkuhl, a friend of many years' standing; and we had a long and happy conversation which ended with handshakes all round. I can still see Torp ruminating quietly while certain points were being discussed, and cutting off bits of chewing tobacco with a hunting knife from time to time and popping them into his mouth. He persuaded us to buy several hundredweight of chewing tobacco to be dropped on Norway, or to be landed in Norway whenever another naval raid was carried out. On the West coast or in Northern Norway, he said, chewing tobacco was a good morale builder. I believe that a large quantity of it was finally imported under my name, and stored in some inaccessible place. I do not know what ultimately became of it. I am bound to say that of all the Foreign Ministers in London none was more active or more pugnacious in his country's interest than Trygve Lie. No one resisted pressure, even Churchill's pressure, with greater vigour and determination. He failed to hit it off with Ernest Bevin, at that time Minister of Labour, but I suspect that that was because they had so many qualities in common, good and bad. With Eden he got on very well indeed. They used to play tennis together; each, I am told, taking it in turns to let the other win, in the best tradition of old-fashioned diplomacy.

Oscar Torp's recommendation that we take chewing tobacco to Norway arose out of the reports he had received after the Navy's raid on the Lofoten Islands in March 1941. The landing party had taken some comforts with them to brighten the lives of the people living under enemy occupation, but chewing tobacco had not been thought of. The party had also brought some prisoners back with them—all Quislings—and most of them were eventually accommodated in one of His Majesty's prisons. They were submitted to the usual interrogation, and eventually I was asked to lend a hand. I found it distressing, distasteful and humiliating. The men were so terrified, and at the same time so truculent that I could do nothing with them, and I had to report failure. Someone with considerable experience of such affairs had advised me to sit well away from the men, to smoke a good cigar or cigarette in their presence and to make sure that the aroma of the tobacco drifted across to them in full strength. They were dying for a smoke, I was told. But my low tricks did not get me anywhere.

Christmas Møller was another difficult character in our collection. I am afraid that his invitation to leave Denmark and to come to London was not properly thought out. Dalton, the Minister responsible, wanted a Social Democrat to come out also, but the man concerned replied he thought he would do better to stay at home inside the Danish resistance movement. So what we got was a Conservative politician, the leader of a minority group who was not particularly popular with his own party, although he was highly respected. It has been said that Møller came over here on the basis of all sorts of promises that were never carried out and that he considered himself, after a while, to have been abandoned and betrayed. I know that he believed that the Danish service of the BBC would keep an open door for him and that he would be free at all times to call upon the Danes to commit acts of sabotage against the Germans. From what I know of British policy at the time, I do not believe that there was any justification for his belief. The British authorities were most anxious not to encourage reckless acts of sabotage; they did not want people to act unless help could be given, or alternatively (as in the case of the heavy-water expedition in Norway) unless vital military interests were at stake. So I do not believe the story that this policy of encouraging sabotage existed at the time, and that it was changed shortly after Møller's arrival, and without any discussion with him.

Møller arrived at Leuchars in Scotland on 6 May 1942. An emphatic warning to the Yugoslavs not to take premature action was broadcast by the BBC as early as on 22 July 1941. So far as I remember this was not a new policy, it was a re-statement of an old policy. But the authorities had no objection to individual acts that might cause irritation but would not lead to general reprisals; indeed, they had no power to stop them. The policy of encouraging sabotage and acts of open resistance in enemy-occupied territory had one dangerous weakness. Some of the Ministers in the *émigré* Governments soon came to the conclusion that their prestige and therefore their ability to influence the British Government turned on the sabotage record of their own people. They believed that if they could report fifteen acts of resistance within a given period they would enjoy greater respect than if they reported none at all. This belief led directly to two different temptations: either to inflate the number of reported incidents beyond the credibility level, or to encourage unplanned acts of sabotage that could easily cut across schemes that had been carefully worked out over a period of months by the SOE experts. And here something more was at stake than prestige: the lives of brave men were also involved. In the latter case a conflict of interests was an ever-present possibility. The situation became much more difficult after the Russians came into the picture. They had nothing like the same scruples as the British Government. They encouraged every kind of recklessness.

I have no doubt that Møller also assumed that he would become the undisputed leader of the Free Danes the moment he arrived in London and that all Danes living abroad would ultimately accept his advice, if not his instructions. But the Danish Ambassador in Washington, Kauffmann, had gone his own way and had set himself up as a sort of independent power in the United States. It was in this independent capacity that he signed an agreement with the United States Government giving the Americans certain rights in Greenland. He was unlikely to take his line from Møller. In London, the Danish Ambassador, Count Reventlow, put loyalty to the King of Denmark above all other considerations and refused to countenance anything that might make the King's position more difficult. The British authorities were unwilling to make any move that might create a civil war situation in Denmark. If a Free Danish movement in London had been recognized as the nucleus of a Danish post-war Government, it would have caused the greatest confusion. It might also have been dangerous; especially since the strongest political party in the country, the Social Democrats, had no representative on the spot. In any case, it would have been regarded as most improper by many people if a Conservative leader had been recognized as the supreme political authority in opposition to the Coalition Government at home. When Møller went up to Newcastle to address a group of Danish seamen, he found that his audience was not altogether sympathetic. They had no objection to him personally; but they did not like his party. His great value to the Danes, the fighting Danes, was that he made people conscious of Denmark at a time when Denmark was very much out of sight and out of mind. When the country was overrun, Kirkpatrick of the Foreign Office refused at first to recommend that any time be provided for broadcasts in the Danish language because, he said, the country had put up no resistance. The fact that there were any Danish broadcasts at all in the early critical days was due to Campbell Stuart who agreed to accept, for a day or two, a cut of five minutes in the time reserved for the German language broadcasts and to allot this time to broadcasts to Denmark.

I was involved in much the same sort of confusion in Moscow in the course of the year 1944. The Danish resistance movement, inspired by Madame Kollontay, had decided to send its own representative to Moscow. He had strong left-wing views and the intention was, I suppose, to balance the Conservative representative in London. The representative's name was Døssing; he was a librarian with no great experience of politics and still less of diplomacy. I saw a great deal of him at the time: I used to call on him at frequent intervals at the Hotel National where he and his wife had two rooms to live and work in. They led a very secluded life; they had neither the means nor the inclination to entertain on the same scale as the members of the regular diplomatic corps. Døssing's position was obscure and ill-defined. He was suspected by many of being a clandestine member of the Communist Party and it was widely believed that the extreme left-wing elements in the resistance movement intended to use him to arrange for much closer relations with the Soviet Union after the war. I thought at the time that this was rubbish, and I still think so. I am sure that Døssing was no more willing than Møller to give a foreign power a foothold in his country. But he was ineffective; his position was equivocal. The Russians did not encourage him: if they had been the least bit helpful they would have found a better place for him to live in. My instructions were to talk to him only in very general terms. In Moscow, as in London, the British Government was most scrupulous about taking sides in internal Danish politics. They continued to regard the Danish Government in Copenhagen as the only constitutional authority. If I found Døssing easier to deal with than Møller it was perhaps because Døssing did not regard himself as being a person of outstanding importance. He was a modest man who laid no claims to eminence.

Møller in London made constant difficulties for us. We tried to keep him in funds in various ways, and we invented all sorts of institutions through which Government money would eventually come to him. But he always found out; and he always made a fuss about it. He did not want British Government money, he said. The Free Danish movement put up a good deal of the cash he needed; but it was apparently not enough and he borrowed the rest from his British banking friends. It was repaid to them by the Danish Government immediately after the war. He objected strongly to the activities of those Danes who were in British Government service, or rather he objected strongly to their failure to keep him informed of what they were doing. The argument that they were in British service and that their first duty was to the British Government did not impress him. He was too jealous of his position; and he could not tolerate any kind of activity in his own country, or about his own country, of which he was unaware. If he had gone straight to Eden or to the appropriate Foreign Office official, all would have been revealed to him and much strain and all bad blood avoided. It remains only to add that the Danish journalists who worked with us during the war were among the best of our colleagues and, I believe, played a major part in reinforcing Danish morale when it tended to sag. I have in mind, in particular, Terkel Terkelsen, now Editor of *Berlingske Tidende*, Denmark's largest newspaper; Sten Gudme, whose skill as an editor was so great that he ultimately played a leading part in the lay-out of all propaganda leaflets, regardless of language, dropped by the RAF; Tillge Rasmussen, later Editor of *Politiken*; Harry Agerbak, now Press Counsellor at the Danish Embassy in London; and Giertsen, a poet of some distinction but of an angular character who later in the war joined the RAF and lost his life.

CHAPTER 9

HUGH DALTON used to come down to Woburn from time to time to inspect the troops. He was a great booming bully; and even at breakfast time his manner was horribly hearty. He used to dress himself in a sort of heavy white jersey, as worn by the best goal-keepers, and call for volunteers to go for a walk with him of a Sunday morning. Walkers became hard to find after a while; people tended to go to earth when they heard his voice: and that could be heard almost everywhere. He was a fast walker, with immense stamina, and it gave him great and perceptible pleasure when he succeeded in driving younger men into a state of breathless exhaustion. He was also a man of courage who wanted others who were not quite so brave to see how brave Dalton was. Occasionally of an evening during the air-raid season, he would invite a subordinate to have a drink with him on the top floor of a Mayfair club which had a glass roof. When the sirens wailed, Dalton remained seated, and so his guest had to stay too. It gave him evident pleasure to see his victim squirm under the noise of falling bombs. His voice boomed away more cheerfully than ever.

The occasions I disliked most were when he thought it necessary to lecture his staff on some aspect of the international situation. We were made to sit in a sort of semi-circle, with Dalton at one end, while listening to him. More than once I detected a look of embarrassment, and even shame, flash across Gaitskell's face as Dalton indulged himself in one of his habitual tactlessnesses. Even Crossman was not too happy, and Crossman is nothing if not robust. One Sunday morning he undertook to lecture us on the subject of *bouillabaisse*. I do not know how it came up, but I suppose Dalton had been talking about Marseilles and the South of France—of the mixed races to be found there, of their links with North Africa, of the *mistral*, of the *Cannebière* and of *bouilla-*

baisse. 'Ah yes, *bouillabaisse*.' He paused for a moment. '*Bouillabaisse*. You know what it is, of course?' Again an expectant pause. 'It's a fish dish, a speciality of the area.' He grinned, secure in his expertise. 'You know, a fish dish—made with saffron and things like that. Ha! Ha!' A booming laugh followed. 'Jesus!' was the only comment that Valentine Williams was capable of when the séance ended. Dalton seemed to us to lack all the antennae that are so essential in the give and take of daily life. It used to be said of him that 'It's no laughing matter when Dalton cracks a joke.' I forced myself to remember that his record in the Labour opposition before the Second World War was outstanding. He was not particularly scrupulous in his methods. Many of us resented his habit of cultivating the acquaintance of very junior members of the staff in order to find out what the seniors were up to and what they were saying. 'I like to be up-to-date and well-informed of what goes on in my own Department,' he used to say with a laugh that rattled the windows in a way church organs often do. His comments in Ministerial red ink on suggestions put up by his officials were models of rudeness.

It seems that Churchill hesitated a great deal before finally assigning responsibility for SOE to Hugh Dalton. The issue was in doubt for some days, and scores of names were mentioned as possibles. The heads of the various intelligence departments—Naval and Military Intelligence among them—apparently knew nothing of what was afoot, and were left for some time in a state of agonized uncertainty. They suspected that Valentine Williams knew something that they did not know, and some of them invited him to a splendid dinner at the Savoy Grill in the hope of wheedling some information out of him. Williams was cautious, above all in his intake of drink. The fact was that he knew nothing, but was determined not to show his hand until he had had his dinner. Half-way through the meal, he was called to the telephone. 'Dalton's got it,' a voice said. Williams went back to his party, but kept his secret to himself until he had had his ration of drink. Then, well content with all their hospitality, he told them what he knew. They were not very pleased.

We had our first taste in those Woburn days of the rush of idealism in the United States and of the suspicions of British motives that seemed to lie behind much of Washington's attitude to London. Robert Sherwood, a special emissary of the President, arrived one day and came to us brimming over with ideas of how to run the British and American propaganda efforts on a co-operative basis. This was thought to be a worth-while proposal. But when Sherwood wanted to expand this Anglo-American effort into a sort of United Nations affair in which everybody would have a say, British officials put up strong resistance. By that time, they had had some experience of running in harness with the *émigré* Governments in London and they knew what the hazards were. They did not think that a Tower of Babel arrangement would work. Nevertheless, I took Sherwood's idea with me when I went to Moscow in the autumn of 1943. I had been given instructions to see if I could come to some sort of propaganda arrangement with the Soviet Government with the ultimate aim of coordinating the efforts of the British Political Warfare Executive, the American Office of War Information and Sovinformbureau. The least we might achieve, so it was thought, was an agreement to coordinate information about our respective propaganda efforts. The official concerned with those affairs at the time was Lozovsky, who was later shot during the course of the anti-Jewish purges. I had instructions to tell the Russians about our joint Anglo-American directives, or propaganda instructions, and to give them copies of specimen leaflets. I was not allowed to refer to our black or underground propaganda, although of course they knew all about it.

After the victory of Stalingrad, the Russians began to make use of some of the German Generals they had captured as the nucleus of an anti-Nazi movement. They began to drop leaflets carrying their signatures to the troops on the Eastern front. I tried hard to get copies of them; and after repeated failures finally succeeded in persuading the Russians to let us have one or two specimens. That is all I ever achieved, in spite of the fact that I passed on to them summaries of the propaganda directives worked out by the Political Warfare Executive in London for the guidance of broadcasters and leaflet-writers. We had no response from the Russians to this. Then one day, the Ambassador was asked to call on Lozovsky. He came back in a fury. Lozovsky had reprimanded him for a recent directive, in which the writers, by way of illustration and explanation, had drawn attention to the points that the Nazis were making against the Russians, and suggesting ways and means of coping with them. Lozovsky insisted that the British

Government were instructing their staffs to carry out anti-Russian propaganda and quoted a sentence from the directive out of context to prove it. He paid no attention to the explanations that were offered; he declined to listen. And so ended our first and only attempt to coordinate our propaganda efforts with the Soviet Information Bureau.

I believe the Russians lost interest in the cooperation when they discovered that the British Government did not control all forms of public expression in Britain, including the newspapers. They could not understand how propaganda could be effective unless everybody told the same story. When I explained to Lozovsky that the press did as it liked, subject to normal security censorship, he did not believe me. I had other discussions on this topic with more junior officials but all found it impossible to believe that our arrangements were as I had explained. I think they believed that the Government wanted to keep one hand free, and to direct one section of what they considered to be a vast British propaganda octopus to attack the Soviet Union while other sections remained friendly. In this way, they thought Churchill and his Ministers would be able to make the best of both worlds. It goes without saying that the Soviet Government itself acted in accordance with this principle. Officially it might well maintain a friendly attitude to the Western powers: the Government newspaper *Isvestiya* would show restraint, but the Party newspaper *Pravda* would be hostile. When Molotov was challenged, he would explain that the Party's views were not necessarily the same as the Government's; and that, in any event, the Ministry for Foreign Affairs had no authority over the Communist Party. Although we knew he was lying when he put up this argument, there was nothing much that could be done.

One of the most distasteful jobs I had to do was to represent the Enemy Propaganda Department from time to time in the company of Sir Maurice Peterson at meetings at the Ministry of Information over which Duff Cooper presided. He always had Frank Pick, his Director-General, sitting next to him; and for some reason or other Pick usually spoke in a whisper. This was just as well, perhaps, for Pick's comments were often most offensive. You could always tell, even if you could not hear, when Pick was being difficult. A vein would suddenly develop on Duff

Cooper's forehead, and it would begin to throb in the most alarming way. Then he might say to Pick: 'Now please repeat what you have just said so that the others can hear.' And Pick would say something unpleasant in a rather louder voice. Usually, it would be at the expense of Professor Ogilvie, then head of the BBC. It was not just the ordinary run-of-the-mill criticism that we all have to tolerate from time to time, but a deliberate piece of barbed rudeness that appeared to be designed to cause pain. And Ogilvie, who was a gentle and sensitive person, was incapable of hitting back. People who knew Pick well told me that it was not his intention to wound, and that he derived no pleasure from it. It was all part of his passion for efficiency, they said. But he did not leave this impression upon me at the time. I came away ashamed and embarrassed. I never discovered what Maurice Peterson thought; he was a singularly uncommunicative person. He had been brought back to London from his Embassy in Madrid to provide a job for Samuel Hoare, and had sulked ever since. The injustice of it galled him. He nursed his grievance with patience and devotion. 'Next to a sum of money down,' Anthony Trollope has told us, 'a grievance is the best thing you can have. A man who sticks to a grievance year after year will always make money of it at last.' Peterson had taken this maxim to heart. He used to come down to Woburn on an occasional weekend and he soon came to be known as Uncle Beastly. He did not recover his good humour or his normal capacity for speech until he was appointed Ambassador to Moscow in succession to Clark Kerr. When I met him there in 1947, he was pleasant, affable and talkative.

Maurice Peterson did not descend upon us until after Stuart had gone, and Stuart went out when Halifax was appointed British Ambassador to Washington. With Neville Chamberlain as Prime Minister, Stuart knew every landmark and every dangerous shoal in Whitehall; but when Winston Churchill came in he lost his bearings. So long as he was head of our Department he used to come down to Woburn at every weekend in the company of three secretaries and many filing cabinets. He never interfered with our work. So long as you had his confidence, he left you alone. He was a master of tactics, with a passion for security. When he called you on the telephone and you heard that characteristic Canadian voice coming over the line you were always prepared for some security warning before he got down to the point. 'I've just been talking to a member of the Cabinet,' he began on one occasion, his voice solemn and sententious. 'He's a Viscount and his name begins with an H.' The H was loudly aspirated, to make the meaning quite clear. 'Do you follow?' It did not take long to work out that Stuart was referring to Halifax. I wonder if the intelligence agents who were presumably eavesdropping were as baffled as he hoped.

Stuart made a great point of cultivating the best possible relations with his staff. He was on nodding terms with everybody. One day he came into the little room that had been allotted to him in the riding school at Woburn and found a man re-arranging a calendar on the window-sill. 'I hope you are happy in your work,' he said cordially, as he shook him by the hand. The man went off to do some other job in another office. Stuart turned to his secretary and said: 'Say, who was that bird?' 'The window-cleaner, Sir,' was the reply. 'There is nothing like flattery,' Stuart used to say. 'When you flatter a person, he is of course aware of what you are up to. He's bound to write it off, at least some of it. But if you lay it on thick, really thick, great layers of it, much of it is bound to stick. It's all for the good of the cause.' I came to have a great affection for this strange, frail-looking but immensely tough character. He had something of the leprechaun about him. His most endearing trait was that he was always prepared to laugh at himself. He did not mind if we joined in.

Many of his exploits had a touch of high comedy about them. He spent a good deal of his time trying to impress the politicians with the work that was being done at Woburn, and with the efforts that were being made to keep all extravagances in check. Herbert Morrison came down, I remember; and Attlee; and Ellen Wilkinson and some others. Stuart would send a car to pick them up either in London or in whatever part of the country they might be staying provided they were not too far away. Attlee, at the time he was invited, was staying somewhere near Woburn and a car was sent in the normal way. Stuart, checking up as usual on the arrangements in order to ensure that there was no slip-up, asked his secretary if the car had gone. 'Yes, Sir.' 'When did it go?' 'About a quarter of an hour ago.' 'What car did you send?' Stuart asked. 'Your Rolls, Sir,' was the reply. 'My God,' Stuart said, 'here we are trying to impress everybody with our parsimoniousness and you send my Rolls. You must be out of your mind. See what you can do.' So another car was sent, a small and mean car in need of overhaul, to overtake the other. It got there after the Rolls had arrived at the cottage where Attlee was staying, and after the driver had made himself known. But the newly-arrived chauffeur had had his instructions. 'Buzz off,' he said to the driver of the Rolls, 'I'm taking the old man back to Woburn.' No one ever knew what Attlee thought as he came out to take his seat in the Rolls-Royce he had seen outside his cottage, and found instead a tawdry little vehicle waiting to take him to his destination. I do not suppose there has been a better act with a car since Harry Tate's day. Stuart did not lose his temper over the incident which was so obviously bungled. Other men would certainly have done so.

When Stuart left us, Leeper took over responsibility for the work at Woburn, with David Bowes-Lyon as his deputy in succession to Valentine Williams who was sent off on a mission to the United States. Walter Adams of the London School of Economics also joined us at about this time, and he made a great impression upon us by his lucidity and integrity. He was a new and stabilizing element among the wild journalists and advertising men at Woburn. His capacity for exposition was considerable; but he preferred to talk to groups of people rather than to individuals. He was shy and reserved. After what I have heard of his work in Rhodesia, my respect for him is even greater than it was. But I am not surprised that he has been criticized. He is inarticulate when it comes to discussing his own actions and his own feelings. I suspect that a stiff upper lip is his most treasured possession; and I do not suppose he told anybody of what he was really trying to do when he was in Salisbury. If he had been completely frank about himself, he would not have suffered from all that ignorant criticism. David Bowes-Lyon who came to us from the Ministry of Economic Warfare was a very different sort of person. He was genuinely interested in other people, relaxed, and not afraid to reveal bits of his personality from time to time. I have never met a person with a greater charm of manner: he would have tempted even a Trappist monk to break his vow of silence. His charm was effortless and spontaneous; it was not switched on and off as circumstances required, or carefully adjusted to the degree of importance of the person to be charmed. He won the affection of President Roosevelt when he was sent over to the United States at a later stage in the war; and within the limitations of his job in Washington he made a substantial contribution to the cause of Anglo-American understanding. When he was at the Ministry for Economic Warfare he used to meet American correspondents in London for tea from time to time. One day, at the end of one of his parties he asked the guests if they would object if his sister turned up next time. The Americans were surprised. One of them told me later that they did not regard these parties as social occasions to which odd sisters could be invited; but they nodded acquiescence. On the following week they were even more surprised when the Queen arrived. Bowes-Lyon always referred to his brother-in-law as that 'perfectly good Monarch'. His sense of humour was infectious, and he was no respecter of persons. Anyone trying to be pompous in his presence was soon deflated by his laughter. He was not intolerant except when dealing with pretentious humbugs. When they were about, a mocking undertone would come into his voice.

He took an intense interest in the production of the leaflets that were dropped by the RAF. This became an immense enterprise after a while and needed a great deal of supervision. Those of us who were involved in these matters were strongly encouraged to put up new ideas and to explore new ways. One very interesting proposal emerged when it became known that the Department had a substantial stock of India-paper on hand. It was suggested that some of it should be made available to *The Times* in return for an undertaking that *The Times* would experiment with the production of a miniature of the Weekly Edition on this thin paper. If they succeeded, copies would be dropped upon selected points in Western Europe. It was known to many of us that people in occupied Europe preferred papers and periodicals produced for the British public to publications specially prepared for them in their own language. It was known, too, that those listeners in Europe who were able to pick up the Home Service of the BBC preferred it to the foreign language broadcasts designed for them. They were so saturated with propaganda by the Nazis that they had come to suspect any package, no matter how good its contents, if it carried the propaganda label. They believed that if they could eavesdrop on what the British people were told, or could read their newspapers over their shoulders, they would be getting close to the truth about the war. By giving them the Weekly Edition of *The Times*, we should be helping to meet this need. After some hesitation, the Manager of *The Times* agreed to take on the job. He hesitated because a quick-printing job on India-paper had not been done before.

The experiment was most successful. From 22 April 1942 until 3 June 1942 the Edition was printed fortnightly by a flat-bed process. Then it became possible to do it on a weekly basis, and this went on until 30 January 1946. The first success went to our heads, and some time later in 1942 I was instructed to get into touch with the Manager of *The Times* once again and to ask him to produce miniature copies of the daily paper in the same way and for the same purpose. I was treated with great politeness, but it was made clear to me that the idea was absurd and impracticable. 'It takes a day or two for the ink to dry,' the Manager said. 'A daily job is impossible.' But the experiments were continued. I did not hear of them at the time because I left the country early in 1943. But a daily Air Edition of *The Times* came to life on 4 August 1944.

When I went to see *The Times* people in 1942 I took with me a copy of a German newspaper printed on something made out of potato haulm. It was much whiter than our normal newsprint, and the typefaces stood out more boldly; but it seemed heavier and rather more brittle than the stuff used by British newspapers. The Manager was greatly interested, and I left the copy with him. Nothing came of it; perhaps the process was too costly in terms of labour to make it worth while. But it was interesting in that it showed the progress the Germans were making with ersatz materials. It showed what could be done if supplies of woodpulp and newsprint dried up.

The need to have access to newspapers published in enemy and enemy-occupied territory faced us with a serious problem. They were regarded as essential both for general intelligence purposes and for propaganda work. We did not expect to find the truth in them; but we did hope, and our hope was justified, to establish what the soft spots were, and to find out, by the comments the papers made and the denials that they carried, what was agitating the authorities and perhaps the public. During the First World War, I was told, all this had been done in a most gentlemanly way.

A man in a bowler hat would go out in a boat into the North Sea with a load of British newspapers; half-way across he would meet another man, also properly dressed, with a cargo of German newspapers. An exchange would be made in silence to the satisfaction of the two Governments concerned. During the Second World War things were much more difficult; the Continent was inaccessible to us and even if aircraft did fly from time to time, to Sweden, for instance, it was always a risky operation. And they probably had more valuable things to carry than newspapers.

So a Press-Reading Bureau was established in Stockholm, responsible for procuring all the most important newspapers published in Europe; to read them; and to telegraph suitable extracts from them to London. These telegrams were edited and cross-referenced at Woburn and printed in pamphlet form every working day under the title of *News Digest*. Some issues ran to 58 pages, size 9½″ by 7½″. They contained an immense amount of information about developments in Europe. A typical issue might contain extracts from newspapers published in Germany, Hungary, Rumania, Albania, Greece, Yugoslavia, Bulgaria, Czechoslovakia, Norway, Denmark, the Netherlands, Belgium, France and Italy. The Stockholm Bureau was managed with immense efficiency and judgment by Cecil Parrott, later British Ambassador to Czechoslovakia. My only association with all this work was that my surname was used as the telegraphic address. I often wondered if the Germans ever asked themselves who this rapacious Barman was who wanted all that information at such great expense.

When David Bowes-Lyon left for the United States, I succeeded him as deputy to Rex Leeper. I stayed only a short time in this job for which I was by no means suited. Fortunately, its importance had been greatly reduced by the time I took over. Much of the work had been transferred to the top floors of Bush House in London where Ritchie Calder and Richard Crossman were the leading lights under the semi-benevolent eye of the Director-General, Bruce Lockhart.

Richard Crossman deserves a section all to himself. It has been said of him that he is a great stirrer-up of hornets' nests. I do not agree. Crossman, it seems to me, is a hornet's nest all to himself. He is one of the ablest debaters I have ever come across, and on those occasions where I have been fool enough to take him on he has crushed me within a very short time. He seems to prefer a good argument to almost anything else in the world: he tends to support lost causes, not because he is enamoured of them, but because of their debating possibilities; he does not mind contradicting even those friends and admirers who are most disposed to agree with him, even if this means making enemies of them. He is never to be found in the same position for more than a minute or two: any new debating point will send him off at a tangent. It is for this reason, I suppose, that his critics maintain that his principles are blurred round the edges. I think this is an unfair judgment. If he had been just a politician on the make, willing to trim his sails to all the winds that blow, he would almost certainly have been given high office in the Attlee Government. Bevin detested him because he was 'unreliable' which is the gravest crime in the trade union calendar. But I cannot regard him as unreliable: the real charge against him is that a good hard-hitting argument means as much to him as drink to an alcoholic. He will make almost any sacrifice to get it.

His argumentative spirit was a heavy cross to bear for his nominal superiors in the Enemy Propaganda Department. An order or a reprimand would automatically become the occasion for a great debate that Crossman would invariably win on points. When his superiors had an order to give they used to call him on the telephone, give the order, put down the receiver very quickly, and hope for the best. Others appealed to senior officials in the Foreign Office for support when it looked as if Crossman was on the point of trampling them down. He has much in common with George Mackintosh, that character in one of P. G. Wodehouse's golfing stories who had been infected by the germ of loquacity. Friends and enemies alike were stunned by a barrage of words after George Mackintosh had taken a correspondence course in elocution. He was not cured until someone hit him over the head with a golf club. Crossman, I am sure, never needed any lessons in elocution. Nor do I believe that either Lockhart or Leeper ever struck him with a golf club, although the temptation to do so must have been almost irresistible at times.

I never had any liking for administrative work; I was not born to be a manager: in many ways the few months between my appointment and my departure for Algiers were among the most troublesome I have ever experienced. I wanted to be on my own again. I began to regret that I had not responded more positively to the suggestion that I might become the Diplomatic Correspondent of Reuter's. I have always found it harder to direct and to supervise the work of others than to do the job myself.

CHAPTER 10

'DON'T LET them put you into uniform,' was the last piece of advice I got from Brigadier Brooks before leaving for Algiers early in 1943. 'They may suggest giving you the rank of Major since you are going into a military area,' he explained, 'but don't accept it. Don't take anything under the rank of Colonel, and I don't suppose they would do that for you. Once you are in uniform you have to listen in silence while Generals talk tripe. If you are a civilian you don't have to. You can tell them just what you think. Better stick to a pair of dirty flannel trousers.' And Brooks was quite right; a good deal of tripe was talked in Algiers by men in uniform, and not least by the Americans in the Psychological Warfare Board to which I was attached for a couple of months. I had been asked to make a report on working arrangements and what could be done to improve them. The British Mission under Harold Macmillan, with Roger Makins as his Chief of Staff, was an oasis of good sense. Shortly after my arrival, Macmillan sent for me. 'There's only one instruction I have to give you,' he said. 'It is this: no one here except myself is allowed to quarrel with the Americans. If you quarrel with them, or if there is any kind of trouble, no matter who is responsible or how innocent you are, I shall have to send you home. If you find yourself in an utterly impossible situation, report to me.' All of us doing any kind of official work in Algiers were given the same warning; and the result was a complete absence of Anglo-American friction on the working level.

Life in Algiers early in 1943 was difficult and hard: and even for the privileged, like myself, it was neither comfortable nor pleasant. I was put up at the Aletti Hotel on the water-front which had the advantage of giving you a good view of the harbour, but with the disadvantage of making you feel that you were in the front line during an air-raid. From my window I could see half-starved Arabs and their families queueing up for milk supplies. My own breakfast at the hotel consisted of some kind of roasted grain as a substitute for coffee, liquid saccharine, and maize bread as heavy as a piece of granite and almost as indigestible. Lunch and dinner which I took at the military mess, consisted of bully beef in various forms—cold, stewed, fried or manhandled in some way—with ample supplies of Algerian wine. When the Americans first got in with plenty of money in their pockets they had bought up practically everything that was to be found in the shops and the place was pretty bare in consequence. British troops and British civilian personnel were not allowed to do this. You were not supposed to buy local produce at all, or local goods. You had to depend upon Army supplies. But civilians like myself who went out into the countryside were not penalized. There were black market restaurants in Algiers itself but we were strongly discouraged from patronizing them.

Real power in Algeria was visibly American, and Macmillan's authority was moral rather than physical. You were conscious of it the moment you touched down at the airport at Maison Blanche. The Commander-in-Chief was American, and so was his deputy. At first the British Government were represented by Harold Mack, a Foreign Office official, described as Political Adviser to the Commander-in-Chief. He had no more influence with the Cabinet in London than any other member of the British diplomatic service; he was demonstrably junior to the President's representative, Robert Murphy, so he had no great influence on the spot. Eventually, Harold Macmillan came out as Churchill's special representative, with the rank of Minister-Resident. Like Robert Murphy, he was formally under the authority of General Eisenhower. Nevertheless, the political backing he received from London, and his own tact and skill soon yielded results. With an eye to post-war developments in Europe, Britain was more conscious of the need to restore France to her rightful place in the world than the Americans were, and Macmillan regarded this as the most important of his tasks. And as Robert Murphy notes in his autobiography, 'when the British moved into French North Africa with the Americans they arrived with an outlook altogether different from ours. To nearly all American strategists, the Mediterranean was a temporary battleground and little more. To our

Navy, the Japanese war in the Pacific was all-absorbing; our Army was intent upon an invasion of Europe from British bases. Our military chiefs had almost unanimously opposed the African expedition in the first place. Now they wanted to pull out as quickly as possible, return to England, and proceed there with preparations for a massive cross-channel attack. To the British, the Mediterranean was an essential link in their imperial system, and they were gravely concerned about what would happen in this area after the war.'

General Eisenhower was bored with the intricacies of North African and French politics; and since Washington could not make up its collective mind about de Gaulle, the initiative soon fell into Macmillan's hands. His attitude to de Gaulle, as well as to Pétain, was sharply defined. He disliked the remnants of Pétainism whenever and wherever they came to his notice; and he was extremely nimble-witted in expressing his disapproval. Sidney Bernstein had come out to Algiers on behalf of the Ministry of Information at about the same time as myself, to make arrangements for an adequate showing of British films in the area. He had managed to organize some sort of gala evening at a local cinema, and Macmillan had agreed to attend it. The Minister turned up rather earlier than expected, and in the company of a group of French officers walked round the lobby looking at the posters that were on display. In the place of honour, so to speak, there was a large picture of Pétain. Macmillan said nothing and went on looking at the other posters. When he had completed his tour he finished up in front of the glassy eyes of Pétain. 'Ah,' he said, 'I understand. *C'est votre Mickey Mouse à vous. Le Mickey Mouse français.*' He turned away to look once more at some of the Walt Disney figures that were also on display. Nothing more was said. But the picture was eventually taken down.

I do not think that the Americans in North Africa, in spite of their well-organized intelligence service, ever came to grips with the Franco-Algerian problem. War and politics, as they saw it, could not be mixed; and so long as the war lasted politics would have to wait. This absence of clear decisions in Washington was undoubtedly among the reasons for all the misunderstandings on the spot, and above all, for the friction with General de Gaulle. The Americans failed to grasp that the régime that had collapsed with the armistice in 1940 was detested by many Frenchmen; and that many people were looking for new men and new methods. Nor did they realize the extent of Anglophobia in the French Navy. It was this Anglophobia that made Admiral Darlan's policy possible and indeed inevitable. In the circumstances of the time, it could not be tolerated by the British Government.

The British Minister-Resident and his staff had no responsibility for the operations of the Psychological Warfare Board. In any case, they were too busy coping with de Gaulle; and with the Anglo-American differences that de Gaulle was helping to create. The Board was under American direction, at least during the period that I spent in Algiers. Its policy meetings were desultory and inconclusive affairs; they often rambled off into nowhere. It was impossible to resist the conclusion that the American soldiers picked for the job of propaganda were not chosen because of their conspicuous abilities, or for their experience in the art of communication or public relations. One of them, a Colonel, told me with pride that he was a senior Cavalry Colonel in the United States Army. Another senior officer, with his home in the Middle West, spoke to me of the pleasure it had given him to discover that he was not being high-hatted by the snooty British as he had feared he would be when he was catapulted into the Psychological Warfare job. The proceedings became farcical when French soldiers were included in the party—a General, perhaps, and a Colonel or two. With the Americans trying to speak French, and the French officers begging them to speak English (or Anglo-Saxon, as de Gaulle might have said) in the hope of understanding what they were trying to say, business never made any great progress.

Nor did I think highly of the security arrangements governing the Board's work. People seemed unaware of the rule that no one should ever be given more information than the minimum he needs to carry out his job. There were long discussions in a room full of people, I remember, about a projected landing on Sicily. I came away with the impression that on the senior level the outfit was not as good as it might be, but that the United States Military Headquarters in Algiers were perhaps not to blame for this. They had far more important problems on their hands. The violent conflicts between various Government Departments in Washington about what to do with General de Gaulle, and how to cope with his tantrums, played havoc with policy-making and therefore with propaganda. So there was perhaps no point in allocating first-class people to the job. At the lower levels, and in the field, there were some people of great ability at work. I believe that Robert Sherwood, who had come to Algiers to look into the American side of things, reached much the same conclusions.

When I returned to London to make my report, I had to travel through Marrakesh where we were held up for several days waiting for an aircraft. The Town Major allotted me 'sleeping accommodation' in a villainous doss-house. I was offered a double bed with filthy unwashed sheets; and I was told that I should be sharing it with a Major who had already spent some days in these horrible surroundings. The doss-house keeper held out his hand: 'That will be fifty francs a night,' he said, 'payable in advance.' I replied that I was not accustomed to sleeping with Majors and that I would have to see what could be done elsewhere. He told me that if I wanted to sleep at all that night I had better make up my mind because beds were scarce in Marrakesh. It is not usual for me to charge about on a high horse; but I thought I should be justified in doing so on this occasion. So I asked to be allowed to use the telephone and got on to the Town Major's office again. I described the situation to the voice at the other end of the line; he was surprised at my surprise. I said firmly that I was not going to share a bed with a Major; and I explained that I was going to Moscow shortly after my return to London, to take up the post of First Secretary at the Embassy there. A Diplomatic First Secretary, I reminded the voice, ranked with a Colonel in the Army. If he would get a Colonel to share my bed with me, I might consider the offer. It sounded to me as if this argument had made some impression upon the voice. Its tone changed, it was not quite so harsh, it eventually became more friendly.

In the end I was given a bed to myself in the Hotel Mamounia where I discovered that I was not the only man in Marrakesh waiting for an aircraft. Only P. G. Wodehouse or Tommy Handley could have done justice to the scene in that hotel: idle Generals waiting for transport and becoming increasingly querulous as they saw their cash resources drying up; junior officers carrying what were obviously secret documents since they never allowed their papers to pass out of their possession. One man had a small bag chained to his wrist; another carried a large envelope, its edges badly frayed, and eventually its contents came sticking out of the corners; a third was hugging a brief-case. He deplored lost opportunities: 'And not even a blonde spy in sight,' he sighed. I was able to get some money at the Villa La Saadia, thanks to Sherwood's introduction. And I recall with the greatest satisfaction that I found it possible to make a small advance, on note of hand only, to an impoverished General. I was given, in return, as good a dinner as an Officers' Mess can provide at GHQ Home Forces when I got back to London.

Villa la Saadia is the 'enchanted castle' where Roosevelt, Churchill and others stayed when they met in or travelled through Morocco. The widow of the American millionaire who owned it had lent it to Kenneth Pendar, one of Murphy's Vice-Consuls (known as the 'Twelve Apostles'), appointed to keep an eye on things in that country. Pendar has described this fabulous place in his book *An Adventure in Diplomacy*. The war must have seemed very far away to men relaxing in the gardens of this Moorish castle at the foot of the Atlas Mountains; and it is not surprising that Churchill was tempted to return to it whenever a suitable opportunity occurred. It was with the help of the people at the Villa, then, that I got my money; and my prestige with the impecunious soldiery at the Mamounia rose sharply when I reported that I had got my cash not from a vulgar bank but from the Churchill–Roosevelt headquarters.

*

I flew to Cairo by way of Bournemouth, Lisbon, Lagos, the Belgian Congo, Uganda and Khartoum. The flight across Africa was made necessary because the Mediterranean was closed to civilian traffic in the summer of 1943. Bournemouth was on my itinerary because it was at Bournemouth that I had to catch the Empire flying-boat, the most comfortable heavier-than-air machine yet devised. The swoosh as you take off from the water, and the glittering spray as you touch down have a glamour and an excitement that no ordinary airport take-off can compete with.

But first a word or two about my preparations which were laborious and in a way rather ridiculous. It had been decided that I should go on from Cairo to Moscow without first returning to this country. So the preparations for my Russian tour had to begin at once. This meant laying in a great store of supplies for my stay in the Soviet Union, where I was expected some time during the second half of September. The Embassy had advised me that I could not go wrong no matter how much I took with me in the way of supplies; and that I should need pretty well everything, apart from a house, if I was going to be comfortable. To lay in a stock of essentials took some doing in the London of 1943 when almost everything was scarce. But as so often in my life, there were good friends to help me; above all Walter Stewart-Roberts, head of the Administration in the Political Warfare Executive. He and his staff got extra ration cards for me and they knew where supplies could be found of everything I needed. All I had to do was to collect the stuff as it became available. I bought three big metal trunks with a water-proof lining; in them I put all the things I had collected over a period of weeks: leather for soling, boot-polish, aspirin, bars of washing soap, buttons, toilet soap, sewing cotton, needles, washing soda, water-softening powders, lanoline, bottle upon bottle of disinfectant, sheets, blankets, adhesive plaster, books, toothpaste, toilet-paper, darning wool, shoe-laces—in short, everything that might conceivably be needed on a desert island except victuals and drink, which I understood were provided on the spot. All these things were finally brought together in the bedroom of my Club where I was staying at the time; and my room gradually came to look and smell like a village shop. The Royal Navy took my trunks to Archangel and from there they were sent on by rail to Moscow. It all seems rather absurd today and even pretentious, but if I had arrived in Moscow without my village shop I should have been a burden on my colleagues. In Moscow there was virtually nothing to be had, except expensive linens at the Diplomatic Shop and fur hats and things like that.

My friends took me to Waterloo to see me off. The station was smothered in posters and placards appealing to people not to travel, and Herbert Morrison's exhortation was very much in evidence. To his question: 'Is your journey really necessary?' the answer appeared to be Yes, since the station was crowded with what I took to be holiday-makers and the train was full. There was not a seat to be had, in spite of my early arrival, so I was given a stool in the guard's van where I sat with my two suitcases while holding tight to my newly-acquired fur coat. I was conscious of the fact that I was making a journey that was unique: surely, I thought, no one before me had ever travelled to Cairo and Moscow via Bournemouth. And no one was likely to follow my example.

Our first stop at Lisbon was an exhilarating experience to me, as it had been to other wartime travellers from blacked-out London. I do not think that city lights and bright shop-windows ever looked so beautiful as they did in Lisbon in the early summer of 1943. We made an overnight stop, and I spent the greater part of the evening strolling up and down the streets in wonder and admiration. I have never been back to Lisbon; this was my one and only visit; and I am told that it is not a particularly beautiful town. But to me, that evening, Lisbon was one of the most enchanting places I had ever seen. We made another overnight stop, this time, I think, at Lagos where I heard a white woman remark that the Africans these days were altogether out of hand. Discipline had gone, she said; people didn't work, now that you could no longer slap their faces. We flew into the Belgian Congo next. There, at least, no one could complain of lack of discipline. Orders were obeyed without question, and prosperity reigned. Of petrol rationing there was no sign; the cars we saw looked spick and span and expensive; and many had brand new tyres on them. The white lords were demonstrably in power and the social order they had created seemed indestructible. On our last stop in the Congo my luggage was searched, just in case I was trying to smuggle out ivory.

There were only a few passengers in our flying-boat and our pilots gave themselves plenty of time to show us the sights, and even to fly short detours when there was something of particular interest to see. They explained that we were now over the country where parts of *Sanders of the River* had been filmed. We flew very low over the Congo River from time to time, and the roar of our aircraft scattered herds of giraffe and elephant and other animals. Gaily-coloured birds made a silent firework display for us as they flew into the sunshine and back again into the darkness of the forest. A broad splash in the river meant that a crocodile had sprung to life after a motionless day half in and half out of the water. Here and there we saw curious open spaces, speckled with what appeared to be heaps of ashes. We were told that the Africans set fire to bits of the vegetation from time to time, in the knowledge that the young shoots that soon spring up attract small game that are easy to kill and good to eat. Then up the Nile Valley, with its ribbons of cultivated green on each side of the River, and endless stretches of what seemed dead and barren land, grey or brown, just beyond them.

The low point of the trip, so far as I was concerned, came at Khartoum. We came down with a splendid splash upon the Nile. The members of the crew told us that we should be spending the night in Khartoum itself, that beds had been found for us, but that we must take all our belongings with us to the hotel as the only possible precaution against pilfering. I picked up my suitcases and my fur coat, and arrived at my hotel on a hot summer afternoon well within the tropics, with a piece of Arctic equipment on my arm. I thought I heard titters and gasps of astonishment as I made my way through the lobby. My flying companions, I am glad to say, were tactful and courteous, although they kept their distance so as not to be too closely associated with a man who was obviously out of his mind. Next morning, with my fur coat on my arm once again, I crept out of the hotel unseen. I had been kept awake much of the night by the sound of lumps of jelly falling from the ceiling. I discovered later that the noise was made by lizards which lost their grip from time to time.

In Cairo I was treated roughly by the customs people. The officer who gave me his undivided attention was sure that I had a camera concealed somewhere: people always had. His eyes fell upon a case hanging by a strap from my shoulder. It was rectangular, three or four inches by four or five, and some fifteen inches long. Of course it held a camera; it might even be a cine-camera. His eyes glistened as his gaze shifted from my person to my case. He pointed an accusing finger at it. 'What is that, then?' he asked severely. 'A thermos flask and a box to hold sandwiches,' I replied. This was too good to be true. He shook with laughter; great waves of it poured down his chest and his belly until I feared his uniform might crack. He drew the attention of an idle colleague to my extraordinary tale. He, too, billowed with delight. 'Open it,' they shouted in unison. I did. When they saw my thermos-flask and my sandwich-container they became furious. They were convinced I had set out to make fools of them. Somebody behind me was tactless enough to laugh. My belongings were submitted to a rigorous search before I was allowed to go; and then only after my fur coat had been carefully examined. I was beginning to regret having bought the accursed thing; even though I had got it cheap from my tailor because the man for whom it had been made died before it could be delivered to him. If I had had the good sense to let the Navy carry it for me, life would have been simple.

My spirits revived when I learnt that Rex Leeper had invited me to stay with him. He had recently been appointed British Ambassador to Greece; and since the Greek Government had established itself in Cairo by then he had gone to Cairo too. His presence in Egypt gave him the added advantage of being near the scene of SOE activities in Greece itself. If Leeper had talked freely to me about all the problems that arose in Cairo, and all the friction that eventually developed between the Foreign Office, SOE and GHQ, I could say nothing about it in this book since I was staying in his flat as his guest. But Leeper did not discuss these things with me since they were no concern of mine. What I did hear came from my association with my Political Warfare friends in Cairo. I soon realized that people in the diplomatic service regarded SOE as being irresponsible. Its officers, they thought, showed no regard for the political consequences of their actions. Some members of the Political Warfare Department tended on the whole to take the Foreign Office point of view. I did. Those concerned with Political Warfare were at least aware of the fact that there was such a thing as public opinion and that if you were going to influence it in any way you had to go with the grain, and not against it. The SOE people, on the other hand, thought that the Foreign Office was deplorably timorous and would always play safe. One senior SOE officer at the London headquarters invariably referred to the Foreign Office as 'the spinsterhood'. General Wilson, at GHQ, was not generally regarded as the most tactful of men, or indeed, as among the most intelligent. Cairo, I concluded, after I had spent a week there, was an unhappy sort of place.

But thanks to Leeper there were many agreeable interludes. His caustic but unmalicious sense of humour stood us all in very good stead. Among his finest qualities, I think, was his sense of loyalty, especially to subordinates. I first became conscious of this in the Woburn days. There were people on the staff there to whom Hugh Dalton took a strong dislike, and he pressed Leeper to get rid of them. Leeper did not refuse to carry out this Ministerial instruction: that was not his way. What he did was to ask the

Minister to get rid of him first, and then to sack the others afterwards. He was among that handful of officials in the Foreign Office to whom Eden owed a great deal for help and support in the appeasement years; but it was a debt that Eden soon forgot. And Leeper was no good at intriguing; he could not join in the plots that were concocted so lavishly by politicians and temporary civil servants during the war. He knew of them, of course; but they made him physically sick. More than most, he was entitled to say: 'I strove with none; for none was worth my strife.'

I was very glad to get away from Cairo, after doing my short stint at the Political Warfare headquarters. I waited for days before I found an aircraft to take me to Teheran. On the first occasion that I was called to the airport, it was discovered that the aircraft was overloaded just as it was on the point of taking off. I went back to bed; and spent another day or two waiting anxiously for a flight. I got away at last; and spent a day or two in Teheran waiting for an aircraft to Moscow. It stopped at Stalingrad on the way. But we were not given time to see anything. We flew off at once after re-fuelling.

PART THREE

DIPLOMACY AND JOURNALISM: MOSCOW

CHAPTER 11

I WENT TO Russia with the determination to learn the language. Instead, I became a good practical gardener. I learnt my trade under the benevolent supervision of the Ambassador.

My intentions, though, were good. I got myself a Russian grammar and a Russian phrase-book and I acquired a modest store of background knowledge in the interval between my return from Algiers and my departure for Cairo and Moscow. Here Sidney Bernstein was most helpful. He told me that there were a number of interesting Russian historical and war films available in London and offered to lay on a studio in Wardour Street where they could be run off for my benefit. I accepted his offer with gratitude and without hesitation, and spent two or three instructive mornings looking at them. I re-read Tolstoy's *War and Peace*, Dostoevsky's *The Brothers Karamazov*, and Conrad's *Under Western Eyes*; and these, and a few other books, followed me to Moscow, including Bernard Pares's *History of Russia*, André Gide's *Retour de l'U.R.S.S.* and *Retouches à mon Retour de l'U.R.S.S.*, and Seton-Watson's *Britain in Europe*. I also sought the advice of Edward Crankshaw, who had got back from Moscow some time before I took off. And, on the recommendation of Tom Brimelow, later British Ambassador to Poland, then third Secretary in Moscow, I bought a copy of Nicolas Berdayev's *The Origins of Russian Communism*. This book made so strong an impression upon me that I have since read most of what Berdayev has written. I soon found out that there was more to be learnt from him about Russia than from Stalin's declarations and the columns of *Pravda*. I am tempted to quote at length from his writings, since they are the foundations for most of my assumptions about Russia and Russian foreign policy. But I will restrict myself to a sentence or two from *Towards a New Epoch*, published in 1949: 'The anti-Communist front in the West prejudices the development of freedom in Russia. Totalitarianism is an old Russian tradition. It existed in a more distant past and under quite other conditions. Ivan the Terrible was convinced that it was his duty not only to save Russia, but also to save souls. In Soviet Russia "orthodoxy" possesses almost the same importance as in the old Kingdom of Moscow, and heresy is also persecuted there. Dialectical materialism is not a science but a faith.' In the year 1943, the cult of Ivan the Terrible was being actively sponsored by Stalin's propaganda agents, in the form of films and books and articles in newspapers and periodicals. And the doctrine of the 'lesser evil' became fashionable at about this time, namely the doctrine that though imperialism was evil, including Russian imperialism, yet the enslavement of primitive peoples by Tsardom led ultimately to their advantage since it made them free men in the Soviet Union which was in the vanguard of culture and enlightenment. To that extent then, their subjection to Russian imperialism did them less harm than if they had been left like sheep or goats that nourish a blind life within the brain.

There were still a few days of summer left when I arrived in Moscow in September 1943. I found Archie Clark Kerr, later Lord Inverchapel, the Ambassador, seated in the garden, stripped to the waist, enjoying the warm sunshine while writing a dispatch to the Foreign Office with a quill as big as a fan. He always used a quill, and he travelled with a big bundle of them. He sat surrounded by chickens. His face and shoulders were sunburnt: he was always sunburnt: his American friends used to say that he had the colour of a cigar-store Indian.

The Embassy itself was still unsettled and even a little disorganized. The diplomatic corps had only just come back from its exile in Kuybyshev, and the members of the British Embassy staff, like those of the others, were in the throes of organizing essential renovation work before moving in again into their old premises. Clark Kerr and one or two other Ambassadors had stayed on in Moscow with only one or two people to help them; and I suspect that they found it a little difficult to readjust themselves to presiding once again over fairly big establishments. The house to which I had been assigned was not yet ready for occupation so I was sent off to the Hotel Metropole to wait my turn. My guide and escort in all this was Eldridge, the Chancery servant, who with his alert Cockney ways seemed to have more influence with the soggy Soviet bureaucracy than any Ambassador. He spoke only a word or two of Russian, but he invariably got what he wanted. He saw me safely into the hotel, he got the photographs I needed for my diplomatic identity card, he saw to my luggage and to all the necessary formalities. He was among the few who were able to get tickets for the ballet or the opera when tickets were scarcest; he had Russian friends, when no one else had, and went away for a weekend occasionally to stay with them on some farm or other. His ingenuity carried him over every obstacle.

Although the diplomatic corps was highly privileged, and was able to get all kinds of foodstuffs as well as fuel not available to ordinary folk, there were things that were very scarce, even to those of us who had access to special shops. We had great difficulty in getting eggs, I remember; but since our allowance of bread was far too high for us, and this at a time when people had to queue up for bread for hours on end, our housekeeper used to trade our superfluous bread for eggs produced by some farmer on his private plot. I found it hard to believe that even farmers were short of bread, but our housekeeper's evidence convinced me. In the strictly legal sense, she was undoubtedly breaking Soviet law; but hers was the sort of criminal activity that authority evidently winked at since it made life less intolerable for a great many people. It has often been said that the Russian planning system would have broken down if it had not been for fixers and middlemen moving from place to place and from factory to factory, offering to trade one product on which they could lay their hands and which was scarce in the particular locality within which they operated, against another that they could divert to an industrial or private consumer who was badly in need of it.

Fresh vegetables, too, were hard to come by; and for about three months of the year some of us spent a couple of hours every day looking after a kitchen garden. The Ambassador had a biggish garden attached to his house, and grew a great variety of vegetables during a short season. A garden also went with the house I lived in together with some of my colleagues, and we grew things like beans and peas and tomatoes and lettuce. There were six of us in the house at any given time: Tom Brimelow, George Berry, a Second Secretary, Arthur Birse, the official interpreter, Scott Burdett, formerly a Consul-General in Manchuria and at that time in charge of the Embassy's administrative services, William Hair, the Embassy accountant. At times—in the absence of any of those already mentioned—we also had with us Moore Crosthwaite, who later became British Ambassador in Sweden, Charles Gifford, the Commercial Counsellor, and George Bolsover, later Director of the School of Slavonic Studies in London. From the very first day Burdett made up his mind to produce the perfect lawn in spite of the Russian climate. I can still see him during the first half hour after lunch, sitting on an old packing case and digging out plantains and daisies with an old penknife. By the end of our very short season he had managed to produce a presentable piece of grass, but in the following spring, when the snow had gone, it was as awful as ever. William Hair and I tried to grow vegetables; and we did manage to get something fresh to eat during the season. Arthur Birse spent most of his time leaning on a spade. When the Ambassador was away, which was only very rarely, it fell to me to keep an eye upon his garden also.

Crosthwaite, then head of Chancery, was a great believer in the virtue of remaining calm in the face of difficulty and even of danger. He worked a longer day than most of us, and used to sleep for half an hour or so after lunch before going back to his desk at the Embassy. The rest of us usually remained at table, gossiping over our coffee if we were not gardening. One afternoon when we had only just got down to things, the door opened silently and Crosthwaite put his head in. 'I don't want to upset you chaps,' he said in a mild and unhurried voice, 'but I rather think the house is on fire.' And with that he disappeared. The house was very much on fire. Clouds of smoke swept through the entrance and up the stairs from a fire somewhere in the basement. Each of us reacted in a different way to the event. One or two of us, including myself, went out into the garden, with the feeling that there was not much we could do. The fire-brigade came within minutes, but not before Burdett had put on his hat with all the dignity of a Consul-General, picked up a valueless occasional table and carried it carefully into the garden while puffing at a cigarette through a large holder. Others rushed upstairs to save what could be saved. Everything turned out well in the end; no serious damage was done; and the fire-brigade people did a splendid tidying-up job.

Arthur Birse, the official interpreter, is the most discreet person

I have ever met. He is not secretive; he never gives you the impression that he has anything to conceal; or that his mind is full of information that must in no circumstances be divulged. He is an extraordinary man, who pretends to be ordinary. His sense of humour is infectious—he never lost it, even at the end of the longest working-day. As an interpreter he was outstanding because he never injected his personality or his views into the job. He subordinated himself entirely to the person for whom he was acting. There are few interpreters who are as self-effacing as that. I recall one Russian interpreter at an international Conference who, when he was translating a speech for his chief, began: 'The Minister says, and I agree with him . . .'. I have been told about another who acted for Stephen Tallents when he was on a mission to the Baltic States soon after the First World War. Tallents became very irritated after a while by the dilatory methods of the politicians he was dealing with and resolved to be firm in future. When next they met he spoke roughly and almost offensively and instructed his man to put over every single word he had used. The politicians listened politely, smiled, and gave way. As they left the Ministry, Tallents turned to his interpreter and said: 'I knew it. That's the way to talk to them. All this soft soap doesn't pay.' His interpreter, young and inexperienced, said: 'I'm afraid that's not quite right, Sir. You see, I did not repeat your piece word for word. I put it more politely.' A comment on the affair in *The Times* in August 1920 did not help matters. 'Great credit is due to Mr. Tallents,' the paper wrote, 'for the tactful and painstaking way he has carried out the work of fixing the Latvia–Estonia border.' Birse could not conceivably have done anything like that. Churchill knew that if he wanted to say sharp things to Stalin, Birse would put them into the appropriate Russian.

The need to look after the Russian staff of the Embassy, the chauffeurs, the messengers, the yardmen and the others, often presented great difficulties. In the eyes of Authority all of them were third-class citizens; their rations were meagre, and such extras as they needed they got from us. Even the cloth for the chauffeurs' uniforms had to be specially imported from London. In the spring of 1944, when everything was extremely scarce and when the ordinary shops were stocked mainly with cardboard cheeses and papier-mâché sausages for display purposes, the Ambassador thought it would be a good idea to help our Russian staff grow their own potatoes. Burdett was asked to make the necessary arrangements, which involved him in long negotiations with *Burobin*, the most obstructive of all Soviet institutions, but the one with which all foreigners were forced to deal if they wanted anything done, all the way from getting the plumbing looked at, to extra rations for distinguished visitors. We called it the Circumlocution Office; and I could never make up my mind whether its delays were due to ill-will or to incompetence. Burdett, who was used to taking procrastination in his stride and without loss of temper because of his Chinese experiences, often came back to the Embassy flushed and angry after a session with *Burobin*. 'If only they had yellow faces,' he muttered, 'if only they had yellow faces. It wouldn't matter to me then, because I'd know what I'm up against.' Eventually, he got a plot of land on the outskirts of Moscow, and a supply of seed potatoes also.

I went out to the field with a couple of my colleagues one Sunday morning to divide it up into suitable allotments for the staff. We had to provide between thirty and forty plots, and we took with us plenty of string and sticks to mark out the land. It turned out to be a tough job since the field was very rough and sloped unevenly down to a stream. In spite of these difficulties, the plots were marked out with great accuracy to avoid jealousy, and we left the ground well marked to indicate the precise extent of each allotment. And then we went home, conscious of a job well done. When we went back the following Sunday, for our formal opening ceremony, we found that all our signs had been moved. We could not quite tell what was wrong, but we could see that everything was wrong. Somehow the field looked even rougher and more derelict than before. Our Russians were there in force and stood about in a high state of excitement waiting for permission to take over. Then Eldridge turned up with the seed potatoes in a lorry and began to shovel them out. A scramble followed; but eventually we got the thing under control and weighed the right amounts on a sort of kitchen scale. Then there followed another scramble, this time for the best plots. There was a good deal of jostling and swearing, but an unarmed Eldridge sorted it all out without bloodshed. Two servants on the Ambassador's personal staff who had taken it for granted that the best plots would be reserved for them were particularly enraged. They found themselves left with the plots nearest the stream at the bottom of the field which were the most likely to be flooded. They made so great a fuss that I withdrew from the argument. Eldridge managed to pacify them. But then Eldridge always did manage things.

I got into difficulties of another kind with the Ambassador's Greek butler, Timoleon the Magnificent. The walls of his room at the Embassy were covered with photographs of the great, most of them autographed. When he threw open the doors into the dining room and announced '*Son Excellence est servi*,' he had the bearing of a worldly priest presiding over a religious ceremony. Only the incense was lacking. No matter how great the difficulties, he always managed to provide a splendid meal for the Ambassador and his guests. There would be no shortage of good food, one felt, so long as he was around. He did not take the easy way out, like hiding an indifferent meal behind a first course of caviar which was easy to come by at the time—so easy, indeed, that we had to ask our own housekeeper not to serve it oftener than once a week. But his ways were peculiar; some of his raw materials were kept in the most unlikely places, as I discovered one day when I had been asked to look over the premises in the Ambassador's absence. In the basement I discovered a contented pig, next to one of the pantries. In the attic there was a flock of chickens. I do not believe that I am particularly sensitive in matters of hygiene, but I thought the pig and the chickens were in the wrong places, and said so. Timoleon was told to find room for them elsewhere, and I dropped several notches in his esteem.

We had a hard-working and most helpful domestic staff in our own house in the Ulitsa Vakhtangova. They were all Volga Germans, descendants of the German peasants and traders invited into Russia by Catherine the Great. They had kept many of their German characteristics, but they were of Russian nationality. They spoke German—a sort of German; and they were clean, tidy and industrious. It was quite plain that they despised the Russians and thought them slovenly, unpunctual and incompetent. Their villages had been oases of good husbandry in the desert of dirt and disorder of the Russian countryside. But our Volga Germans were uneasy, extremely touchy and sometimes morose. This was not surprising since most of their people had been deported far to the East because the authorities suspected them of being politically unreliable, to the extent even of preferring German to Russian rule. I have no doubt that there were people in 1941 prepared to pay a high price to escape from Stalin's clutches; and that this explains, in part, the speed of the German advance to the outskirts of Moscow. One Communist who spent many years in Siberian labour camps before the war, the Croatian A. Ciliga, has recorded that, among the internees, conversation turned often to the prospect of being liberated by the Germans or the Japanese. The greater part of the non-party intelligentsia, he wrote in a book published in 1949, thought on these lines, as well as most of the peasants. Only the urban working class was immune to these ideas. He observed also that the great purges of the mid-'thirties were undertaken in order to punish people for crimes they had not yet committed, but which they would be almost certain to commit, given the opportunity. The Volga Germans, then, were deported not for what they had done, but for what they might do.

I soon became embarrassingly conscious of the fact that in a country where even bootlaces were a luxury, the things we brought back with us from the rich West must have been a source of constant temptation to our domestic staff. We tried not to flaunt our opulence. We did not stoop to the vulgarity of checking our supplies at frequent intervals; and I have no doubt that if there had been any noteworthy pilfering we should very soon have become aware of it. Never before have I encountered greater honesty. I noticed the same honesty at the Hotel Metropole where I lived for about ten days immediately after my arrival in Moscow. When they gave me tea in the hotel, I was always given a dozen or so lumps of sugar to go with it. Sugar was very scarce in Moscow in those days; and since Russians are very fond of all kinds of sweets this must have been a great hardship to them. I was given so much sugar that most of it was left in the dish at the end of my meal; but the chambermaid who removed the tea-things always took care to leave the sugar behind. It remained untouched and at the end of a week I must have accumulated well over half a pound of the stuff. When I left the hotel I did what so many others had done before me: I gave the sugar to the girl. I did not dare to catch her eye as I did it. It was a horrible experience. I wished she had taken it all while my back was turned. Not everybody would support my statement about Russian honesty. One member of Moscow's diplomatic corps found himself trouserless one morning while travelling in an overnight sleeper to Moscow. He had left the carriage window slightly open during the night and someone had managed to steal his trousers while he slept. He was so distressed that he was tempted to abandon his diplomatic career.

It would be untrue to say that I went about Moscow with a perpetual feeling of guilt because I was so much better fed than the Russians, so much better housed, so much better clothed. Yet somehow one was always aware of the gap between our living standards and theirs. The party bosses, the administrators, the ballerinas, the leading authors and journalists and their fellow time-servers, did themselves extremely well, and I do not suppose that the word 'shortage' figured in their vocabulary. They had shops of their own at which many of the unobtainable things could be bought at a reasonable price: 'Surplus-Value Stores', one of my Marxist friends used to call them. But even these highly privileged people made it obvious at times that their appetite for better goods and more of them was almost an obsession. A friend of mine who had a luxuriously produced American mail-order catalogue in his possession was persuaded to lend it to a senior official in the NKVD (as the security police were called in those days). He took it home to his wife, and admitted later that the illustrations had made her giddy with envy. The lives of most other people were overshadowed by hunger and poverty, and, in the winter, cold. We once heard an old woman staggering under a load of firewood mutter to herself: 'Thank God Capitalism has been abolished.' I can still see in my mind's eye that hungry old man, his eyes dimmed by a thousand humiliations, looking at all the delicacies in the diplomatic shop that were not for him to buy, even if he had had the money; and that nice-looking middle-aged woman, her pride broken, as she begged one of our party with tears running down her cheeks, to buy an orange for her so she could gratify the whim of an old sister who lay dying at home. Nor can I forget the gnarled hands of the old, old women, their faces blue with cold, as they stretched out their arms for charity while crouched on the icy steps of a dilapidated and abandoned Church. All this made a much deeper impression upon me than the sight of a couple of famished bodies lying in the gutter of a side-street in Teheran. The authorities did not want foreigners to know about the extent of destitution in the Soviet capital; and when I returned there in 1947 to report the four-power Conference for the BBC I was told that beggars and down-and-outs had been picked up by the police, put into Army lorries, and dumped into the countryside some fifty miles out.

It was at about this time—in the late winter of 1947—that Clark Kerr's successor at the Embassy, Maurice Peterson, was having trouble with the authorities over a consignment of supplies addressed to him and intended for the whole Embassy staff. There had been calls without number upon the officials of *Burobin*, but all to no purpose. Finally, the Ambassador asked Vyshinsky himself to use his influence. He did not insist upon anything; he did not demand anything; he just wanted a little help, a word spoken in the right place. Vyshinsky nodded. The Ambassador ended the conversation with the remark that he and his staff were now running short and that they were genuinely in need of the supplies that were being held up, apparently by the customs people. In order to show his goodwill, he would be delighted to give a substantial part of the consignment to the poor of Moscow. Vyshinsky's face lost its fabricated good humour. 'There are no poor in Moscow,' he said sharply. At the time of the interview, bread was so scarce in Moscow because of the shortfall in the 1946 harvest that there were queues outside the bakers' shops and angry scenes when supplies ran out, as they often did. Everything was scarce in 1947. 'Many people in Moscow,' the *Manchester Guardian* reported on 27 February, 'are beginning to show clear signs of malnutrition'—which is the customary euphemism for starvation. On the previous day, the paper had noted that the 'Russian civilian is having a much harder life today than a year ago, or even during the latter stages of the war. The price of bread has been increased 3½ times as compared with the year before.' It was not unusual for people to finger our over-coats as they passed us in the street and to mutter their admiration at the quality of the material. Even the diplomatic corps was made to feel the pinch of scarcity: there was only one hotel in the whole of Moscow, the Hotel Moskva, where the delegations to the four-power Conference had their headquarters, in which white bread could be had at the time. In the war years, the privileged had had no such difficulty.

Two years after a victorious war, the Russians were very near the end of their economic tether. Stalin was almost certain that there would be an economic breakdown in the West also. In January 1945, while Roosevelt was still alive, Molotov asked for a reconstruction loan from the United States in order, as he put it, 'to save the United States from a post-war depression'. From the Russian point of view, reconstruction credits, and things like Marshall Aid, were of greater importance to the economy of the United States than to the needy peoples of Europe. The Parliamentary correspondent of *The Times* made almost the same point in a comment published on 7 June 1947. Marshall Aid, he wrote, 'is also partly due to a growing anxiety in American business circles that the failure of European markets, combined with falling prices at home, might lead to a slump'. In April 1947, in a conversation with Governor Stassen, Stalin asked whether an economic crisis was expected in the United States. There were reports in the American press, he said, that an economic crisis would soon arise. Objectively, as the Russian Communists no doubt argued, Marshall Aid was designed to bolster up the American capitalist system, and was therefore of necessity anti-Russian. It would have made the Russian predicament more tolerable, and easier to explain to the Russian people, if the West had been plunged into crisis in 1947; it would have made it simple for Stalin to argue that people must put up with present difficulties since they were universal; but that a happy future, based on the ruins of the old economic order, was just round the corner, with Russia leading the way to it. But Stalin found no consolation in the evidence available to him. The economist Varga was disgraced for failing to predict the fall of capitalism. Perhaps Molotov's repetitive insistence upon reparations from Germany to the value of $10,000 millions at pre-war prices was dictated, in part, by the pressure of an unhappy and disillusioned people for some tangible proof of victory. A few months later, Stalin boycotted the Marshall Plan and carried Russia and her satellites into another nine years of destitution. If he had co-operated with the West, the Russian glacier might have slipped off to an unknown and unforeseeable destination. Held against a doctrinal wall of his own making, Stalin had no other way to go but back into the past.

Of equal inportance in this connection, is that when the Marshall Plan was launched, the struggle between the Communist Party and the Russian peasant had been resumed. It first began with Stalin's forced collectivization programme and has by no means ended yet, in spite of all the conjuring tricks performed later by Khrushchev. During the war with Germany, there was a kind of uneasy armistice between the Party and the peasant. The peasants were encouraged to step up the output of food from their private plots and were allowed to charge high prices on the open market for such things as eggs, butter, cabbages, cucumbers and fruit. In practice, this privilege applied only to those peasants who had plots of land so near the big towns that they could travel in with their produce without too much loss of time. They were not allowed to hire anybody to sell it for them. From time to time, we caught a glimpse of the rich pickings that fell into their grasp during this profiteering period. They used to come into the Commission Shops, or Government-run pawnbroking establishments, to turn their roubles into ancient fur coats, or household fittings, or bits of bric-à-brac, or odd pieces of jewellery or something else of what was left of the property of the dispossessed classes, often some treasured family heirloom without great intrinsic value, and offered for sale by those who hoped their chattels would produce enough money to keep them from starvation for another month. A peasant would pull out a fat bundle of filthy bank-notes from under his smock or tunic, thousand-rouble notes among them, pay for something he appeared to prize and walk away in triumph with his acquisition. The terms 'melon millionaire' and 'cucumber millionaire' crept into the language; and their antics were the stock-in-trade of the clowns in Moscow's circus.

But all this cucumber money was not spent on trinkets. Much of it was hidden away at home. It represented vast purchasing power at a time when there was nothing to buy. No doubt the peasants hoped that by the end of 1945 or in 1946 they would be able to spend it on something they really needed, a sewing-machine, perhaps, or if that was too ambitious, some cotton-thread and needles to sew things by hand. All this money represented a threat to the stability of the régime which now found itself faced with people no longer vulnerable because they were living on the edge of destitution, but with enormous purchasing power at their disposal. Stalin disarmed them by revaluing the rouble. The savings vanished overnight, and the Party renewed its campaign to bully the peasant into acquiescence. With much of the purchasing power that might have been used to pay for consumer goods destroyed, Stalin was able to resume his drive towards a highly developed heavy industry, without thought for the consumer. This policy could not have been squared with the aims of Marshall Aid; it is impossible to believe that the United States Congress would have been prepared to vote aid-money for Russia, or for the satellites, if it had been used mainly to strengthen the foundations of Russian heavy industry, not to mention Russian nuclear research, while the consumer continued to go short. Marshall Aid would have been acceptable to Stalin only if it allowed him to maintain what was basically a war economy which also made it much easier to exercise control over the population. When ration cards have to be presented as you buy food or articles of clothing; when residence permits are required before you can get a bit of floor space in Moscow or one of the other major towns, then police control is easily exercised. But once ration cards are abolished, with food becoming more easily available, a greater force of security police will be needed to keep the sort of order and discipline that a totalitarian régime requires. There were occasions when I imagined that Stalin deliberately pursued a policy of scarcity in order to maintain his grip upon the country. Some of the relative laxity now apparent in Russia and in Eastern Europe must surely be due, in part at least, to greater relative plenty. Revolutions are made by people with full stomachs; a starving rabble is capable of little more than a riot.

The Russian authorities not only did all they could to hide the evidence of famine, they also terrorized their people into denying that it existed; except, of course, in such places as Leningrad where the privations of ordinary folk during the siege made good propaganda. And yet even in Leningrad one heard some strange stories. In the summer of 1944, I visited Leningrad, in the company of John Balfour and his wife, and a member of the staff of the Canadian Embassy. Balfour was Minister at the British Embassy at the time, under Clark Kerr. The siege had been lifted some four months earlier, and things were only just beginning to get back to normal. We were met by two very helpful women from Intourist who guided us through the town and its environs and who took a great deal of trouble to make our stay comfortable as well as instructive. At the end of our tour, we wanted to show our gratitude in some practical way. Money we could not offer; that would have been an insult. Fortunately, Mrs. Balfour had brought some chocolate with her. 'No thank you,' said our guides. 'No thank you. We don't eat chocolate.' Then

Mrs. Balfour remembered that one of the women had spoken of her children. 'Oh well,' she said, 'give it to your children. They will like it,' The answer came without hesitation. 'We have plenty of chocolate at home.' The gift was refused; and the façade of icy self-sufficiency remained without blemish. Officially, there were no shortages in Russia, not even in Leningrad, now that it had been liberated.

Yet all was not stoicism and harshness, even when things were at their worst. Among the elderly in Russia were numbers of foreigners—British, French and other nationalities—who had stayed on in various capacities after the Revolution. Leningrad had its quota of genteel French governesses who continued to exist in spite of difficulties that would have overwhelmed less determined characters. In Moscow, there were people who had had businesses of their own before the Revolution. They had lost everything; but they stayed on working in offices or factories that had once been theirs or under their management. There was one old Scots couple I heard of who just managed to keep going with the help of occasional supplies from the Embassy. The ration for elderly people, incapable of hard physical labour, was derisory during the war; it was regarded by many as tantamount to a sentence of death by slow starvation. My acquaintances used to say that when they stood in their long queue to get their meagre rations, they could always tell whose turn had come to die. His face would seem grey one week, they said; then slightly yellow and rather puffed. And that would be the last time the man was seen. No one asked after him, of course; to make inquiries about people who disappeared was to invite the police to take an interest in you, and that was something no Russian in his senses would ever do. One day, so I was told, a party official called upon the couple and gave them a ration card. 'But I already have one,' the old man said. 'We know,' was the reply, 'but you stayed with us after the Revolution and helped us to run one of our factories. We have not forgotten that. We want you to have that extra card.'

CHAPTER 12

IF OUR privileges created a barrier between ordinary Russians and ourselves, the authorities not only seemed well satisfied with this state of affairs, but did their utmost to increase the discrepancy. Our clothes, as I have already mentioned, set us apart, even if we did not utter a word in a foreign language. We suffered from a sort of apartheid. I know that in a peasant community, the guests of the house are often treated as if they were feudal lords. A generation ago, if a small-holder in the poorer part of Norway invited you to share a meal with him, his wife would serve the best the house could offer, and make you sit down at table while she and her husband stood about ministering to your wants, without touching a bite of food themselves. Russian hospitality was even more embarrassing. In the autumn of 1944, the whole of Moscow had one solitary bar. It was open from about twelve noon to about seven o'clock in the evening; and the rule was that there should never be more people on the premises than there was seating accommodation for. Perhaps the policeman who invented this rule had picked up the idea in Washington where it is illegal to drink while standing up. In Moscow, the effect of the regulation was that there was always a group of people outside the premises waiting hopefully for a vacant seat and a glass of Caucasian brandy, or champagne, or vodka, or some strange mixture whose secret was known only to its maker. When an obvious-looking foreigner joined the queue, the policeman on duty would go into the bar, tap a Russian on the shoulder and tell him to get out. His place would then be taken by the lucky foreigner. If there were two or three foreigners anxious to get in, two or three Russians would be thrown out. They left, so far as I could see, without a murmur of protest; and the people in the queue watched impassively.

If you went to the Bolshoi Theatre you were also given preferential treatment. Tickets for the better seats were available only to privileged persons, members of the diplomatic corps, distinguished visitors and foreign journalists, and, if Russian, to officials of appropriate rank, or worthy members of some trade union or other. The people waiting to leave their hats and coats in the cloakroom were brushed aside when a foreigner arrived, and he was given priority treatment. The same thing happened at the end of the performance, no matter how many people were waiting. The Ambassador in his ancient Rolls-Royce was invited by the authorities to break all the traffic rules, if he felt that way inclined: to drive on the wrong side of the road, or to ignore the traffic lights if he was in a hurry. The police, they told him, would see to it that all would be well. These and other privileges made it virtually impossible to establish any real contact with ordinary citizens.

Things are not so rigid today; people seem quite willing not only to talk to foreigners, but to air their grievances in public. When Harold Wilson went to Moscow in the summer of 1966, I was with the party of journalists who flew to Russia to report the visit. We had been working rather late one evening, and we found that all the restaurants in our neighbourhood were crowded out; so we wandered about in the hope of finding a vacant table somewhere. Then, in a well-lighted corner café, we caught sight of three or four unoccupied tables. When we tried to go in, we found a tough-looking doorkeeper in the way who told us that the door was locked and that they were not, at the moment, open for business. He explained that they were keeping one or two tables free for people who had been to the Moscow Arts Theatre and who would soon be turning up. My friend, who spoke fluent Russian, argued with the man, but to no purpose. He told the doorman that we were hungry; that we had called at several other restaurants and found them all crowded out; and he mentioned casually that we were foreigners. This was a magic word twenty years ago, and would have opened almost any door to us. Its only effect on this occasion was an outburst of anger. 'They are building hotels and restaurants for foreigners all over Moscow,' the man shouted, 'while we are still living four to a room. All for the sake of foreigners. Come back in ten years' time, and then perhaps there will be a table for you.' People would not have dared to talk like that in Stalin's day, at least not in the big towns. They would have been afraid of denunciation by spies and snoopers.

It was no doubt this fear of coming under suspicion that led those Russians we did meet on formal occasions, the officials and the privileged journalists and authors, to refuse all our invitations. Among the few who found it possible to come on his own to a meal with foreigners, was Ilya Ehrenburg. I met him for the first time at the house of the Australian Chargé d'Affaires who had invited him to dinner. Ehrenburg's vocabulary, on this occasion, seemed modelled on one of *Pravda*'s less inspiring leading articles; his main topic was the need for a second front, and when he thought his conversation needed a little comic relief, he made ponderous jokes about the reluctance of a great seafaring nation to launch an invasion fleet across the Channel. We soon got bored with him and let him prattle on. We understood why the authorities found it unnecessary to restrict his movements: a man with such a fine ear for official doctrine would be quite safe among heretics and foreigners. Even in 1946, you could still detect references to the second front in Russian conversation and to the cowardice of the British in refusing to face the Channel. In the late autumn of that year, Ernest Bevin led a British delegation to a four-power conference in New York. He travelled in the old *Aquitania*; and a group of British diplomatic correspondents accompanied him, myself among them. Also on board were several members of the Russian delegation to the Conference. On our first evening out, while still in the Channel, we exchanged a few words with the Russians as we stood on deck watching the waves tapering off into a slow swell upon the horizon. Suddenly, one of the Russians had an idea. 'We too,' he said, 'we too, have waves on the Volga.' The inference was obvious: the waves on the Volga had not frightened the Red Army. The waves in the Channel had deterred the British.

Ehrenburg, then, was safe enough as the mouthpiece of the Kremlin and he was therefore allowed to move around with comparative freedom. But in the ordinary way, if we invited a Russian official to lunch or to dinner, or for a drink, although he might well accept, he would fail to turn up, or he might bring half a dozen or so friends with him who would be in a position to assure authority that nothing indiscreet had been said. Among the few who managed to come to terms with the Russians, and to talk with them more or less on equal terms, was Brigadier George Hill. This extraordinary man went underground as a secret agent in

Russia in 1917–18 at the time when Bruce Lockhart was arrested. He had made all his arrangements well in advance. He had a false passport in the name of Bergman, and lived as an ordinary Russian. He got himself a job on the night shift of a newsreel studio at a time when the Bolsheviks were offering a reward of 50,000 roubles for him, dead or alive. When his name was put forward in 1941 for the post of liaison officer with the NKVD, Molotov promised to make inquiries. When next he saw Stafford Cripps, who at that time was British Ambassador in Moscow, he told him with a smile that they knew all about Hill. He raised his arm: 'We have dossiers that size about him,' he added. And in due course, Hill came to Moscow.

He wore his Tsarist decorations with his DSO and his MC, and no one took it amiss. His Russian friends probably welcomed this piece of boldness at a time when Stalin was stirring up memories of old military glories, and restoring Tsarist Generals to the Russian Pantheon. He even succeeded in persuading two high-ranking NKVD officers to accept Clark Kerr's invitation to dine at the Embassy. They acted their part to perfection; that is to say they behaved as I had always expected secret service people in a thriller to behave. They parked their car some hundred yards or so away from the Embassy, well out of sight, and arrived on foot trying to look like men without a care in the world, out for an evening stroll. I, too, was on my way to the Embassy that evening, and I had noticed a strange-looking car on the point of parking just ahead of me. I saw two men in black uniform get out, inspect their car to see that all doors and windows were locked and look carefully round to see (as I thought) if they were being followed. By that time, I had passed them. And then I got the impression that I was the one who was being followed. I felt all the more sure of this when they walked past the outer gate, a point beyond which no Russian would dare to penetrate unless he was on Government business, and into the Embassy itself. I bounded upstairs to tell the Ambassador about the invasion. 'There are two NKVD Colonels or something on my tail,' I began. 'They're actually in the building.' 'Of course,' was the reply, 'I've invited them to dinner, along with Pop and yourself.' Pop was our name for Hill. It had been given to him by Philip Jordan because of his extraordinary resemblance to the key figure in the strip cartoon of the name carried by the *Daily Sketch*. We had a pleasant and amusing dinner, and the conversation was light-hearted. The security Colonels discussed politics rather in the way Jesuits might have argued about certain lay aspects of the Faith.

During the course of a party at Hill's flat one evening, he happened to run short of brandy. I suppose the time must have been around ten o'clock, and no shops were open. Hill picked up the telephone, dialled a number and got an immediate answer. He spoke a few words, and within half an hour a man in a black uniform arrived with a case of the stuff. I wonder whether M I 5 would have been equally helpful if a foreign Embassy in London had run short of liquor. We had been talking at the time about Hill's hope to get permission to be dropped behind the German lines in Poland, just to get an impression of what was going on. He was bitterly disappointed when his superiors turned down his application. I am sure he would have found it as easy to pass himself off as a German as he had found it to look and speak like a Russian some twenty-five years earlier.

Others did not find it so easy as Hill did to get supplies of what they wanted and at the right time. When Churchill warned the Embassy that he was coming to Moscow in September 1944, the Ambassador remembered that there was one kind of Russian champagne that the Prime Minister very much liked. I should perhaps explain that the ordinary Russian champagne is not very good, although we were only too glad to have it at the time. But this particular champagne had something special about it, and the Ambassador was determined to lay in a case or two against the visit. When the usual list was made out of the extra supplies that would be needed for the occasion, which included a dinner party for Stalin as Churchill's guest at the Embassy, a request was made for this special quality. One of the secretaries thought he knew its name, but he had got it wrong. Another suggested that it would be best to describe the label on the bottle when ordering, but no one could remember what it looked like. A letter went off to the manager of the Diplomatic Shop. The reply came back almost at once: no one had ever heard of the stuff; perhaps it did not exist. Someone got on to the Ministry for Foreign Affairs and asked for help. The officials professed ignorance; they did not respond; there was, it seemed, nothing that could be done; was the Embassy sure that this champagne actually existed? The Ambassador was sure that it did and remained determined to get it. Finally, he wrote a personal letter to Molotov explaining the circumstances; and expressing the hope that Churchill would be in a position to offer Stalin the same splendid champagne as Stalin had given Churchill at a party in the Kremlin. At the very last minute, a case of it appeared at the Embassy without a word of explanation.

Hill, I believe, was the only man on the official side who managed to get on easy personal terms with the Russians, although everybody tried hard. Among journalists, the most successful were Ed Stevens of the *Christian Science Monitor* and Alexander Werth, then of *The Sunday Times*, whose books on Russia enjoyed a well-deserved success. These two were exceptions to the general rule; most of us were kept at arm's length; although we were, of course, invited to the great formal parties at which we were expected to wear white ties. There was no nonsense about equality on those occasions. Guests were carefully graded, and those who were regarded as being of particular importance, such as the British and American Ambassadors, were given extra-special VIP treatment. They were allowed to go into a sort of inner room where they found Molotov and Mikoyan and Voroshilov and other leaders. They were given the best sort of caviar; and the best champagne and the best vodka. The rest of us were kept moving in the outer rooms, where only pressed caviar was on offer, or worse still, red caviar, and where supplies tended to run out rather too soon.

The first official function to which I was invited in my capacity as First Secretary at the British Embassy took place in November 1943, on the day of the twenty-sixth anniversary of the October Revolution. By that time, all the Embassy staffs had got back from Kuybyshev, and diplomatic life was back to normal. The tide of war was turning; and this gave added importance to the party. I remember walking in a sort of queue into one of the great reception rooms where Molotov and Vyshinsky and other Ministers and senior officials were standing, poised to shake hands with their guests. After a while I noticed that people were staring at me with critical curiosity. I felt guilt-ridden and inferior. Perhaps my white tie had come undone: I fingered it nervously. I had not been able to tie it myself and it had been done for me by one of my colleagues. Perhaps I should have come in through some other door. All sorts of unpleasant and embarrassing thoughts occurred to me. When I finally got though my ordeal and had completed my quota of handshakings, I turned to one of my colleagues and asked, 'What's wrong? You've all been glaring in the most unpleasant way.' He looked at me with pity. 'You've made a jolly good start in Moscow,' he said. 'You came in with the Japanese. Perhaps you don't know that we are at war with them.'

Molotov was in a light-hearted mood on this occasion and seemed to have a smile for everybody. He proposed toasts to victory, toasts to the Alliance, toasts to post-war friendship, toasts to a happy future, toasts to Uncle Tom Cobley. He soon moved off into the private room taking Averell Harriman with him. When the British Ambassador appeared, Molotov wedged him into a sort of corner between himself and his interpreter. Harriman managed to get away fairly early, but Clark Kerr was caught. At one point the Swedish Ambassador tried to inch his way into the company. He could see that Molotov was in a mellow mood. Molotov gave him a shove. 'You're a Swede,' he said, 'you're neutral. And I don't like neutrals. Now my friend Kerr here,' and at this point Molotov slapped the Ambassador hard on the back, 'my friend Kerr would have been a partisan if he had been Russian.' The humiliated Swede disappeared, and Clark Kerr was eventually allowed to escape. Molotov tottered away, unable to stand without help, half carried by two secretaries. Clark Kerr woke up next morning with a cut on his forehead. No one dared to ask any questions. There were hushed voices in the Embassy throughout that day.

The Russians liked to see how much drink their guests could take. They were always asking you to take more vodka, always insisting that you drained your glass when you drank a toast with them. I still cannot make up my mind whether these promptings were inspired by a spirit of generosity, or whether they were just a vulgar plot to make you drunk. They themselves usually took good care not to overstep the mark, and the November 1943 party is the only one at which I have seen Molotov overcome. Some of us suspected that the Russians wanted to make fools of their foreign guests. The Australian Ambassador in Moscow at the time, a former trade union leader who knew what he wanted and usually got it, became extremely suspicious after attending two or three Russian parties. He noticed that while the guests often came away drunk, the Russians usually stayed sober; and he promised himself to get to the bottom of the mystery at the first opportunity. At his next party, the Ambassador was Mikoyan's guest; and Mikoyan, as usual, proposed a great many toasts, all in vodka. The Ambassador waited until his host was engaged in conversation with the man sitting to the other side of him, then he took a quick sip at the glass that Mikoyan had been using. It contained a thin Caucasian white wine. The Ambassador called upon the interpreter to pay attention, and then denounced Mikoyan in a loud voice. 'It's a strange sort of hospitality you have here in Russia,' he said. 'You keep the best drink for yourselves and give the guests the next best thing.' He pointed at Mikoyan's glass as he spoke. Mikoyan laughed without any sign of embarrassment. He had all the *savoir-faire* of a super salesman. He could have made a highly successful career for himself in any country, under any kind of social system. He could have made a fortune as a Wall Street operator; or as a manipulator of markets; or as a commercial-traveller. He was a superb fixer; he fixed even Castro for a while. But always, it seems, a lone wolf. He fell into the hands of the British military force in the Transcaucasus in 1918, together with other Bolsheviks. Some of them were shot. But Mikoyan got away. Throughout his career he has always managed to get away; his timing has been perfect.

It seemed to me that there was always far too much drinking at these official parties, although Churchill in his accounts of meetings with Stalin and his Ministers has denied it. When vodka became more plentiful again after the war, the toiling masses, to use *Pravda*'s term, took to the bottle in a big way. At one time it was possible to buy a glass of vodka from special kiosks dotted about the streets of Moscow. After a while the Party press in Moscow as well as in the provinces began to denounce the crime of heavy drinking and wrote about its bad effects on industrial output and on country life where farm workers took advantage of every possible feast-day in the calendar to souse themselves in drink. A generation earlier, Henry Ford had argued in much the same terms when he strove to step up efficiency and output in his factories in Detroit. Then came the day when Khrushchev launched his temperance campaign. It was at its height when Macmillan and Selwyn Lloyd visited Russia in 1959; and it led to an interesting scene at the British Embassy when Khrushchev,

Mikoyan and others came to a reception in honour of the occasion. Khrushchev was seen stalking about the room with some sort of soft drink in his glass. He stopped in front of Mikoyan. 'I cannot understand it,' he said, raising his eyes to heaven. 'The voice I hear is the voice of Mikoyan; the man I see looks like Mikoyan; but it cannot be Mikoyan since he is drinking whisky.' Mikoyan answered him with a laugh: 'When I go to a party at the Chinese Embassy,' he said, 'I eat snakes. When I go to the British Embassy, I take whisky. Prosit.' And he raised his glass to his leader.

The effects of Khrushchev's temperance campaign were felt even in Kiev where our party stayed for a day or two during the course of the Macmillan visit, and where we were made to trudge through the mud of a collective farm as part of the sight-seeing programme inflicted upon foreign visitors. The ordeal had no attractions for any of us; and as I stood looking at Selwyn Lloyd across a bale of straw, I saw a twitch in his eye rather like a wink. On the following day, I was having lunch with some of my colleagues when I saw that my decanter of vodka was empty. I had had the normal hundred grammes, but I wanted some more. One of our party who knew rather more about the rules than I did told me he was sure no more vodka would be provided for me, but he encouraged me to try. I called the waitress and asked her to get me another hundred grammes. She went away and came back with a severe-looking female dressed all in black. She could hardly believe her ears when she heard me repeat the order. She looked at me with disapproval. 'Mr. Khrushchev he say,' she said in her strange English, 'that one hundred grammes enough.'

There were no obtrusive signs of temperance when the British Parliamentary Delegation led by Lord Coleraine was entertained by a group of collective farmers, mostly wine-growers, near Tiflis. The BBC had managed to get me attached to the delegation and I travelled widely through the Soviet Union with its members in October 1954. When we came to Tblisi (Tiflis), it was easy to see that the Georgians had made up their minds to outdo the Muscovites in their hospitality. The highlight of our visit there was an alfresco meal served on an immense trestle-table overburdened with food and drink of various kinds. Half-way through the proceedings, one of the farmers produced a huge drinking-horn, filled it up with wine and drank it off in one great gulp. He expected his guests to follow suit. Some of us, including myself, had seen what was coming, had prudently left the table and were hiding as best we could behind some nearby trees. Stanley Evans, who jumped to fame in the first post-war Labour Government as Featherbed Evans, was not quite quick enough and they caught him. The drinking-horn was pushed into his hand; it was filled with wine; and he was told to drink, to drink it all. He did his best, but was not entirely successful. Some of the wine poured down his shirt. He came to the surface coughing and spluttering; but at least he could claim that he had not let the side down. When it was all over, and we had settled back into our cars for the long drive back to Tiflis where another banquet awaited us in less than three hours' time, we saw our hosts rushing towards us shouting and cheering, and waving swords at us, or what looked like swords. When they got nearer we could see that the swords were spits with chunks of meat skewered on them. They shoved their swords through the windows of our cars and insisted upon our having a little more to eat. Since we were helpless, we did as we were told.

George Wigg, who was also of the party, suddenly rebelled against all this hospitality. On our arrival at Kiev he heard that a ballet had once more been laid on for us, and the thought of yet another load of culture followed by yet another banquet dismayed him. So the chill he had caught during the preceding day took a turn for the worse, and he decided that the best thing he could do was to go to bed, and have a small snack in comfort in his bedroom. I thought it my duty to keep George Wigg company; so with Wigg in bed and myself sunk comfortably in an easy-chair by his side, we spent a happy evening gossiping. I rang the bell and ordered champagne; Wigg, I thought, was delighted. I ordered some more; and I hope and believe it impressed the patient. My enjoyment was especially keen because the champagne was on the house. Neither the BBC nor I myself would be called upon to pay for it. I thought it wise to let Wigg know this, otherwise he might have got the wrong ideas about how the BBC spent its licence money. The members of the Parliamentary delegations were the guests of the Soviet Government. The BBC paid my normal expenses; but owing to the peculiar system of accounting then prevailing in Russia I was able to get my drink without charge. The usual thing when going to Russia is to pay in advance for your board and lodging; you then get a receipt in the form of sheets of coupons. Each sheet is divided into sections: one section for breakfast, one for lunch, one for tea, and one for dinner. If you want a drink with your meal you pay for it in cash, but only in Moscow and Leningrad. Or so at least it was at the time. Outside these two cities the drink goes with the coupon and you can order what you like without any outlay. This great discovery stood me in good stead in Kiev, as I explained later to Wigg. After that hilarious evening, I came to regard Wigg as in the best tradition of the English eccentric. Whatever his critics, and he has many, may say about him, public life in this country would be poorer without him. He had, in those days, a weakness for publicity; and I am sure he put on a bit of ham acting at times in the hope of getting his name and picture into the papers or on the television screen. He stepped out of an aircraft once carrying a bucket in the hope that the camera-men would be interested. Some of them were.

The hospitality in Leningrad was at least as great as in Tiflis, although not so boisterous. And in Leningrad it was the Duke of Wellington who was the star turn, not Stanley Evans. We had been taken to the ballet, as usual; and we were expected to say, as they always expect you to say in Leningrad, that the show was far better than anything we had seen in Moscow. They do not try to hide their contempt for the Muscovites in this Northern city which looks like a capital whereas Moscow is a sprawling market town. The pity is that the outlying parts of this sub-Arctic place are being ruined by shoddily-built tenements; in twenty years' time the environs will consist of little more than blighted slums. At the ballet, the members of our Parliamentary delegation were given seats in a special box; and at the end of the performance, the Duke of Wellington went on the stage to thank the dancers for their performance. He spoke a few words in Russian. He told his audience that as a young man he had served as an Attaché in St. Petersburg; in other words, that his recollection of Russia went back to the days of the Tsar. His words brought the house down. I thought the cheering would never stop.

In a country whose citizens were offered blueprints instead of bread, and where people's happiness remained always upon the horizon and never within reach, the past had some evident attractions whereas the present had none. Tsarist Russia may well have been a terrible prison, as the revolutionaries used to say. But at least life was not always grey in those days and it held something more for people than statistics. Past glories were always sure to get a cheer in Moscow, as Stalin found when he restored some freedom to the Orthodox Church, when he re-introduced the disciplines and standards of the officer corps, and when he encouraged a re-interpretation of Russian history. I remember the almost hysterical enthusiasm when Tchaikovsky's 1812 Overture was played in Moscow for the first time since the Revolution. It happened, I think, in the early part of 1944 and the Red Army Band was responsible for the performance. The men had brought guns into the Tchaikovsky Hall for the occasion and great church bells: the sound was deafening. But they had not been allowed to play that part of the Finale in which the Tsarist hymn gradually overcomes the Marseillaise: this had been doctored, and instead of the hymn we got an air from one of Glinka's operas. Still, the magic worked; and the audience was delighted.

CHAPTER 13

THE WORST thing about life in Moscow during the war was the feeling of isolation—a sort of apartheid, as I have already noted—and the knowledge that all you said and did was constantly being reported on by spies and snoopers. We tried to take a light-hearted view of things and to look for the comic lining in every cloud. When things were slack, I used to while away the time by writing leading articles in the *Pravda* style. I soon found myself able to produce passable imitations by making copious use of such expressions as 'the toiling masses, democratic elements, fascist hyenas, capitalist warmongers, social democratic class enemies' and so on. They were rather easier to write than leading articles in *The Times*. But sometimes even the acknowledged experts got it wrong. Ilya Ehrenburg, the Talleyrand of Soviet intellectuals, missed his target badly in the spring of 1945 when he wrote an article in the best Vansittart style denouncing all Germans as people without hope of redemption. Policy had just changed but Ehrenburg did not know it. Stalin had come to the conclusion that there were some good Germans after all. Ehrenburg was muzzled for some weeks after the publication of his piece. I do not know what happened to the Editor of *Pravda*.

We even tried to laugh at the snoopers and to get them to join in our laughter. When I celebrated my fortieth birthday in the Aragvi Restaurant in Moscow in December 1943, one of my guests suddenly left the table in the private room where we were dining, took his chair with him, drew it up against the wall and climbed on to it. He turned his back on us, to face the grating high up in the wall. Then he recited a verse or two from Pushkin. When he had come to the end of his exercise, he called down the ventilation shaft: 'Take that you blighters,' and resumed his seat at table as if nothing had happened. I myself tried to help the snoopers by providing them with secret documents of various kinds. I had taken with me to Moscow a rubber stamp with the lettering 'TOP SECRET' and a red-ink-pad. When I found something interesting in the London papers, I cut it out and pasted it on a sheet of plain paper. This I stamped TOP SECRET and left it under a bundle of shirts in the cupboard of my bedroom. I did the same thing with harmless documents of various kinds. So if my belongings were searched, and I felt sure that they would be searched at some time or other, the secret police would always find something. I did not want to send them empty away. In their disappointment they might have turned against our invaluable Volga Germans.

I do not want to leave the reader with the impression that most of us came to the Soviet Union in a hostile and critical mood, always anxious to put the worst possible construction on things. This would be quite wrong. Clark Kerr would not have tolerated such an attitude for a moment. Rabid anti-Communism with a high emotional content was anathema to him. He was determined to get on with the Russians; he tried to establish relations that would make it possible, in future, to talk things over without friction. Churchill thought at times that he went too far; and so did some of his colleagues in the Foreign Office. In spite of great provocation, he rarely lost his temper, so far as I know. I can recall only two occasions when he came back fuming after calling upon the Ministry for Foreign Affairs. I have recorded on another page what happened when he saw Lozovsky. Vyshinsky's behaviour, at another interview, made him angrier still. He had gone to tell him that the British Government had decided to make some naval craft available to the Soviet Government, for use in Arctic waters. They were now in harbour in Scotland, and perhaps the Soviet Government would let him know when suitable crews would be sent over to sail them home. Vyshinsky was astonished. They could not spare men for that sort of thing, he said. He reminded the Ambassador that the Soviet Union was fighting a war against Germany.

If relations between Britain and the Soviet Union worsened steadily after September 1944, for reasons which I hope to explain on a later page, the fault was not Clark Kerr's. No British Ambassador is remembered as Clark Kerr is remembered in Moscow: with respect and admiration. The secretaries on his staff, the younger men who were in the Embassy when he took over or who joined him later, had open minds, and they were prepared for difficulties and wanted to overcome them. If only the Soviet authorities had treated them a little more intelligently, if only they had been a little more cooperative, a little less offensive and high-handed, a little more willing to open up, they would have found a friend in every member of the British Embassy staff. The same can be said about the United States Embassy under Averell Harriman and George Kennan. But Stalin would not allow Soviet officials to behave like human beings. Many of the men who had served in Moscow therefore came away disappointed and sick at heart. They felt that they had failed in one of their most important duties: the duty to get to know the people in the capital to which they had been appointed, to make friends with them, to get on the sort of footing with them that would make it possible to deal with difficulties between their two Governments without formalities, Notes, protests, *démarches*, representations and so on. It was not for want of trying: they all tried, but they were just frozen out. It led to many misunderstandings and eventually to hostility.

Another difficulty was the discrepancy between the propaganda façade put out by Stalin and his agents, and the facts of life in the Soviet Union. In the light of Russian claims to perfection, one could not avoid making comparisons between their hospitals and ours, their social services and ours, their medical services and ours. When we had an opportunity to investigate them, we found that things were no better, and sometimes a great deal worse, than in other countries at roughly the same stage of economic development. One got very tired of hearing about the Moscow underground as if it were one of the wonders of the world. No established industrial country would have expected the foreign visitor to go over a power station or a textile mill equipped with antediluvian machinery as part of the routine of sight-seeing. One was taken only to the show places, of course; to factories or farms that were not typical, but unique; but even these were not very exciting.

I am convinced that one of the great Russian secrets was that there was no secret: there was nothing to show, nothing worth showing. That is why the movement of foreigners was restricted; and that is why Russians were discouraged from talking to them. All the barren nothingness of things might have been revealed.

Moreover, foreigners might be talkative; they might make remarks, not out of malice or ill-will, but just casually in the course of a conversation that would raise doubts about the veracity of the Russian claims to perfection. When Russian soldiers got back to their families with their loot from Eastern Europe, they brought with them all sorts of things proving that the capitalist world was not a poverty-stricken backwater tyrannized by a handful of rich gamblers. They were able to tell their friends and families that things like well-made and inexpensive wrist watches, handbags, cosmetics, decent clothes and shoes were nothing out of the ordinary there. This gave the lie to what the newspapers, Moscow Radio and the Party agitators had been saying for years. And it seems to me reasonable to conclude that among the reasons for the tough Stalinist policies after the war was the realization that the men in the Red Army who had spent so much time abroad had seen too much. They and their families had become politically unreliable. They needed a period of re-indoctrination; and that made it all the more necessary to keep foreigners at arm's length. If Stalin had allowed any relaxation at all, the whole fabric of lies on which his authority rested might have collapsed.

It takes a little time before one becomes conscious of how the whole of Soviet life is saturated with lies. The Russian nineteenth-century novelists said the same thing about the Western way of life, but the order of lies in Russia is different. It is often a lie played out for foreign consumption and it seems to involve a great many people, at all levels. When we were in Leningrad, on the occasion of Macmillan's official visit, we saw a lie performed for our benefit with all the precision of a ballet. One Sunnday afternoon we were all going to the Hermitage Museum. Some of us decided to go early, and when we got there, we were surprised to find that it was shut and the doors locked. We saw one of the attendants standing near and we told him we were members of the Macmillan party and that it had been arranged for us to visit the place. He unlocked the door. The moment it opened several inert figures came to life and began madly photographing the exhibits. Others brought a hand to the brow in silent contemplation of some favourite work of art. Clearly we had arrived too soon; if we had come at the right time the actors would have been at stations, and we should all have drawn the appropriate conclusions about the high standard of popular culture in Russia.

Journalists were as badly affected by this atmosphere as people in the Embassies. Vernon Bartlett who went out in 1942 with the Beaverbrook mission was dismayed by all he saw and heard and by the lies spread like a blanket across the facts. The only reason why he did not speak out in public when he came back about all the evils that shocked his liberal soul was that the war demanded the greatest possible degree of Allied unity. His silence, I know, caused him almost physical pain: Vernon Bartlett is not the man to remain dumb in the face of abuses and injustice. At the turn of the year 1944–45, while on a quick visit to London, Clark Kerr got in touch with several distinguished radical journalists and begged them to subordinate their understandable and natural anti-Stalinist views to the overriding need to defeat the enemy with Russian cooperation. This help was still badly required as the German thrust into the Ardennes had shown. Clark Kerr pleaded for understanding and sympathy, and for the sort of patience that he himself was showing in his work in Moscow.

So the Russian accusation that the British Government encouraged anti-Soviet propaganda at the time, is yet another of Stalin's lies. If the Government erred at all, it erred in the opposite direction. A great many things were left unsaid that might well have been said, with the aim of enlightening public opinion about the nature of the difficulties facing the British Government in its dealings with Moscow. But that would have brought comfort to the enemy. Because of this concealment, Soviet prestige in Britain, and elsewhere in the world, was immeasurably high in 1945. If Stalin and Molotov had pursued an intelligent foreign policy, if they had shown a reasonable degree of honesty and some tact, they might have achieved great things, even at the expense of British interests, since British public opinion was so largely on their side. When the British Government acted openly against Communism in 1944, and therefore in the popular imagination against our Russian allies, there was an outcry. Owing to British intervention at the end of that year, Greece was saved from the fate that overtook other States in Eastern Europe a short time later, but not many people saw things in that light. Even President Roosevelt failed to do so. He still regarded British imperialism as the great evil. Elliott Roosevelt recalls how his father reacted to the British Government's action: ' "Fighting against the guerillas who had fought the Nazis for the last four years." He made no attempt to conceal his anger. "How the British can dare such a thing," Father cried. "The lengths to which they will go to hang on to the past." '

The memory of three encounters in Moscow will long remain with me. The first was with Molotov, in September 1944, at the time of the armistice negotiations with Finland. They had been going on for some time in the Soviet Government's official guest house, which we called the Spiridonavka, after the street of that name in which it was situated. In this building there was cleanliness and luxury. There were cakes of fresh Yardley soap on the edge of the washbasins which had all been made in England. This sort of soap was virtually unobtainable in London at the time but was apparently plentiful in the United States. There were also clean towels and plenty of them. When the talks had ended I was sent for in order to be told of the arrangements that had been made about the publication of a communiqué. It was to be released, so the Ambassador said to me, in the early hours of the following morning. I realized that unless the texts could be given to the British correspondents without any delay, it would be impossible for their telegrams to get to London in time. I was then told that this could not be done, and that the correspondents would have to wait. I replied that on that basis, very few morning papers would be able to carry the story. 'Don't tell me,' Clark Kerr said, 'tell Molotov.' So I went up to Molotov and asked for his help. I told him that I wanted the correspondents to have the communiqué at once, otherwise they could do little with it. At first he refused to make any change: all the details had been approved by Stalin, he explained. But after a while he relented, and said that the texts would be made available within an hour or so, for transmission to London and elsewhere. I replied that even then there would be difficulties. 'Why?' 'Because your censors are too slow,' I replied. His answer was unexpected. 'You think our people are too slow? Very well, go and do the job yourself. I will tell my people that every press telegram carrying your signature submitted during the next twelve hours is to be transmitted without delay. But don't make any mistakes. If you do,' and here he looked with a meaning smile at Clark Kerr, 'if you do, we'll exile you to Poland. We have plenty of friends over there.'

Molotov's sense of humour was not resilient enough to take a joke that went against him. When the results of the British general election in 1945 were received at the Potsdam Conference, Clark Kerr seized the first opportunity to congratulate him on the outcome. 'Your friends have done very well,' he said. 'They've doubled their representation in the House of Commons.' Molotov beamed at him. 'And how many Communists are there now in the House of Commons?' he asked. 'Two' was the answer.

Then there was my evening with Stalin—on the occasion of his dinner at the British Embassy in October 1944. The whole place was in a state of siege. It had been searched from top to bottom earlier in the day. There was a searchlight somewhere on the roof; and the street outside was bright, in spite of the blackout. In fact, the rigid blackout in Moscow ended on that day, and while the Russians themselves still had to be careful, privileged foreigners left their lights on, and their windows unshaded without any hesitation. And perhaps I should add here that I never heard a shot fired in anger, or a bomb dropped from an aircraft during the whole of my two years in Moscow. The only explosive noise I heard was the sound of the guns firing salutes in honour of almost daily victories. Nor did I ever see a badly wounded serviceman in all the time I spent in Moscow. The blind and the maimed, the armless and the legless and the faceless were kept carefully out of sight. But when Stalin came to dinner, all was light round the Embassy. All traffic had been stopped in the neighbourhood; and the route across the bridge from the Kremlin was guarded by security police.

The only guests at the dinner party itself were the great men and the most senior of their staffs. The rest of us were invited to some sort of reception to be held after dinner. I remember waiting in the Embassy ballroom for Churchill and Stalin to appear. At last the doors to the dining room were thrown open. We could hear the soft murmur of voices; a faint cloud of cigar smoke trickled slowly out of the room. We waited eagerly, and none more eagerly than myself since I had never seen Stalin in the flesh. Then the Ambassador's private secretary came up to me and asked me to work out a few lines for a communiqué about the dinner. There was a Russian official waiting downstairs for me to talk to. We worked away at this innocuous communiqué for what seemed to me to be a very long time. It gave nothing away, of course, yet my Russian colleague made all sorts of difficulties. Finally we had our three or four lines and they were approved. I went upstairs again to the reception. All was over. Stalin and Churchill and the others had gone to earth in another room, a tough-looking NKVD Colonel stood with his back to the door to ward off all intruders. And all I could do was to slink off home to bed.

I was more fortunate in my third encounter, this time with Edouard Herriot who came to lunch at the British Embassy in April 1945, together with Lady Churchill. Herriot had just been released from a German camp by the Red Army, and Moscow was his first port of call on his way home. He had been a fat man when I had seen him in France before the war. Now, as one might expect, he was a good deal slimmer: meals in a German detention centre could not have been up to the standard to which he was accustomed, especially in Lyons of which he had been Mayor for many years. Food was one of the major hobbies of this Radical leader, and at times his doctor had insisted upon his keeping to a strict diet so that he might live to eat another day. During the course of one of these fasts, he had been invited to dine with some friends in one of his favourite restaurants. He ordered almost everything on the menu, to the dismay of his secretary who was of the company. 'You mustn't forget what the doctor said,' he murmured. 'Of course not,' Herriot replied, and called back the waiter. 'Please remind me of what I have ordered for dinner.' The waiter went through a long list. '*Bon*,' said Herriot, '*supprimez la salade*.'

The meal at the Embassy gave him obvious satisfaction. At the end, he rose slowly to his feet. As a simple Frenchman, he began, he would like to put into words some of the thoughts that had been with him for so long. Then came what he called a modest tribute to Winston Churchill, generous in spirit, noble in style. He spoke of what the world owed to Churchill, and France above all; his magnanimity and sense of history turned what might have been just an after-luncheon speech into a great occasion. If Herriot was on the edge of tears at times, some of us at table were well beyond it. But what puzzled me about this affair was the presence of Madame Herriot. Surely, I asked, the Germans had no valid reason for arresting her? Herriot, no doubt, was a dangerous politician, but the same could not be said about his wife who, so far as I knew, had never played any part in politics. 'They did not want to arrest me,' she replied. 'But I asked them to take me away with them. My husband is so impractical, often so helpless, that I could not allow him to go off on his own, even to a place of detention. Let me give you an example of the sort of thing he is capable of,' she went on. 'After the Russians had released us, they took us away in one of their cars on the first lap of our trip to Moscow. When we had been driven for half an hour or so through all the horrors that I'd sooner not think of, my husband said: "I've forgotten something. We must go back." So the Russians took us back. And do you know what my husband had forgotten, and what he went back for? To say "thank you" to the Commandant of the centre for treating him with courtesy.'

CHAPTER 14

THE REASON why I went to Moscow in 1943 is that Clark Kerr told me he needed someone to contradict him. 'You didn't hesitate to contradict me in Stockholm,' he said, 'and then you were only a journalist. Now come to Moscow and see what you can do. The regulars in the service are not always very good at opposing an Ambassador unless they are very sure that he is very wrong. They are too tactful.' It was in this ambiguous way that I was made First Secretary at the British Embassy in Moscow, with the words 'local rank' carefully added to my letter of appointment. There was no difficulty about procuring my release from the Political Warfare Executive. Much of the maid-of-all-work I had been doing in the early days had been taken over by other people. The department was in a constant state of reorganization, and the Scandinavian section was now headed by Brinley Thomas. There had been pressure on the head of the Political Warfare Executive, Bruce Lockhart, to establish some sort of liaison with the Soviet propaganda people, in the hope of associating them in some way or other with the joint Anglo-American enterprise in London.

There were occasions, during my two years in Moscow, when I was forced to say to the Ambassador that I could not agree with some course of action that he proposed, or with his interpretation of the facts. Usually, he took my contradictions with high good humour: he either met them head-on and pushed them aside; or he hesitated, reflected, and perhaps changed his mind. At times he would be upset by my contrariness; and there was no point in my reminding him that I was only doing my duty in that state of life to which it had pleased him to call me. He would avoid me; he might not speak to me for a fortnight or more, especially if by some lucky fluke I had been proved right. Then, after a suitable interval, he would catch hold of me in the corridor. 'What's the matter with you?' he would say. 'Have you been sulking? I haven't seen you for days.' And with that remark, our diplomatic relations would be restored.

Our most important difference, so far as I remember, was over the Lublin Poles. These were the Poles who had been handpicked by the Soviet leaders to govern the country in the interests of Russian security. It became clear, in December 1941, during Eden's visit to Moscow, that the Russians had strong ideas about Poland and were going to enforce them, in spite of the views of the British and American Governments, the special commitments of the British Government to the Polish Government-in-exile, and the efforts made by that Government to meet Stalin's wishes. The Lublin Poles, including the formidable Bierut, Hilary Minc, and the seedy Osubka-Morawski, came to the British Embassy in the summer of 1944 and we spent long hours listening to them—the Ambassador, John Balfour, the Minister, Arthur Birse, the interpreter, and myself. They outlined their plans for the future, they spoke of conditions in Poland at the moment, and they finished up with a plea for British and American help. It was a very laborious conversation, if that is the word for it, since they did most of the talking, rather like children who have learnt a long recitation off by heart. The Poles spoke in Polish; this had then to be translated into Russian by an interpreter provided by the Russian authorities. This meant, of course, that Stalin had his own personal agent in the room. The Russian version, in turn, was translated into English by the incomparable Birse. What it meant was that each hour with these Poles amounted only to some twenty minutes of talk.

There were two reasons for their visit. In the first place, they wanted to convince Clark Kerr that they, and not the Polish Government-in-exile, were the genuine future leaders of Poland; they claimed to represent the people of Poland; and said that they would control any general uprising when the time came. They described how their country had been devastated and mutilated by the Germans; and they reminded us that in spite of German terrorism, the Poles were fighting on and were resisting the Nazis at every conceivable opportunity. They told us that while the present was important since it involved such things as fighting the Germans, cooperating with the Red Army and establishing some sort of order in the areas that the Germans were abandoning, the future mattered even more. Above all, they said, 'We must think of our young people, the generation that will create the Poland of tomorrow.' They told us that they had underground schools and underground universities to keep alive the language and culture of Poland; and this in itself involved them in a running fight with the Germans who were trying to stamp out all that was Polish. 'The list is endless,' they said. 'We need everything, everything. What we are doing now, we are doing with our bare hands because we have nothing.' The Ambassador looked up after a moment's reflection. 'It would help me,' he said, 'if you could be specific. I cannot do very much with general statements; the Polish plight is no secret, and I do not have to tell my Government about it. But if you will go into detail about the sort of help you need, and how urgent that need is, with some indication of priorities, I will pass on everything you say to my Government.' Hilary Minc, the man who later brought Poland to ruin for the second time with what he called 'bold Bolshevik planning', answered without much hesitation: 'Let me give you an instance. We need skeletons for our medical schools.' 'Dear me,' Clark Kerr murmured, 'I should have thought there was no shortage of skeletons in Poland.' 'All they need,' he reflected after they had gone, 'is a spade or two.'

They made an unfavourable impression upon some of us, these Poles. I could see that Clark Kerr was none too happy himself and that he was making a great effort to understand them and, if possible, even to sympathize with them. After Poland's unique record of uncompromising hostility to Nazism, it was heartbreaking to meet Poles who were prepared to sell out to Stalin even to the extent of denying the fact of the Warsaw rising. This was an obvious point for me to make, and I made it. I suppose if I had been given a day or two to reflect my comment might have been different. I should have known that Tsarist Russia pursued precisely the same kind of policy towards Poland as Stalin was now doing. In the latter half of the nineteenth century the Russians encouraged industrial development in Congress Poland. And since Russia was the chief market for such industries as emerged during this period, the new middle-class associated with the new trend found they were more interested in Russia than in Polish independence. The Tsars brought an industrial middle-class to power, whose pocket-books depended on Russia: Stalin brought a bureaucratic class to power, whose lives depended on Russia. This is yet another example of the continuity of Russian foreign policy.

I might also have remembered that Poland cannot afford to antagonize Russia and Germany at the same time; and now that Germany had become enemy Number One, some sort of understanding with Russia, even at the price of surrendering certain Polish national interests, was unavoidable. Clark Kerr was anxious to know what we all thought about them and their story. 'What do you think?' he asked me. I was still shocked by the harshness of Bierut, the steely insensitiveness of Minc, and the obvious mediocrity of Osubka-Morawski. On the spur of the moment I blurted out: 'I can't stand Bierut and Minc. They are horrible. As for Morawski, he'd be lucky if they gave him a job playing the piano in a brothel.' This was not a popular remark, and I was made to feel it. Nor, I suppose, was it particularly helpful; but I was too angry and too depressed for proper reflection. 'And where do you think you ought to be?' Clark Kerr asked. I could think of nothing better to say than: 'here'. He looked at me and said, 'You flatter yourself.' To another member of his staff who was also critical, he retorted angrily, 'The trouble with you is that you have never got beyond the stage of thinking that the most important thing in life is to play golf at Biarritz at the right time of the year with the right people. There are other things in life, you know.' And with that, he left the room. This particular debate was never resumed.

I suppose that the Lublin development, or more accurately, the future of Poland as an independent State, was the chief cause of friction between the British and Soviet Governments from 1944 until the German problem came to the top of the European agenda. Early in 1945, the United States became involved in the quarrel, with a consequential cooling off in Soviet-American relations. It was not the Marshall Plan that proved to be the turning point in our relations with Russia, nor yet the takeover of Czechoslovakia in 1948. I believe that the cold war goes back to the Polish question, to the determination of Stalin to have his own way in Poland; and to the failure of London and Washington to comprehend that Poland was, so to speak, the political arch in the Soviet Government's security system. Stalin warned Roosevelt, only a very short time before the President's death, that if the

United States Government carried its support for the Polish Government to the same extremes as the British Government had done, then Russo-American relations could hardly fail to be affected. I find it impossible to believe that Churchill and Eden could have done much more than they tried to do. George Kennan was undoubtedly right when he told the Senate Foreign Relations Committee early in 1967 that the Sovietization of Eastern and Central Europe was part of the price paid for our ability to defeat Hitler.

Short of war, nothing that the Western Powers might have done would have helped Poland. Churchill came to Moscow in the autumn of 1944 in the hope of saving something from the wreckage. Mikolajczyk was also there and attended some of the Anglo-Russian talks with other Polish leaders. When Churchill and Eden went on their own to the Kremlin they reported back to the Poles who were kept informed all along of how the conversations were going, and how hard the British Ministers were being pressed to accept the Lublin group and the cession of Lvov. Some of the scenes between Churchill and the Polish leaders were very stormy. Mikolajczyk recorded in his autobiography that on one occasion Churchill turned on his heel and walked out of the room. I was not present at any of these talks; but a Polish friend who knew all that was going on at the time told me that Churchill had exploded with a string of four-letter and six-letter words. My friend added: 'We very much admire your Prime Minister. We know that he is doing all he can for us. But he does use some very rude language at times.'

By their own actions, the Poles in Moscow made unnecessary difficulties for themselves. They talked too much; in view of the high stakes for which they were playing, and the risks they were running, they were terrifyingly indiscreet. As a child I had learnt that the Norwegian expression for an unruly group of people was a 'Polsk riksdag', that is to say, a Polish Parliament. I now understood that the term had its point. What made this garrulity so awkward was that the British Ambassador had asked the Russians to take off the censorship on all press messages dealing with the Polish negotiations. (Just as the British Government were to ask for the censorship to be lifted in 1947 on all press messages reporting the four-power Conference in Moscow.) Foreign correspondents in Moscow were therefore able to telegraph home all that the Poles chose to tell them. I thought after a while that the situation was getting out of hand and might easily get the Poles into serious trouble; so I told the Ambassador that I proposed to call upon the Sovinformbureau people that very day and ask them to reimpose the censorship—in other words to return to normal—in the hope of protecting the Poles against the consequences of their own indiscretions. 'I am not asking you for your approval,' I said. 'But if you do not want me to do it, please tell me.' I was given no instructions, so I went off to Sovinformbureau whose officials did as I suggested. That same evening, over a drink with the Foreign Secretary, the Ambassador pointed to me and said: 'Do you know what he's been up to? He's asked the Russians to put back the censorship on Polish news.' Eden offered no comment. I felt myself at the time that my action was right; and I still hold to this opinion. We were all sympathetic to the Polish point of view; we wanted to help them as far as we could. But their flamboyant rashness had catastrophic possibilities. When I think of the Polish resistance to the German invasion in 1939, I see in my mind's eye a cavalryman in scarlet uniform charging down with a lance upon a German tank.

Eden himself became emotionally involved in the question of Lvov. He felt it would be wrong if the British Government were to give way to the Russian demand for this ancient Polish town. He seemed unhappy and uneasy. One evening he came back to the Embassy very late after a long session with Molotov and the others. He seemed exhausted and depressed as he came into the Ambassador's room, where one or two of us sat talking over the day's events. Eden walked through the room without a word, into his bedroom which lay just beyond it, and reappeared in a dressing-gown with his shirt-collar open. The first thing he wanted was a stiff whisky and soda. He strode up and down the room for a while before he began talking about the day's conference and some of the difficulties he had encountered. Suddenly he stopped: 'If I give way over Lvov,' he said, 'shall I go down in the history books as an appeaser?' He did not wait for an answer. First he put the question to the Ambassador, and moved on. Then he came to my colleague and put it again, and moved on. Then he put it to me. At no time did he wait for an answer. Perhaps he did not want an answer. It was clear enough that he was plagued almost beyond endurance by the need to make what he regarded as an unreasonable and unjust concession. The word appeasement has haunted him like a ghost ever since 1936. I suspect that the full-page cartoon that appeared in *Punch* on 19 May 1954, on the eve of the Indo-China Conference, touched him to the quick. It showed Anthony Eden, complete with rabbit-teeth, stepping down from an aircraft at Geneva airport. The clothes he wears are Neville Chamberlain's. His briefcase is labelled Munich, Berlin and Geneva.

I felt at the time that I had caught a glimpse of the real Eden, the person behind the impeccably-dressed young man who was hardly ever ruffled. The Eden I saw then was an artist more than a man of power, but perhaps a rather vain artist, more concerned with what people would say about his actions than about the actions themselves. I imagined him to be nagged by the thought that he had failed to stand up and be counted when the Nazis remilitarized the Rhineland; with his eye constantly on the history books, on the part played by other Foreign Secretaries in England's history and how the historians would compare his role to theirs. The question 'What will the history books have to say about my action?' is only another way of asking 'Can I pull this one off without being found out?', or 'Will this short-term defeat come to look like a long-term victory?'. I went to bed that night in a mood of great depression. I felt that there was something unbearably tragic about Eden's predicament.

Russo-American relations were equally affected by the Polish crisis, and by American attempts to safeguard Polish independence. Harry Hopkins, who had served Roosevelt so well, came to Moscow in May 1945 at the urgent request of President Truman in order to plead Poland's case. He was a sick man at the time, and nothing but a sense of public duty could have induced him to make this trip with all the arduous negotiations that went with it. He worked out a formula with the Russians under which three Poles from London and three or four from Lublin, 'all of whom had previously been approved by the British and American Governments', were to form an administration. Stalin would not, or could not, understand why Britain and America were so determined to 'interfere' in Polish affairs. In order to overcome American suspicions, which Truman expressed with great pungency, Stalin gave Hopkins all sorts of assurances. He told him that even the Polish leaders, some of whom were Communists, were against the Soviet system and that the Polish people did not desire collective farms. Gomulka, the Polish leader, was disgraced and imprisoned some years later for taking precisely this line. 'Our democracy is not similar to Soviet democracy,' he said in November 1946, 'just as our social system is not similar to the Soviet system.' Stalin went much further in 1945. 'Poland,' he said, 'would live under a parliamentary system which is like that of Czechoslovakia, Belgium and Holland. Any talk of an intention to Sovietize Poland is stupid.'

It was quite safe for Stalin to refer in these terms to Czechoslovakia in 1945. The business of undermining the country's constitutional and parliamentary practices was in the capable hands of Fierlinger, then Czechoslovak Ambassador in Moscow. I suppose that Benes thought he had established himself securely in Moscow's eyes in 1941 by signing a treaty to govern post-war relations between his country and Russia. His was the first Government to do so, and he no doubt calculated that he had made a shrewd tactical move in setting this good example to the peoples of Eastern Europe. The mistake he made, a mistake made by many others, was to trust Stalin without having enough force to impress him. When he and Masaryk came to Moscow in early April of 1945 on their way to Slovakia, they found that their position had been undermined. Masaryk came to dinner one evening at the Embassy and I was fortunate enough to be among those invited to attend. At the end of the party, I walked with him down the steps to the main entrance. 'How are you getting on with our Russian friends?' I asked him. 'My boy,' Masaryk said, 'I am sick to death of the lot of them. One of these days I shall get up and denounce them.' All this was said with the greatest vigour. He used words that would not look well in print so I have paraphrased his remarks. He often expressed himself in rather crude and jocular terms with the result that there were people who did not take him seriously; but I think myself that he had a far better political nose than Benes had. His forebodings about the cold war and about the paralysis that would overtake the United Nations found succinct expression in a comment he made to King George VI. The King thought that Masaryk would have made a good Secretary-General of the United Nations, and told him so. And he added: 'You would make a perfect bridge between East and West.' Masaryk's answer came without any hesitation. 'Sir, I don't want to be a bridge. You know what happens to bridges: men march all over them and horses drop things on them.'

In spite of Masaryk's strong language in April 1945, he did not get out. He stayed until he was driven to suicide, or murdered. We shall probably never know what happened in those dramatic days in Prague. What would have been the consequence if he had carried out his threat at the time, if he had resigned from the Czechoslovak Government and denounced Russian interference in the affairs of his country? His words would probably have fallen on deaf ears. Russia had earned such prestige throughout the world that the cries and warnings of those who knew the truth about what was going on would have had little or no effect. Even Masaryk might have been written off as just another crank, or as *Pravda* might have said, a Fascist beast. He had probably reflected upon the campaign of abuse directed against the British Government for its intervention in Greece in order to forestall a Communist take-over there. That may have convinced him that there was no way out for him. He was not the sort of man that cantankerous refugees are made of.

The atmosphere in Moscow, in spite of all these difficulties, was still reasonably cordial, in so far as that expression could be used. But I believe the last occasion to which it could be applied was in connection with the reception in honour of Harry Hopkins. He looked very frail; but he talked with animation to those who questioned him about the new men in Washington. Madame Kollontay was among the guests; and attracted much attention. The most formidable of Soviet diplomatists who had dared to tell even Stalin that he was mistaken was now in an invalid chair. She had lost nothing of her old fire and her eyes sparkled with mischief as she got Marshal Voroshilov involved in an argument that seemed beyond his depth. We often referred to the Marshal as the Playboy of the Eastern world: he looked the part in his well-cut cavalry uniform; his face pink, prosperous, and glowing with after-shave lotion. He did not owe his position in the Soviet hierarchy to his intelligence or his political acumen, but to his subservience to Stalin. It was said that during the great purges, when Stalin felt himself in constant danger and surrounded by enemies, Voroshilov drove his car for him.

There was something grotesque in the eventual involvement of the United States Government in the Polish crisis. When the frontiers of Europe came under discussion in a preliminary way at the Teheran Conference, Roosevelt professed interest only in the German question. And when Stalin and Churchill opened up a discussion on Poland, he withdrew from active participation in the debate, except for an occasional word. Stalin drew a podgy finger down Russia's Western borders, marking a line corresponding roughly to the Curzon line. That was the border he wanted. That was the border the Poles ultimately had to accept, with 'compensations' as they were called, at the other end of the map, in East Prussia. In all this Roosevelt played only a minor part. It was not until 1945 that he understood the full ramifications of the problem and not until after relations between the British Government and the London Poles had cooled off because Churchill saw he had no alternative but to give way to the Russians and had told the Poles so. When Harry Hopkins came on the scene, acting under Truman's instructions, it was too late for minor concessions. Poland had to be written off.

While I do not believe it lay within the powers of the British and American Governments to save Poland, I am nevertheless convinced that they made things unnecessarily easy for the Russians. By conceding that the Kremlin had the right to demand that the Governments established on their borders must be friendly, they legitimized interference of all kinds in the affairs of neighbouring States. Even the Finns were victims of their attentions under this general formula. Moreover, by acquiescing in the use of the word 'democracy' when applied to the domestic and foreign policies of the Soviet Government, they made it possible for Stalin to seize the initiative in the process of so-called democratic reform, which, by common consent, was badly needed in many parts of Eastern Europe. At the Potsdam Conference in 1945, Stalin declared that 'a Government that is not Fascist is democratic'. The slogan set the tone for all subsequent Russian propaganda, and sanctified every murder, and every labour camp, in Eastern Europe. Under its shelter, there grew up throughout the world a multitude of anti-Fascist leagues and anti-Fascist societies, all Russian-directed or Russian-inspired and all serving Russian national interests.

Since Bierut in Poland, Rakosi in Hungary and Gottwald in Czechoslovakia were all anti-Fascist, it followed automatically that they were democratic, just as Stalin was. Those who opposed them were therefore Fascists. The Western leaders might have avoided this trap by taking greater care over the drafting of their communiqués. Language only could not have prevented the Russian take-over in Eastern Europe. But a more careful choice of words would have made it possible to strip Russian imperialism of its disguise, and so stopped it from strutting upon the world stage as a crusader for freedom. All the warm emotive words in the history of the West—words like democracy, freedom, peace—were transmuted by Stalin's alchemy into ignoble weapons designed to sow confusion and to spread doubt. In the West also the language has been debased. Many of us still squirm at the recollection of Foster Dulles's denunciation of 'atheistic Communism'; especially those of us who have had the good fortune to attend crowded church services in Moscow and Leningrad. The young people we saw there were risking their careers, unlike their compeers in the United States. Nor is it easy to remain silent when Western politicians include Spain and South Korea and Formosa among the 'free nations' of the world.

There was yet another error that might with advantage have been avoided with a little more forethought. In the normal course of events, the British and American Ambassadors in Moscow dealt with Molotov or with Vyshinsky, his chief assistant. They never got very far with either of them, except on ordinary routine matters, such as getting an extra supply of flour for a teaparty given on the occasion of the Archbishop of York's visit to Moscow in the autumn of 1943, or a special brand of champagne for Churchill. When it came to something of substantial importance, Molotov usually stone-walled. On the state of play being reported back to London and Washington, the British and American Governments would instruct their Ambassadors to seek an appointment with Stalin, either jointly or severally, in the hope of inducing him to over-rule his Foreign Minister. Sometimes, they were able to persuade him to ask Molotov to yield an inch or two; but the effect of this style of diplomacy was to elevate Stalin into a sort of Super-Arbitrator. He was not just the head of the Soviet Government dealing on equal terms with the British and American leaders: that was done by Molotov. He became instead the Supreme Authority to whom the British and Americans finally turned when they got into difficulties with the Soviet Government. The skill with which the Russians took advantage of this development provided them with considerable diplomatic benefits: all too often the Western representatives came away contented from the battle after Stalin had awarded them about a quarter of what they had asked Molotov for. And in Molotov's diplomacy, anything put forward as a 'basis for discussion' was seized upon at once, and retained, as a concession.

It seems to me, too, that the Western Governments did not take sufficiently into account that there were Russians who chose to regard the Second World War as merely a continuation of the First; and that Europe had in fact suffered a twentieth-century Thirty Years' War, broken only by an uneasy armistice, in which Teutons fought against Slavs and Slavs against Teutons for supremacy. In the earlier part of this war, so ran the argument, Russia collapsed and was unable to regain her footing among the great powers, largely owing to the ill-will of her former allies. In the second half of the period, France collapsed, but was soon restored to honour, although not without some friction, and not without pursuing certain blackmailing tactics that might have caused Stalin to chuckle. Did not Stalin commit himself to this principle of continuity when on declaring war with Japan he spoke of wiping out the defeat of 1905? If the promises made to Russia during the early stages of the Thirty Years' War had been carried out, Stalin would have controlled not only the Baltic States and Eastern Europe as he came to do, but Constantinople and Northern Persia as well, as he tried to do. In other words, in restricting his claims to Eastern Europe he showed moderation. I believe these factors were very much in Russian minds at times, and that they accounted for some of their hostility and some of their suspicions when they observed Western reactions to their policies.

Churchill's sense of history made it easy for him to perceive this and to regard Russia as a normal imperialist power, with normal predatory instincts. If he had been left to deal with the Russians on these lines, things might have taken a different turn. He realized that Stalin began to think in post-war political terms so soon as he got over the first shock of the German invasion. Roosevelt's judgment was warped by the conviction that the October Revolution had wrought a fundamental change in Russian aims, and that it had halted for ever the Russian drive towards empire. Woodrow Wilson and his Ambassador in London had some equally curious illusions during the First World War. They appeared to believe that 'democracies' were peaceful and unwarlike; and that the military and undemocratic type of Government that prevailed in Germany in 1914 was responsible for the war. When the Americans came to grips with the power problem after the First World War it was too late. During the Second World War, also, the Americans suffered from certain romantic illusions, notably the illusion that the October Revolution had put an end to Russian imperialism. 'You know,' Roosevelt told Frances Perkins (his Secretary of Labour) late in 1943, 'I really think the Russians will go along with me about having no spheres of influence and about agreements for free ports all over the world.' When the Americans realized their error, it was again too late. Over the one country where an 'imperialist deal' was made, Greece, Stalin kept his word because the British position was backed by force. It is true that if the Communist Party there had gained the upper hand, Stalin would have won in the end. Perhaps he was sure it would win. But he did not intervene. To that extent, the spheres of influence policy had worked. Roosevelt hated it, except, of course, when applied to Latin America.

Very near the end of the war, when the collapse of Germany seemed only a week or two away, our minds began to turn to the post-war world and to the problems that would face the principal powers. One could hardly fail to notice that the Americans were becoming increasingly conscious of their strength, and increasingly resentful of Stalin's high-handed way of dealing with them. 'They can't push us around like this,' said Averell Harriman one day, in a fit of justifiable anger, 'we're a great power, too.' It took time for Stalin to understand that there had been a shift in the American attitude and that the days of Roosevelt's *bonhomie* were over. As another straw in the wind, there were the remarks made during a long discussion with some of the members of the Commonwealth Missions in Moscow. Few of those who took part in it had any doubts about Britain's economic strength. A distinguished Canadian insisted that British industry had acquired new techniques during the war, and greater efficiency. Added to American know-how, which had been freely communicated, it would face American industry with very severe competition. It appeared to be the general belief that Britain would emerge from the war, not richer, but with a greatly enhanced economic potential. It seems probable that some of our post-war difficulties, including the recurring stop-go policies, were due to this general over-estimate of British power in Ottawa and Washington and no doubt in Australia and New Zealand also. The British attitude to France in the immediate post-war years sprang from this same misconception.

PART FOUR
THE DANGEROUS PEACE

CHAPTER 15

THERE WERE looks of disbelief upon the faces of the courteous women who preside over the flowers and telephones in the main lobby of Broadcasting House when I reported for duty in mid-January 1946. The time was 9.30 precisely. I gave them my name; I told them that I was joining the Foreign News Department; and that I had been instructed to turn up at 9.30 on the dot. There was an undertone of polite scepticism in the voice of the woman who answered me. 'Half past nine?' she repeated. 'Nobody turns up until ten o'clock. By all means go up: we'll get a Commissionaire to show you the way; but you'll find nobody there.' The corridors were silent and deserted as we came out of the lift. There was not a charwoman in sight.

I got another shock when the Administrative Officer announced that a personal secretary had been appointed to help me, but that unfortunately she would not be available until the following day. I told him that I was grateful for the postponement. I explained that apart from a short period during the war, I had never employed a secretary in my life, and that I felt sure there would not be enough work for her. In the Paris Office of *The Times*, I added, we had had very efficient help in the person of a male telephone operator who handled all our communications with the editorial office in London. He typed letters for us, if we happened to write any. But he was not a secretary. When I heard all this patter about secretaries I had visions of being pursued all day long by women begging me to dictate letters to them, and always wanting to know how I spent my time if I was not actually seated at my desk in the office. I had not the slightest desire to dictate letters, or articles, or telegrams or pieces for broadcasting or anything else to anybody. I was quite capable of typing my own material. But if somebody could be found who would be willing to answer telephone calls and to type out occasional expense-sheets in a form that would be acceptable to BBC accountants, then I should be content. What I needed, I said, was someone who would do the equivalent of about two hours' work a day for me. The Administrative person was not impressed by my arguments. He made it plain that there was no alternative: I had to have a Secretary; it was, he said, Standard Corporation Practice. These are sacred words in the BBC: they represent the ultimate. Once they have been pronounced all discussion has to stop. I had been warned about this well in advance so I did not transgress. I gave way. Eventually, I acquired two secretaries.

The door into the BBC, like the door into *The Times* some fourteen years earlier, had been opened for me by Arthur Barker, then the BBC's Foreign Editor. He had visited Oslo in the very early 'thirties as Special Correspondent of *The Times* while on a general Scandinavian tour, and I had been of some help to him at the time thanks to my friendship with the head of the Press Department at the Norwegian Ministry for Foreign Affairs. We had kept up a desultory sort of correspondence since those early days. He joined the BBC some years before the war to help organize the foreign language broadcasts that were just beginning and I had written occasional pieces for this new service from Paris. Shortly after the end of the war he said to me that the BBC was expanding its Foreign News Department and went on to tell me that there would be one or two jobs that might perhaps interest me. I had hoped to get back to *The Times* after the war; but I found the going very sticky. I was as much out of sympathy with the foreign policy of the paper in 1945 as I had been in 1938; I found its attitude towards the British intervention in Greece to be wholly mistaken. I regretted that Dawson was no longer Editor since he, at least, would have appreciated that British interests were directly involved in the Eastern Mediterranean; whereas Barrington-Ward, who was then in control, was in a sense an unpractical romantic when it came to matters of this kind. I went to see him just before going back to Moscow early in January 1945 and I found his mind throbbing with a sort of Rooseveltian optimism. All my arguments about the predatory nature of Russian foreign policy he dismissed with a wave of the hand.

No doubt I made my views a little too obvious. Whatever the reason, the fact remains that no job that could be regarded as attractive appeared on the horizon, even though I waited patiently for some months. So I was grateful to have Arthur Barker's help once again. It led to my appointment as the BBC's Diplomatic Correspondent after a trial period of six months. Some of my friends in journalism and politics warned me strongly against taking it on. Whatever you do, they said, you will be wrong. Some people will acuse you of being little more than a Whitehall stooge; others will say that you allow your personal views and prejudices to intrude into your material. The neurotic attitude of both political parties to the BBC was another hazard. I was told that at Transport House, as at the Conservative Central Office, people with hard faces sat about with stop-watches measuring the precise time given to the Labour Party's point of view on matters of public importance, and checked it against the time allotted to the Tory attitude; and vice-versa. If the discrepancy was greater than a second or two, an uproar would follow. A. P. Ryan, then Editor of the BBC's news, had an effective technique in dealing with angry and verbose people. He would listen patiently while they shouted their complaints over the telephone; and then, in a gentle voice, would ask them to repeat what they had just said in order to make sure that he had all his facts right before passing them on to the staff. The accuser would draw a deep breath and then discover that he had lost the thread of his argument. The incident was closed.

The prospects at the BBC seemed exciting because the expansion of the Foreign News Department was just getting under way. So far as I can recall, the BBC had only three staff correspondents abroad at the time: Thomas Cadett in Paris, Norman MacDonald in Berlin and Anthony Wigan in Washington. It is true that the opportunities in those early days were not as great as they have since become. We were not expected to do a lot of broadcasting ourselves: we wrote bits for the news bulletins, one hundred words or so, to be spoken by the news reader. I found it hard to write pieces of that length that were intelligible as well as accurate after my experience of having five or ten times that number of words to play with while on *The Times*. I was surprised to discover that the BBC found it possible to take journalists like myself off the peg and plunge them straight into broadcasting without any previous experience: the written word, after all, is a very different thing from the spoken. The management made no effort to train us in the new technique, not even in the technique of television at a later date, and it was all very much of a hit-and-miss affair. The training of staff in the News Division is something that did not come until many years later; and even now I have the feeling that it is inadequate. I remember with dismay the innumerable mistakes I made in my broadcasting manner in those early days; and I have good reason to be grateful to BBC listeners for their patience. I had plenty of candid friends who kept on saying: 'God! How awful you were last night.'

It has often been put to me that the rule that BBC correspondents must not express personal opinions is a serious obstacle to worth-while reporting. The rule was strictly applied when William Haley was Director-General. There was one occasion when a senior member of the editorial staff, after looking at a piece I had just written, said in an agonized voice: 'This is a violation of the Charter.' All our pieces were closely scanned for any evidence of a personal view. The first talk I ever did for the Third Programme had to be done all over again because some busy critic in the office had discovered two opinions in it, opinions of which I had been completely unaware when I wrote my piece. And because of this restriction, journalists on the staff were regarded as very dull fellows by most other departments. They were not allowed to have views; they were not allowed to be controversial, and since controversy is regarded as the essence of good broadcasting, at least by producers, it was thought that whatever contribution staff correspondents made to output would send any broadcasting audience to sleep. There was therefore a general tendency never to employ BBC staff for other than purely News Division purposes; which meant, in effect, that the opportunities normally open to journalists to write long and reflective pieces were denied to my colleagues and myself. I found this a hardship. I found an outlet for my views in some modest extra-mural activities, in the form of occasional contributions to the *Spectator*, and the *Atlantic Monthly*, under the pseudonym of G. B. Thomas.

Nevertheless, there is much to be said for the Haley rule in the matter of day-to-day reporting. A news service whose reporters are for ever ventilating their personal views and prejudices soon loses its credibility, Charter or no Charter. The real danger to honest reporting lies not so much in giving expression to a personal view, as in the way selections are made from a vast mass of facts. It is always possible to dig up a comment from some obscure newspaper somewhere that can be quoted in support for a view that the reporter holds. The BBC, in Haley's day, had a weakness for newspaper quotations; it did not seem to occur to anyone in authority that they could be used to justify the wildest heresy. I myself soon discovered that while it was impossible to point to possible flaws in some aspect or other of British foreign policy so long as I was reporting from London in my capacity as Diplomatic Correspondent, the operation became quite simple the moment I was abroad. There was always someone who spoke or thought as I did; and it was not against the rules to quote him. Still, even with all these disadvantages, the Haley rule did ensure a high standard of reliability; a standard that the public has the right to demand from a monopoly service.

Under Hugh Greene, many of the old rules have lapsed; and I find it difficult on occasion to distinguish between news and comment. Moreover, the treatment of foreign news has become more superficial than it was in Haley's day. Fifteen or twenty years ago, foreign correspondents on the staff of the BBC, like foreign correspondents on the staff of *The Times*, were permanencies and they might well be kept in the same posts for years on end. They therefore acquired an intimate knowledge of the country in which they were working, its history, its politics, its legal system, its social strains, its politicians and business men and trade union leaders, and possibly even its literature. I was not a foreign correspondent myself and I was stationed in London. But I was singularly fortunate in that the BBC allowed me to go abroad even if there was no urgent news to be reported, in order to help me to understand what was going on and to get the background right to possible developments in future. Now, the whole business has become one-dimensional. The foreign correspondents are still there to do the daily bread-and-butter job; but the tendency is to send out a man from London on a lightning visit when a story develops. He arrives without any particular knowledge of the country in question; he gets a glimpse or two of the obvious; and goes back to London none the wiser. Nor, I suppose, is his audience. Since the reporter will not be sent on a foreign mission unless there is something sensational to report, it means that he is reduced to reporting a massacre, or an earthquake, or a revolution, or a battle, or a kidnapping. Foreign news therefore tends to become news about human wickedness and natural catastrophes. Thanks to the demands of television reporting, above all in the longer feature programmes, the term Darkest Africa has become more apposite than ever.

What also came as a surprise to me when I joined the BBC was to discover that remnants still existed of the close war-time relationship between the BBC and the Foreign Office. The Editor confirmed that he and his Foreign Editor were anxious to get rid of them as quickly as possible. I found that almost any junior in the Foreign Office considered himself entitled to telephone direct to the BBC's News Room if he thought it necessary to complain about some item or other in one of the news bulletins. By the time we had got to the year 1946, very few people in the News Room paid any attention to these calls; they knew, if the Foreign Office did not, that war-time practices were out of date. Such complaints as were made were entered in a log-book open to inspection by senior editors. Otherwise they did not have much effect. But they did lead to ill-will and friction. Conscientious people in the News Room felt they were constantly being shot at by irresponsible snipers in Whitehall and they did not like it. They therefore tended to ignore comments or suggestions that might well have been reasonable. The Foreign Office concluded that there were too many hob-nailed rustics in the BBC unaware of the finer points of diplomacy.

So the first thing we did was to ask the BBC's sub-editors to ignore all calls from the Foreign Office unless they came from its News Department. The next step was to ask the head of the News Department to communicate only with the Diplomatic Correspondent. We agreed that if the Foreign Office felt it necessary to make complaints in future, the News Department should make them to the Diplomatic Correspondent's office and to no one else. Only when this approach failed was a formal complaint to be made to the Director-General. We got things right in the end: the number of complaints fell almost to vanishing point; and the BBC's News Room eventually came round to the view that there might perhaps be some quite decent people in the Foreign Office after all.

Haley was not involved in any of this. I sometimes doubted, in those days, whether Haley really existed. I had been taken to see him formally before joining the staff; I had seen him at lunch one day at Broadcasting House; and I had heard him address a mass-meeting of staff. Apart from these three occasions, I did not set eyes upon him in the BBC. There were others who had never seen him at all, and they used to say that to believe in the existence of Haley required as great an act of faith as to believe in God. My own faith, I must add, was strengthened from time to time by seeing Haley in the flesh at cocktail parties and at other social functions. He was most conscientious about not recognizing his staff on any of these occasions. When a malicious friend of mine became aware of it, he took pleasure in introducing me to my Director-General at the most inappropriate times. In the presence of a small handful of people, Haley's silences and reserves were glacial. In a large gathering, he was articulate and friendly. I saw him at his best when he addressed a staff meeting at Broadcasting House. I saw him at his worst at a dinner-party given by the Irish Ambassador in honour of De Valera. Haley had left the BBC by that time to become Editor of *The Times*. The whole point of the Embassy party was to persuade De Valera to talk; and to listen to his views. The only man who tempted him to talk, and to talk brilliantly, was A. P. Wadsworth, the waspish Editor of the *Manchester Guardian*. Haley said hardly a word: he sat somewhere in the shadows, grey, reserved, silent. If there had been an aspidistra in the room he would no doubt have hidden himself behind it. He did not nod to me as I came into the room; nor did he exchange a word with me during the whole of that exciting evening. Lord Simon of Wythenshaw, then Chairman of the BBC, more than made up for Haley's silences. He tried hard to get to know members of the staff, and used to have groups of us in to lunch in his flat in Westminster together with one or two of the Governors. Simon was the most friendly of men, but he was not given to unnecessary extravagances. He would turn to you soon after you had joined the party and ask: 'What will you drink?' As you paused for reflection, he would say quickly: 'Lager or bitter?' There was no nonsense about cocktails or sherry. He was always asking questions about how you did your job, and what you thought about this or that person in public life. When I was asked how I spent my time as Diplomatic Correspondent I replied rashly: 'I spend most of my time gossiping.' A female Governor drew in her breath sharply and quickly changed the subject.

Every afternoon, after joining the BBC, I went to the News Department of the Foreign Office for a good gossip. There is something soothing about that long corridor that faces you as you come in through the main entrance. It is cool and quiet on a hot summer's day and would make an excellent cocktail bar; it echoes to footsteps in the same way as a congregationless Cathedral. Halfway down the corridor there is the entrance to the News Department, just at the point where there stands a statue of Lord Salisbury with his back to the wall, dressed apparently in a loose-fitting dressing-gown. A little beyond him, there is a picture of Queen Victoria, with an expression of near-disgust upon her face. Either the drains have gone wrong, she seems to think, or there is a journalist somewhere within smelling distance, but one cannot tell for certain what is worrying her. At the end of the corridor is the Permanent Under-Secretary's Office; past those grand stairs that lead to the Ambassadors' waiting room and the Foreign Secretary's office on the first floor. When the newspapers or the BBC announce that there is intense diplomatic activity in Whitehall it need mean no more than that two or three juniors have been seen running up the stairs with bits of paper in their hands.

By mid-January 1946, when I took over my job, the illusion had been shattered that the Labour Party was better qualified to deal with the Communist leaders in Russia than the Conservatives were. During the general election in 1945, Stafford Cripps was responsible, with others, for launching the slogan about Left speaking to Left. 'I feel convinced,' he said on 3 June 1945, 'that the Labour Party could handle that matter (of Anglo-Soviet relations) better than any other party in the country because they are basically more sympathetic to the Russian objectives than the other parties, who have constantly expressed their dislikes or fears of them.' On 1 July 1945, he said it again: 'It is absolutely vital to have in this country a Government which fully understands and appreciates the outlook of the people of the Soviet Union, and that can only be a Labour Government.' A few weeks later, *Pravda* published some very sour comments on Britain's new Foreign Secretary, Ernest Bevin. Anyone who had followed the relations between the Russian Communist Party and Socialist parties in other parts of the world knew that its leaders regarded Social Democrats as the most dangerous of enemies. And they treated them as enemies except during the very short Popular Front period when Stalin was prepared to sup even with the evil to save his skin. So far as Bevin was concerned, *Pravda* of course had a case. He had fought Communism so often and so strongly in his own trade union that he did not change his order of battle when he became Foreign Secretary. At the four-power Conference held in London in the autumn of 1945 he lost his temper with Molotov and came very near to accusing him of using Fascist tactics. Molotov got up from the Conference table and was on the point of leaving the room when Bevin's apology brought him back. The two men never hit it off: Molotov regarded Socialists as class enemies; and Bevin knew that Communists were plotters and intriguers. He carried his trade union experiences with him into the diplomatic world. This fact struck me with particular force when the problem of recognizing Communist China came up for discussion between us. Bevin had been talking calmly about all the arguments for and against when he suddenly raised his voice. 'Non-recognition!' he exclaimed, 'non-recognition! You've no idea how terrible it is, how humiliating, how much it hurts. In the old days in Bristol some of the employers refused to see me because my union was not recognized. It was terrible.' His voice was heavy with self-pity.

No sooner had I settled down with the BBC than I was asked to go and see Eden, then deputy-leader of the Opposition. When I called on him in his room at the House of Commons he suggested to me that I might be interested in a job at the Conservative Central Office, on the publicity or public relations side. He wanted to know how I would respond if an offer were eventually made to me. I did not give him an answer on the spot. I said I wanted a day or two to think things over, and that I hoped he would allow me to discuss the matter with one or two friends. He agreed to wait for an answer until the following week. On reflection, it occurred to me that while I had never had the slightest difficulty about holding strong views on a variety of topics, they were never the same for very long. Indeed, twenty-four hours after expressing one view, I might find myself defending the opposite opinion with even greater vigour. I found it easy to be a passionate Tory one day and a fervent Socialist the next. I do not believe I have ever voted for the Government in power at election time; my instinct has always been to vote against the party in office. I realized that I could not possibly transform myself into a reliable partisan of any particular political party. And then another thought came to me. After the fiasco of the 1945 general election, I felt sure that some of the members of that curious group that surrounded Churchill were a political liability rather than an asset. I made this point to Eden when I saw him again, and he took it very well. He waved away my objections. 'Don't trouble yourself about that,' he said. 'The Old Man won't be there much longer. The people you have in mind will go with him.' This was all too hypothetical for my liking. Still, it made no difference; I had made up my mind by that time that journalism was much to be preferred to politics. But it was not until 1953 that the Old Man withdrew from the political scene.

Harold Nicolson also thought that I ought to go into politics. He spoke to me often about the thrill of being an MP; and how much he regretted that he could no longer walk into the Chamber and take his place on those familiar benches. He wrote a letter to the Deputy Chairman of the Conservative Party with a strong recommendation that the Central Office should give me its support if I decided to put my name forward as a Conservative candidate. A very encouraging reply came back. But here again, I thought it best to say no thank you. It was not only that my views were and still are absurdly inconsistent. There is also the fact that I find it hard to distinguish between our two great political parties, except at their respective extremes. I have often felt equally critical of both. It is possible, I suppose, that among the reasons for our economic difficulties is that there is no genuinely Radical element in British political life at the moment, no group prepared to dig things up by the roots regardless of vested interests. All too often, the electorate is invited to choose between two equally conservative policies. I have done a fair amount of lecturing in different parts of the country over the years, and I have found that the coal miners of County Durham are as conservative as are prosperous middle-class people on the South Coast. Where they differ, is in their definition of what constitutes a reasonable standard of living.

My twenty-one years with the BBC were happy years. I was given a great deal of freedom; more, perhaps, than would have come my way on a newspaper. I was not constantly driven to turn out a half-digested story. I was given time for reflection, although there were, of course, occasions when events moved so quickly that I had to rush ahead without much thought, relying instead upon instinct. I have no doubt that the BBC is among the best employers in the country. People not on the staff may suspect that its rules and regulations have an inhibiting effect and that they tend to encourage caution rather than initiative. I can only say that I was not often conscious of being cramped and confined. The introduction of a competitive television service has encouraged the spirit of enterprise, and has created a greater willingness to experiment and to take risks. In this particular respect, the television staff has had every encouragement from Hugh Greene, the Director-General. Where there have been excesses, it is because young producers to whom he has given so much liberty have taken advantage of his tolerance; and perhaps the BBC's greatest weakness today is to be found in the devotion with which some of them pursue the lowest common denominator. It is, I suppose, another and less happy consequence of the pressure of competition.

If the race between the BBC and the ITA is to be run solely in terms of viewing figures, then the programmes designed for the mass audience are bound to be very much the same, or rather to contain much the same ingredients. All non-mass-audience output will be held over for off-peak hours where it will not interfere with the sale of detergents. It has been said that never in its history has the BBC more accurately reflected the mood of the nation than it does today. I am not convinced that this is a good and praiseworthy development. The present mood of the nation is one of doubt and disillusion and frustration. To see all our worries, contemptible sins and petty crimes mirrored in the television screen is neither helpful nor particularly entertaining, or so it seems to an old servant of the Corporation like myself who still clings to the view that some standards are worth maintaining and some ideals worth defending even in a popular television programme.

The BBC is not alone in this almost pathological desire not to be a spoil-sport, not to be a moralizer or a purveyor of uplift, but to be With It. The Church of England is setting an even better example. Not content with transferring its interests in Hell to Harley Street, it is now busily engaged in dismantling the image of God the Father and God the Son. In the end we shall be left with only the Bomb to hate or to worship. Every generation, I suppose, must have its own ideology and its own ideals to fight for. The Swedish philosopher Victor Rydberg, in a cautionary tale written at the turn of the century, described the reactions of two people to changes that had taken place over three centuries. They had been given the opportunity to go back in history and to see something of the ferocity of the struggle between the forces of Reformation and Counter-Reformation. They saw whole towns in flames and Calvinists and Lutherans burnt alive to the greater Glory of God. A *fin de siècle* member of parliament watches the scene with surprise and disgust. 'How lucky we are,' he says, 'to be living on the threshold of the twentieth century. Why are all these madmen killing and murdering? Why are they setting fire to property worth many millions in hard cash? For matters that have no relevance in the modern world. They must be mad; there can be no other explanation. If some practical issue were involved, I could understand it, although I might well deplore it. Something, for instance, like the customs tariff between Russia and Germany; or the duty on pork with its strong arguments for and against.'

I have never felt other than awkward when speaking a piece for the television camera, especially when the piece took the form of an interview. The first time I did it, I was given a great quantity of gin in the hope that I should feel dashing and care-free. I did not. It is true that I received a commendation on my performance from Norman Collins, then Controller of BBC Television; I thought he was just being tactful and I could not believe him. I suppose that if I had had a rigorous training as an actor I might have pulled it off to my own satisfaction. To appear natural when the butterflies are hammering away at your stomach requires acting skill of a high order. I prefer to forget all those interviews, with Selwyn Lloyd at London Airport, Maudling in Paris, Makarios in Athens, Hammarskiöld and Adlai Stevenson in London and many others. The thought of them still makes me feel embarrassed and ill-at-ease. I may act like a noisy fox-terrier among friends, but in public I am as docile as any sheep. I am unable to put the harsh penetrating question in the manner of a successful barrister; I am much more of an usher. Nevertheless there are aspects of some of these interviews that I can recall without embarrassment or humiliation.

When Makarios was released from his internment on the Seychelles in April 1957 and was on his way to Athens, the BBC decided that I should fly to Athens to interview him. I got in touch with the Greek Ministry for Foreign Affairs so soon as I arrived and its officials promised to help me as far as they could. I called also on the British Embassy where I was given to understand that this business of interviewing Makarios was not a Good Idea. The BBC staff correspondent who was in Athens at the time was in one of his parsimonious moods, and when he was asked to book a room for me decided that the time had come to do some solid cheese-paring. It would be grossly extravagant, he considered, if I were to stay in the expensive hotel in the centre of Athens; so he found a room for me somewhere on the edge of the town, well away from the hotel where Makarios had his headquarters. When I got in touch with the Makarios people, I found Robin Day staying at the same hotel: he was then with Independent Television News. He was strategically placed on the first floor; and he had his door open to keep an eye on the goings-on in the Makarios camp. In the event, he got an interview with the Archbishop long before I did; and it was shown on the ITN screen while I was still negotiating my way to a meeting with him. No sooner had this piece of news been broken to me than I telephoned to London suggesting that I should return at once without wasting any more time. But I was not allowed to take the easy way out. I was told to stay and to do the job. And I finally succeeded. It was all very tiresome and frustrating; but it is the sort of thing that happens to you at times in the world of journalism. One tries to forget about it as soon as possible. There is always the hope that one's luck will turn one day.

I came upon Robin Day again, this time in Moscow on the occasion of Macmillan's tour early in the year 1959. Day was still with ITN. The ubiquitous television cameras had become a source of irritation to British and Russian officials alike, and they decided to persuade the television crews to be more restrained. They summoned them to a meeting at the British Embassy at which it was agreed that there was to be no filming when Macmillan went to the Bolshoi Theatre for the *Romeo and Juliet* ballet on 25 February. Macmillan went to the theatre and everything seemed to be going according to plan when suddenly someone heard the whir of a camera. Robin Day, who was in the audience, was furious. He soon found out that the camera belonged to a television company which provided television film for the BBC, and when he saw me the next morning he protested violently. I could only tell him that I bore no responsibility for what had happened. I did not even know that an agreement had been made to restrict output since I had not been present at the meeting at which the BBC had been represented by the television producer. By some oversight, the Embassy had failed to invite the representatives of the outside agency to their conference, so they were in no way committed. Day said he was making a very strong protest to the Foreign Office, in the hope, no doubt, that an attempt would be made by officials in London to stop the BBC from showing the film. I replied mildly: 'I thought you liked scoops, Robin,' an answer that seemed to vex him. I felt sure that the Foreign Office would have the good sense not to interfere in this matter, so the threat of a protest did not trouble me. But I thought it just as well to telephone the BBC's News Room and to tell people there what had happened. I added that if the Foreign Office proved to be misguided enough to make what are euphemistically called 'representations', they should ignore them.

This Moscow trip, as I heard later, had not proved to be 'good television'. There had been no action; no quarrels in front of the cameras; the fact that Khrushchev sulked and refused to see Macmillan on the grounds that he had toothache could not be shown on the screen. I was persuaded against my better judgment to talk to people with the walls of the Kremlin in the background—just a bit of 'local colour' as the producer said—but it had no effect at all upon our British audience. I heard later that viewers had not paid the slightest attention either to my questions or to the replies given by those Russians who knew enough English to follow what was being said. All they noted was that I was not wearing a hat in what appeared to be very cold weather. Robin Day was more successful in his attempts to generate television excitement. At a press conference given by Macmillan on the eve of his departure for London, Day asked the Prime Minister if he could say something about the date of the next general election. Macmillan pointed an accusing finger at him. 'You are the wrong man, asking the wrong question, in the wrong place, at the wrong time,' he said. That was about the only piece of 'good television' we got out of our trip. Even Malcolm Muggeridge, who was also of our party, had the air of a chastened man.

The ingredients of my interview with Hammarskiöld in April 1958 were largely generalizations and clichés as they so often are on these occasions. But our private conversation was more interesting and informative. Hammarskiöld had only recently been in Moscow, and naturally enough I asked him what he now felt about the views and policies of the Russian leaders. I reminded him that the Russians seemed to be doing exceptionally well in the space-race and that their influence in the world—at that time—seemed to be unusually high. Might they not have gained enough self-confidence, I asked, to make it possible for them to be more accommodating? Their intransigence was understandable so long as they were regarded as inefficient and incompetent and treated as outcasts. But now? Hammarskiöld hesitated. Then he said quietly: 'Sometimes, you know, it works the other way. There is a point where self-confidence is transformed into rashness.' He left me with the impression, although he did not say so explicitly, that he had brought with him from Moscow impressions that were disturbing and perhaps even alarming. Later in the year, there came Khrushchev's ultimatum on Berlin.

If most of my interviews were routine affairs, my encounter with Adlai Stevenson was not. I called at the United States Embassy in London during the afternoon of 14 July 1965 and recorded an interview with him at a quarter to five for use in that night's Ten O'clock programme on the BBC. We talked about the war in Vietnam, about which it was widely believed that Stevenson's views did not altogether coincide with those of the Administration of which he was a member. But he did not go beyond his official brief. He seemed to me to be a disillusioned man: he was friendly enough, but his smile was forced. He gave me all the stock answers, with the conventional conclusion that the United States would have to go on fighting in order to persuade North Vietnam and China to negotiate. The only alternative was capitulation. There was no point in asking the United Nations to take over, he said, unless there was a disposition in Hanoi to accept United Nations mediation. And *that*, he added, the North had rejected. Stevenson seemed tired and a little absent-minded. I thought he had the look of a man who needed a holiday in the sun. By the time I got back to the BBC I heard that he was dead.

He had collapsed a few minutes after I had left him, and a death certificate was issued less than an hour after the interview with him had been recorded. There were long discussions in the BBC about whether or not to broadcast his remarks; and finally it was decided that it could be done. I very much regret that his last recorded words were orthodox sentiments on the subject of Viet-nam. Although he did not in any way confide in me, I came away with the conviction that the liberal in him did not altogether approve the actions of the Johnson Administration.

CHAPTER 16

MY FIRST important assignment after my return to journalism was to report the Conference in Paris in 1946 at which the terms of the Peace Treaties with Italy, Hungary, Rumania, Finland and Bulgaria were formally negotiated. Vyshinsky, it seemed to many of us, was at his worst; and the members of some of the Western delegations came to hate him. We used to go round the Conference Room after each sitting to inspect the doodles with which some of the delegates had whiled away their time while the deputy-head of the Russian delegation was lecturing them. One evening after Vyshinsky had been more than usually vituperative and garrulous, we found that a member of one of the Western delegations had drawn a gallows upon his blotter, with something that looked rather like Vyshinsky dangling from the hangman's rope. Molotov was another speaker one came to dislike. His invective was icy, carved out of a glacier; whereas Vyshinsky's was more like molten lava. As he piled insult upon insult, Molotov would sense the growing hostility around him, and his stammer would become more pronounced. He would blink as his consonants halted the smooth flow of his speech. His long and beautifully-proportioned fingers would play nervously upon the edge of the desk before him as he stood stiffly to attention. ('His real name is Scriabin, you know,' Macmillan once said to us. 'He comes from a family of musicians. He is an artist. I am sure I shall get on with him.' The Russians knew him as 'Stone-Bottom'.) The eyes behind the harsh pince-nez were expressionless: there was no hatred in them, no anger, not even irritation.

Some of us also found Field-Marshal Smuts hard to like. He was a master of the wrong word and the misplaced sentiment; and his speeches were stuffed with hollow clichés. His manner was urbane, statesmanlike, philosophical, remote and well-intentioned. As I saw him upon the speaker's rostrum I understood how he had come to be described as 'Stroking Jesus' in Arnold Bennett's *Lord Raingo*. He was loudly applauded at the end of his speech; hardened politicians like a touch of sentiment at times, provided it is expressed in terms that will not set the Thames on fire.

It was not until we heard De Gasperi, then Prime Minister of Italy, that the Conference came to life, and the voice of Europe became audible. It was a stirring moment; and even those of us who could understand little more than an odd word of Italian were moved and impressed by the performance. One felt that the ideal of Europe was beginning to take shape, a feeling that frightened many Labour Ministers and their supporters at the time. De Gasperi was a Roman Catholic, and the spectre of a clerical Europe dominated by De Gasperi, Schumann of France and in due course, no doubt, Adenauer of Germany was enough to frighten any Protestant or Socialist. Ivone Kirkpatrick, who later became Permanent Under-Secretary at the Foreign Office, and himself a Roman Catholic, played upon these Labour fears in his opposition to the European ideal. He told Bevin that if Britain played too active a part in the development of a European Community, he might live to see confessional parties in this country of the same kind as on the Continent. Did he want a Roman Catholic Party in Britain and a Protestant Party? Bevin had seen enough of the battles between Papists and Orangemen in Liverpool—'all for the Love of God', as he once said to me—to want any truck with that sort of thing. Kirkpatrick's argument helped to close his mind to the thought that Britain might one day lead the movement towards European unity. In a speech to the Transport and General Workers' Union on 17 July 1947 he said: 'I hear talk of the United States of Europe. It is no use trying to unite the world if you have predominant in your mind political unification. The war has accentuated racial and national difficulties.' These remarks accurately reflected opinion in Whitehall at the time, in the Foreign Office, the Treasury and the Board of Trade. Two months later, again in a speech to the Transport and General Workers' Union, Bevin said it was very difficult to accept a customs union in Europe 'as a panacea of our difficulties. I hope that the Commonwealth, and certainly the Empire, will agree as to the possibility of a Customs Union for the British Commonwealth and Empire. I do not think we can avoid any longer common defence and acceptance of certain economic principles if we are to avoid constant recurrent crises.'

I believe myself that some form of European Union led by the British Government, on terms acceptable to the British people and probably to the old Commonwealth also, was well within the Government's grasp in 1946 and 1947. The Americans would have supported it; and they might even have financed it, for to them the goal of a Europe united under British direction seemed eminently desirable. Western Europe would have accepted British leadership since the Attlee Government enjoyed immense prestige. No British Government since 1945 has had a higher standing. But Attlee and Bevin had not the will, and the Civil Service at the time was too insular and too lacking in perception. Some of its members argued that it was all very well for the nations of the Continent to merge their identities in some sort of European Federation; after all the war must have proved to them that nationalism was not enough. But things were different on this side of the Channel: the British victory in 1945, the civil servants said, was a triumph for nationalism which could not now be obliterated in some nondescript amalgam. And so the European spirit that had waited in the wings of the Paris Conference was driven off. Instead of European security and European unity, the leading powers became more concerned with German security and German unity. I shall have more to say on this subject in a later chapter.

It was in Paris, too, at this first great post-war Conference, that I became aware of the tensions that led eventually to the breach between Stalin and Tito. I remember discussing with one of the senior members of the Czechoslovak delegation—a man who later lost his life in one of Stalin's purges—the action of the Yugoslav Air Force in shooting down an American aircraft near Klagenfurt. News of the affair had spread gloom over the negotiations and there was some wild talk of American reprisals. The Yugoslavs were more Stalinist than Stalin himself in those days; and it was generally assumed that their action had been carried out with Soviet connivance, if not actually at Soviet instigation. I said I could not understand how the Russians could have allowed the Yugoslavs to act so rashly; it must have done a good deal of harm to Moscow's relations with the United States. My friend gave me a look which said plainly that I was being unusually obtuse. He told me that I did not understand the position. 'When a small country is allied to a great power,' he added, 'it is usually the small country that calls the tune in matters of this kind. The Yugoslavs did not bother to consult Moscow before they acted. They knew that the Russians would be forced to support them for the sake of appearances. Given the differences between East and West, the Russians are bound to do all they can to preserve the façade of unity in the East. And the Yugoslavs are trading on the fact; indeed they've been trading on it for a long time. But no doubt the Russians are giving them hell behind the scenes.' A minute or two later I saw Molotov walking down the corridor with Kardelj, speaking earnestly, gesticulating, and apparently trying to convince his companion of the validity of whatever case he was making.

Charles ('Chip') Bohlen, whom I had got to know in Moscow during the war and who was on the United States delegation to the Conference, was of enormous help to me in taking a sensible view of all the conflicting opinions that had to be sorted out at noon every day and again in the evening. We had our BBC microphones installed in a studio within the Conference building, with direct access to the news rooms in Broadcasting House at fixed hours of the day. In the morning we had to outline the shape of things to come to our colleagues in London so that they could make the necessary arrangements for accommodating the material in the news bulletins. Vague hints were of no use to them; we had to provide them with something firm and definite. Speaking without a note, and often without much preparation, I found the going very hard. If it had not been for the friends we made among the delegates and for the help we got from them, the job would have been impossible. Bohlen's advice was especially valuable. He had been at the Teheran and Yalta Conferences with Roosevelt, and at Potsdam with Truman and he knew as much about the negotiating techniques of the Russians as any man alive. Unlike some other people in the State Department, he had an open mind and a gift for putting himself in the other man's place. We were discussing one afternoon the growing difficulties of dealing with the Russians: every day, it seemed, they were becoming more intransigent. Bohlen did not think there was much that the United States Government could do at the moment. It would be best, he thought, to sit back for some fifteen or twenty years, and see how things developed. In that long waiting period, the United States should develop its economy and help the Governments of Western Europe to strengthen theirs. In due course, 'the Russians and their friends will be looking over the fence to see what is happening: they'll be interested, they may well be impressed.' Then, Bohlen reflected, it might be possible to talk. If we add fifteen or twenty years to the year 1946 we come to 1961 or 1966. The Russians and their friends have been looking over the fence for some time now. Bohlen's forecast was not far wrong.

The BBC European Service sent off a fairly big staff to Paris to report the Peace Conference since its proceedings were of the greatest interest to people all over Europe. The Talks Department signed up Harold Nicolson to do a series of commentaries; and his diplomatic experience, going back to the Treaty of Versailles, was of enormous help to us. We used to hold an editorial conference every afternoon to discuss the day's work, and how it was to be handled, and how duplication between the various language services could best be avoided. Nicolson used to play a very active part in our proceedings. In the hot weather he took off his coat and a stream of rags would float out from his shirt upon the conference table. We were still in the days of clothes rationing, and Nicolson wore his shirts beyond the point where they could be used as dusters. The rags hanging from his elbows made effective fly-whisks, but they were too flimsy to cover that part of the human frame that was visible to us. He took his broadcasting very seriously; and by common consent he was an excellent and persuasive performer. So far as I recall, he was committed to recording two talks a week; and on those days he was careful about everything. He did not smoke until after his work had been done. In the studio, he was seen to gargle in a restrained sort of way with the help of a liquid which I discovered later was port. He was still writing his weekly article in the *Spectator* at the time, and I remember his telling us that he found broadcasting far more difficult than writing, and far more demanding.

In 1946 one still had the feeling that the European situation was fluid, that some sort of settlement would yet emerge that would not be too intolerable, but that an immense amount of patience would be needed in working things out. And patience is something that politicians do not usually possess: they want quick results; they want to show that they are at all times in tune with public opinion, whatever that may mean. With the wisdom of hindsight I am now convinced that all those great Conferences from 1946 onwards were an obstacle to agreement rather than the the other way round; and that if only there had been a bit of quiet diplomacy out of range of television cameras and reporters something might have been achieved, in spite of Stalin. But with politicians striking attitudes one afternoon, and nailing their colours to the mast on the following day while hurling moral platitudes at each other, the scope for compromise disappeared. Yet in 1946, the picture still seemed fairly simple. It is true that the Russians were being obstructive but most of us thought they could be made to budge a little. It would be necessary for the Western Powers to take into account the strains and stresses caused by the terrible losses the Russians had suffered during the war, and their almost pathological need not only for security, but also to be accepted as an equal among the 'respectable powers'. If the Western Governments would do this, then the Russians might yet prove open to arguments and persuasion.

It was not until the Moscow four-power Conference early in 1947 that I first became conscious of another and equally important factor in the post-war political situation: the American guilty conscience. It was not put into words until Foster Dulles became United States Secretary of State, and then only in an oblique way. The guilty conscience was a major ingredient in Senator McCarthy's campaign of abuse and persecution that bedevilled American public life for years. I did not perceive any of this at the Paris Conference in the summer of 1946; not at the New York Conference later in the same year. It occurred to me like a flash at the Moscow Conference in 1947. I suddenly realized that the Americans, as Bevin might have said, were hawking their consciences from Conference to Conference. They knew that the Russian encroachment into Europe proper was a direct consequence of the unwillingness of the United States Government to take political factors into account while the war was still being fought. 'The trouble with Churchill,' Roosevelt said to his son Elliott, 'is that he is thinking too much of the post-war period and where England will be. He's scared of letting the Russians get too strong.' Once the Americans had grasped what had happened, they set about trying to retrieve the situation. The result was a curious reversal of roles. After the 1914 war, it was the Germans and the Russians who were determined to upset the status quo; after the 1945 war, it was the Germans and the Western Powers led by the United States. In a war-weary Europe, no one was prepared to think beyond the status quo, at least not if it entailed the risk of war. When Eisenhower and Dulles fought their election campaign with the slogan, among others, of liberating Eastern Europe, they were playing straight into Russian propaganda hands, as they had done so often before, and were to do again and again. All they achieved was a massacre in Budapest in 1956, whereas by tacitly accepting the status quo they might have secured tolerable terms for Berlin.

In the sort of political poker game that the Russians played, that Churchill would have been more than willing to play, but which the Americans refused to play, winner takes all; there is not much point in complaining later about unfairness and misunderstanding. It was partly because the Americans kept on saying 'we wuzz robbed' and partly because of their guilty conscience that every international Conference went sour almost on the opening day. Moreover, in defending the arrangements agreed at Teheran, Yalta and Potsdam against critics at home, the Americans had been driven into arguing that the Russians at the time had carefully concealed their true intentions, and that it was not until the Polish crisis in 1947 and the later Czechoslovak crisis that their machinations were revealed. The Americans then made the further mistake, or so it seems to me, of describing Russian imperialism as Communism, thereby giving an ideological reason for resisting Russian power. Once an ideology is evolved, the ordinary big-power compromises are ruled out. You cannot compromise with the devil, as both Martin Luther and Foster Dulles have reminded us. Nor can you be neutral. Neutrality roused Dulles to passionate anger.

It struck me also at the time that there was a striking parallel between American policy in the early cold war years and Anglo-French policy in the nineteen-thirties. In the pursuit of appeasement, the British and French Governments were motivated not by wickedness or the lust for profits or for imperial power. They were just frightened, as were so many people in Europe. They were terrified of war, and they feared that once war came, only Communism stood to gain. In precisely the same way, American policy after the war was based on fear; the fear of Communism.

But whereas the fear of Communism drove European leaders in the 'thirties into retreat and compromise, in the post-war period it led the Americans into resistance and defiance. After the successful launching of the Marshall Plan and the conclusion of the North Atlantic Alliance, their foreign policy became a matter of responses, not of constructive initiatives. In the light of Stalin's callous blunders, the American reaction up to about 1950–51 was inevitable. But after that year, a more imaginative and less rigid approach might well have paid off.

It is because of their ideological rigidity that the Americans have failed so signally to persuade foreign peoples of their good intentions in the post-war world? No nation has a better record of good deeds than the United States. Marshall Aid saved Europe from collapse; the North Atlantic Alliance restored European political and military confidence; military aid to Europe and economic aid to former colonial territories have been on an incredibly liberal scale. These acts of generosity have not prevented the growth of anti-American feelings and vicious criticisms of United States policies. While the Americans have offended Conservative opinion in some European countries by pursuing strongly anti-Colonial aims, they have failed to win reliable friends among the new States in the underdeveloped world. The loss of Indonesia, the Congo, Suez, and French North Africa has left deep scars on some European minds. The part that United States pressure played in these developments is not likely to be forgotten. And yet among the liberated peoples there is no gratitude. Some ten years ago, a senior officer in the United States Diplomatic Service told the Senate Foreign Relations Committee that the United States appeared cast in the role of Louis XIV, 'the most reactionary of régimes; and this is by no means exclusively the achievement of Soviet propaganda. The moralistic attitude of some American policy makers, and the urge to make over the world in the American image, combined with a puritanical zeal to stamp out Marxian socialism have substantially contributed to this development.'

Yet this is only part of the story. Why is it that the Americans who are so good at selling things, are so bad at putting over ideas? Why is it that the Central Intelligence Agency, which no doubt has many useful deeds to its credit, always seems to be associated with failures and blunders in the public mind? Why do so many

American Embassy buildings in foreign capitals tempt us to compare their style to the monstrosities in Eastern Europe? What leads the Americans to believe that propaganda which concentrates upon power and wealth is likely to endear them to foreigners, and above all to the peoples living in the under-developed parts of the world? The Russians, I know, are deeply impressed with material achievements. No doubt that was why Stalin took great care during the war to conceal, as far as possible, the extent of American aid to the Russian people. But those nations upon whom the Americans are particularly anxious to make a good impression do not worship size and power in the same way. As for the unpopularity arising out of the American involvement in Vietnam, of which General de Gaulle as well as the Russians have made such skilful use, it needs only to be said that almost all the raw material for anti-American propaganda has been provided by the Americans themselves. The horror photographs, the war films, the eyewitness bombing reports have all been provided by them or sponsored by them. It is as if the Second World War had been reported mainly in terms of the killing of German civilians in air-raids upon Berlin and Hamburg and Dresden. More than one Foreign Minister in Western Europe, knowing something of the anti-American feelings raging among his own followers and in his own country, has personally implored the Americans to reconsider their present policy on war reporting. It has been suggested that some American Generals would look rather better dressed if they wore muzzles. None of these arguments seems to have had the slightest effect.

It was at the Moscow Conference early in 1947, then, that the cold war became an acknowledged fact. It was at the Moscow Conference, also, that the French Government found it necessary to align themselves with the policies of the United States and British Governments in order not to fall into complete isolation. Up to that time they had tried to play a mediating role; but in 1947 they came off the fence. They understood that it would not be possible for them to come to terms with the Russians on the basis of a German settlement equally satisfactory to Moscow and to Paris. Their policy remained as it had been defined by General de Gaulle on the eve of the Yalta Conference in February 1945. He then declared that the 'separation of the territories on the left bank of the Rhine and the Ruhr basin from what will be the

German State, and the independence of the Polish, Czech, Austrian and Balkan nations, are conditions which France judges to be essential.' He said much the same thing in an interview with the Paris Correspondent of *The Times*, published on 10 September 1945; adding that if the Ruhr and the Rhineland were internationalized 'they would become the focus of European cooperation. In the hands of one power they are an instrument of domination.' De Gaulle counted upon Anglo-French cooperation to achieve these aims, extended, in due course, to include the Soviet Union in spite of his unhappy experiences in Moscow in December 1944. In the event, Britain moved even closer to the United States, while the French for a while tried to come to terms with the Russians without British help. They failed, so they sought shelter in the Western camp, although not without bitterness as de Gaulle has since reminded us.

Nevertheless, their new situation left them with a feeling of insecurity. Once again, as in 1919, they were at the mercy of the Anglo-Saxon powers whose European interests were not necessarily the same as theirs. They had no faith in the stability of United States foreign policy, and they were afraid lest a Russo-American *rapprochement*, over the question of Germany, endanger French security. Alternatively, and here they shared the fears of the Poles, they perceived that an Anglo-American understanding with Germany could always be achieved at their expense and Poland's. They remained suspicious. In May 1948, the United States Ambassador in Moscow had a long conversation with Molotov with the aim of defining the position of his Government on several controversial points. He then left for a fishing holiday. While he was travelling, and therefore out of touch with his Embassy and the State Department, Molotov put out a communiqué which implied that the Americans had agreed to open bilateral talks with Moscow. The first reaction in Paris was one of panic-stricken fury. When the communiqué was first shown to Bidault, then Foreign Minister, he broke into a long series of angry expletives. He believed, and he was not the only one, that France and Europe were about to be sacrificed on the altar of Russo-American reconcilation.

Although General de Gaulle had withdrawn into private life early in 1946, and the Moscow Conference was therefore held without his guiding hand on French policy, Bidault formally proposed the internationalization of the Ruhr on Gaullist terms. He got no support from Bevin or Marshall. London and Washington had drawn the lines by then and since Western Germany had to be on the right side of them, nothing could be done that would upset its leaders, in spite of French fears and hopes. The only concession the French got out of the Conference was the integration of the Saar with what Marshall called the economic and financial system of France, after Bidault had pointed out with passion that so soon as German steel output exceeded French, the security of France would be endangered. The French noted, incidentally, that some of the changes in Eastern Europe, notably the transfer of Königsberg to the Soviet Union, were final, in spite of the absence of a Peace Treaty; in the West all was left open. Naturally enough, the feeling persisted among them that all hopes should not be abandoned of a Franco-Russian *entente*. Each step away from this nebulous hope, and many such steps became inevitable over the years, made the French uneasy, difficult, and increasingly critical of Anglo-American policies. As late as 1951, Adenauer was still worried about the pro-Russian and anti-German tradition at the Quai d'Orsay. 'I had myself experienced and observed,' he wrote in his autobiography, 'how difficult it was, especially in the first years after the war, to work against this tradition, particularly the tradition of advocating ties between France and Soviet Russia which I was afraid was still very much alive.'

The French had not the same scruples about taking reparations out of current production from their zone of Germany as had the two other Western Powers. They were not represented at the Potsdam Conference, so they were not strictly bound by the agreement that the proceeds of German exports from current production and stocks were to be made available in the first place for the payment of essential imports. Once they began to collect reparations their example was quickly followed by the Russians, who, of course, were committed by Potsdam but who discovered good reasons for ignoring the terms of the agreement. Molotov and Vyshinsky fought what I can only call a vicious battle for reparations at the Moscow Conference; and got some very sharp answers from Bevin and Marshall in return. The debate injected a new and bitter ingredient into the cold war. I believe myself that the arguments used on that occasion had lasting effects on the political situation in Europe. The hopes of East-West reconciliation became more remote than ever, or so it seemed to me. Curiously enough, the Russians were not yet willing, early in 1947, to admit that things had gone completely wrong. When I was quoted by the BBC as saying that the Moscow Conference had been a failure, I was sharply criticized for my pessimism in the Moscow press. Yet the facts seemed plain enough to me.

Those of us who reported the Conference went by Bevin's special train which had been laid on in order to save the Foreign Secretary from a tiring and boring flight his doctors had warned him against. We left Victoria early in March and travelled from Dunkirk via Berlin, Warsaw and Brest-Litovsk, where we had to change trains because of the different gauge. From Brest to Moscow were were accommodated in splendid coaches going back to Tsarist days. The dining car, in particular, was a model of Victorian comfort and luxury. There were twenty journalists on the train, so far as I remember, mostly British but some representing Commonwealth newspapers, and three Americans as well. Among these last was Helen Kirkpatrick, one of the most distinguished of American reporters, who insisted upon singing the Marseillaise in a very loud voice as the train passed out of West Berlin into Eastern Germany. I do not suppose anyone heard her except those of us who were in the same coach.

When we got to Warsaw, we were met by a high-level reception committee whose members invited us to join them in a sight-seeing tour. Others have written about the destruction of the Polish capital, and of the efforts of the Poles to rebuild it. All I want to do here is to underline the political and psychological consequences of the rejection of reparations in the light of the Polish situation. We toured Warsaw for an hour or two and saw the Poles digging into the snow, and clearing away the rubble with their bare hands. They had no mechanical equipment, so far as I could see. The rubble was loaded by hand on drays, and these were drawn by horses which could barely stand upright for lack of food. Their ribs stuck our like scaffolding round a building undergoing repair. It seemed clear to us that it was going to take the Poles many years to do a job that might be done in months, perhaps in weeks, if only they had had the machinery, and perhaps a little more food and fuel. When we got back to the train, we were asked to take our places in a special dining-coach that had been added to it, well away from our own compartments. The doors were locked, and we were given a sumptuous meal as the train steamed slowly through a desolate and snow-covered countryside. Here and there, not far from the track, haggard figures waved listlessly to us. Perhaps they knew that we were the guests of the Polish Government.

It is against this background of destitution and possibly despair—although the term despair seems hardly applicable to Poland at any time—that this debate on reparations must be seen. It is true that Poland was offered Marshall Aid some months later, in precisely the same way as the other States of Europe, but that Stalin told Bierut to turn it down. To that extent the Russians were responsible for the difficulties that followed. But at the Four-Power Conference held in Moscow early in 1947, at a time when the whole of Europe was suffering from an exceptionally severe winter, there was yet no suggestion of Marshall Aid. The starving Poles in their blackened ruins could now read in their newspapers that Germany would not be asked to pay, and this at a time when Polish needs were greatest. Germany was to be restored with Western help, their papers told them, while Poland got nothing. In accordance with the Potsdam Agreement, the Russians were made responsible for collecting reparations on Poland's behalf; so that if Russia did not get any neither would the Poles. I wonder now if the situation might not have been handled with greater tact in the hope of persuading Poland and the other countries of Eastern Europe that the Western Powers were as interested in their welfare as the Russians were. Bevin and Marshall kept on equating the German problem with the Polish, and vice-versa, at least in economic terms; and their speeches seemed to imply, to the Poles and to the Russians, that the concessions Stalin had squeezed out of London and Washington during the war would have to be reconsidered, now that the war was over. There is a great deal to be said against the Polish acquisition of Breslau and Stettin, but to view these territorial changes from the German angle, in 1947, seemed tactless and therefore politically unwise. Marshall told the Moscow Conference that he wanted a commission to report 'on Polish re-settlement and German settlement in the areas (the so-called Western territories of Poland) and the best means to ensure effective utilization of such areas for the economic well-being of the Polish and German people and of Europe as a whole'.

The sentiments were unexceptionable, but were unfortunate in the context of the time. Could one really discuss Polish and German economic well-being in terms of a joint operation after what had happened between 1939 and 1945? The public relations people attached to Marshall's delegation at the Conference made every effort to persuade us that their Secretary of State had offered a sensible and humane solution, and that its acceptance would not only put an end to the problem of German refugees, whose presence was a crushing burden on the military administration of Western Germany, but would also help to solve the terrible food shortages in Eastern Europe. The wide discrepancy between Polish living standards and Western still rankles in Polish minds. As recently as the summer of 1966 a Polish official referred to it with the greatest bitterness. 'I would make almost any sacrifice,' he told me, 'to have the sort of living standards and economic opportunities that people have in the West.' And I believe this attitude, although not usually expressed in these extreme terms, goes some way towards explaining the vicious anti-German propaganda in Poland. The West German economic example is so tempting, and has so many attractions that it is essential for the Polish régime as the guardian of Polish souls to denounce it in the same fierce terms as theologians once denounced the world, the flesh and the devil.

As for the specific problem of reparations, to which the Polish problem became linked during some of the discussions at the Moscow Conference, Bevin explained matters in the House of Commons some time later. The British Government, he said, 'had had to borrow precious dollars from America and deprive our own people of what these dollars could buy in food in order to finance the import of food into Germany.' In the British view therefore, the first charge on Germany's foreign exchange resources, once Germany's essential needs had been met, should be, not reparations from current production, but the repayment of the sums advanced to Germany to pay for basic imports. On this point Bevin undoubtedly carried British public opinion with him; and, so far as I was able to judge at the time, opinion in Western Europe also. But he was on less firm ground when he went on to explain the more positive aspects of British policy towards Western Germany. 'Meanwhile we are going to push on to raise the German standard of living in accordance with our promises, to rehabilitate their industries, always remembering that we must not push Germany ahead of the liberated countries.' Among the smaller States of Western Europe, the reaction to this part of Bevin's statement was unfavourable; as they saw it then, Britain was repeating the mistake she made after the First World War; backing Germany against Russia this time, while a generation ago it had been Germany against France. In Eastern Europe, where people had no greater liking for the Russians than for the Germans, the report that the rehabilitation of Western Germany was high on the list of Western priorities came as a great shock. I thought at the time that something might perhaps be done to give a friendlier aspect to Western policies, and when the idea for a Council of Europe first came up for discussion (it came into existence in August 1949) I proposed that there should be an empty chair in the Council Chamber marked 'Poland'; and that the Polish Government should be invited to send a representative to its meetings whenever they felt so inclined. I argued that it would show that people in Western Europe regarded the Poles as worthy of full membership in any Western club. Nothing came of my idea. It died peacefully in Whitehall, as so many ideas do.

The West's relations with Eastern Europe might perhaps have taken a different turn if the good example set by Sweden in 1946 had been followed. During the course of that year, the Swedish Minister of Trade, Gunnar Myrdal, negotiated a credit of around £60 millions to the Soviet Union, for the purchase of £12 millions-worth of goods a year over a period of five years, to be repaid after fifteen years. Because of later economic difficulties in Sweden, this transaction was much criticized. Yet from the international point of view it seemed a most constructive move. In essence, it was inspired by the same spirit as the Marshall Plan: namely the desire to tide a less fortunate neighbour over a difficult period while at the same time maintaining or opening up a market for exports. It differed from Marshall Aid in that it was a loan, not a grant; but it left the recipients free to spend the money how they liked without reference to others, or to a master-plan.

Its importance lay in the assumptions that inspired it. It implied that Russia was 'one of us'. Churchill's visits to Russia in 1942 and thereafter carried the same implications. The Russians had been treated as outcasts since 1917; but even before the Revolution they had been held at arm's length. The correspondence of Walter Hines Page, American Ambassador in London during the First World War, throws an interesting light on the attitude which then prevailed. Among the ominous consequences of victory, he wrote, would be that Russia would have to be admitted to what he called 'the society of nations'. During the Second World War, Franklin Roosevelt apparently tried to bring Stalin into the magic circle; but I do not believe that his schoolboy *bonhomie* had the effect he seemed to hope for. There is something almost nauseating about his own account of how he dealt with Stalin at the Teheran Conference, where he met the Russian dictator for the first time. Frances Perkins, who was Roosevelt's Secretary of Labour, in her book *The Roosevelt I Knew*, quotes Roosevelt as explaining to her: 'then I said, lifting up my hand to cover a whisper (which of course had to be interpreted) "Winston is cranky this morning, he got up on the wrong side of the bed". A vague smile passed over Stalin's eyes, and I decided I was on the right track. As soon as I sat down at the Conference table, I began to tease Churchill about his Britishness, about John Bull, about his cigars, about his habits. It began to register with Stalin. Winston got red and scowled, and the more he did so the more Stalin smiled. Finally Stalin broke into a deep, hearty guffaw, and for the first time in three days I saw the light. I kept it up until Stalin was laughing with me, and it was then that I called him "Uncle Joe".'

Who can doubt that Roosevelt went the wrong way about it? This sort of banter did not mean that the Russians had been admitted into the inner circle of the great powers. They may well have thought it was Roosevelt's way of keeping them out of it, in the same way as a child is kept at arm's length in the presence of adults talking serious business by someone reciting a nursery rhyme for its entertainment. To recognize Russia as an equal meant recognizing her as an ordinary great power with normal imperialist appetites. And that was something that had not been done since the Congress of Vienna. In 1815, Tsar Alexander played a leading part in the European settlement; although even then, as Tolstoy has told us, there was no confidence between East and West. 'Austria is betraying us,' says Anna Pavlovna in

War and Peace. 'England with her commercial spirit will not and cannot understand the Emperor Alexander's loftiness of soul. The famous Prussian neutrality is just a trap. Russia alone must save Europe.' In 1945, Stalin was given no opportunity 'to save Europe'; he was excluded from all areas that he failed to take by force or by stealth. If it had been found possible to accept Russia as an equal, enjoying the same rights as Britain and America to assert her authority in, say, the Eastern Mediterranean, or anywhere else for that matter, it would have involved the maintenance of Western forces in strength until a European settlement had been reached, including a German settlement. But in the event, the Western Powers made the worst of both worlds: they did not accept the Russians as equals and so provided Moscow with a grudge; at the same time, they failed to maintain adequate forces in those areas where they wished their own influence to be felt. Roosevelt's idealism, and his conviction that the October Revolution had altered the essential character of Russian foreign policy, made a great-power deal impossible. Stalin, of course, did what he could to achieve equality of status with America. His demand for three votes in the United Nations, and his willingness to concede three votes to the United States also, showed that he was thinking in terms of a Russo-American condominium. The British Government were the first to resist this master-plan, first under Churchill, then under Attlee. The production of an independent British nuclear deterrent followed inevitably. France and China took the same road to independence in due course; it was only the return to power of General de Gaulle that prevented the French nuclear deterrent from becoming a joint Franco-German affair. Franco-German technical and financial talks for this purpose were well on the way in the last days of the Fourth Republic. De Gaulle demanded complete French independence in this matter, as in so many others. Yet the Russians have not abandoned their determination to come to some sort of global understanding with the United States. It is not hard to understand why both the French and the Chinese have argued so strongly against the terms of a treaty to prevent the spread of nuclear weapons.

But the Moscow Conference was not without its lighter moments. When Vyshinsky laid on a press Conference for the visiting journalists, he was floored by a perfectly proper and sensible question put by the elder statesman among the Diplomatic Correspondents, W. N. Ewer, then of the *Daily Herald*. We had been treated to a long and bitter diatribe on the employment of former Nazis in West Germany when Ewer drew attention to recent reports of former Nazis employed in East Germany. Vyshinsky had not got an answer ready; nor had his assistants who sat with him; so he became offensive. One realized that if this notorious Public Prosecutor had been forced to operate in a normal Court of Law, the story of the great purge-trials might have taken a very different turn, even if the evidence had not been fabricated. His insolence angered me, although I was not its victim. I did not think that anyone had the right to talk to us, to one of our colleagues, in the way he did. So I suggested to Ewer that we should all walk out in protest, and leave Vyshinsky in possession of an empty room. 'No,' said Ewer, 'I don't think we should do that. We are the guests here, and we must remain polite.' So we stayed. My own experience in dealing with authority in Moscow is that firmness, combined with the utmost politeness, usually paid off.

I discovered one day that one of my Conference cables to the BBC had been heavily censored. I had been charged in full for the number of words I had written although about one third of them had been cut out. Yet the cashier at the Telegraph Office had not offered to refund any money. I was told by the resident foreign correspondents that this was a common practice, and that the Soviet Government appeared to be making a handsome profit out of the practice. I made up my mind to get a refund, although I was warned by all the old hands that the thing was not worth trying. When I made my claim, the people in the cashier's office shrugged their shoulders. They didn't understand. I told them that I was quite prepared to wait until they had made up their minds to be honest. In the event, I got my way. Then there was the occasion when I asked Ilyachev, at the time head of the Press Department at the Ministry for Foreign Affairs, for the correct address of Moscow Radio. He said that he would send it to me through the post. This is one Russian way of saying no. So I insisted upon getting it then and there. I also asked him to write it out in Cyrillic characters for the benefit of my chauffeur. He looked at me sternly, as I settled back comfortably in the chair opposite him, to emphasize that I had plenty of time upon my hands. Finally, he gave way and grudgingly handed over a piece of paper. I found him just as disagreeable to deal with as Vyshinsky. He later became head of Agitprop (Agitation and Propaganda) and a thorn in the flesh of Russian poets and novelists. Experience has taught me that Soviet officials always take an experimental view of you. They want to see how far they can drive you, how often they can put you off, without provoking a reaction. If you become offensive you are lost. You are then accused of being an uncultured person; which I suppose is the Russian equivalent for the word 'cad'. But if you give way, or agree to come back tomorrow, you are lost also.

One evening at a diplomatic reception for Conference delegates, I was told that when Bevin raised the question of an extension of the Anglo-Soviet alliance of 1942, Molotov argued that there was not much point in trying to improve Anglo-Soviet relations by an extension of the Treaty unless something was also done about the attitude of the British press. It seemed that he was asking for some form of Government control aimed at preventing the publication in British newspapers of any material that the Russians might regard as inimical. This was much the same point that Soviet Information Bureau officials had put to me in 1944 when we discussed the possibility of concerting British and Russian war-propaganda, so I knew how strongly the Russians felt about all this. I also realized how important it was for our people to resist Russian pressure at the very outset. But since the information had been given to me in confidence, I could not use it.

When next I met my informant, he told me that the Russians had not given up hope of getting something out of their talks with Bevin. They wanted a general reference to press relations included in a revised and extended version of the Anglo-Soviet Alliance, I was told. My friend suggested that I should report the facts to the BBC to ensure their becoming known to the widest possible public. I replied that unless I could see the actual wording the Russians wanted to insert into the Treaty there was nothing much that I could do. I added that if he could get me a sentence or two from the text—on the explicit understanding that I could quote it verbatim—I would at once pass it on to my news room. He told me to meet him in the course of the following afternoon in a quiet square well away from the Conference area. There, he promised, he would hand over a slip of paper with the text upon it. We met in a ridiculously surreptitious sort of way. Our efforts at secrecy must have been apparent to a junior boy scout; but I got my few sentences and I was able to report fully to the BBC.

When the facts were broadcast by the Overseas Service, which was of course heard in Moscow, one or two members of the diplomatic corps began to make inquiries. One of them tackled a member of the British delegation. He said he had heard this report about press control on the BBC; he understood that it had been sent by the special correspondent who was once on the staff of the British Embassy. He therefore surmised that the report was 'roughly accurate' as a reluctant Ambassador might say when facts are brought to light that senior officials would much prefer to keep secret. In the British delegation they were obviously anxious to find out how much I knew and how I had got my information. They told me that they had been questioned; they told me also that they had assured anxious inquirers that while Tom Barman was quite a good chap, he no longer had access to official sources of information; the inference being, of course, that I had got my facts wrong. This annoyed me. My vanity got the better of me and I stupidly blurted out: 'Come off it. I have seen the text.' The only effect of my impetuosity was that every member of the British delegation was asked to declare in writing that he had had no truck with me, and that he had told me nothing about the Treaty negotiations. There was no difficulty about that. I did not get my facts from anyone in the British delegation. I got them from a source that was not less well-informed.

CHAPTER 17

IF THE Moscow Conference of 1947 was a failure, the London Conference in December of the same year was a disaster. The Western Foreign Ministers and Molotov differed openly and publicly on almost every point; and the press Conferences that were called to keep us in touch with the turn of events were inspired by much ill-will on all sides. When the Conference was nearing its end, Molotov tried to score a propaganda point with the suggestion that a group of Germans should be invited to address the Ministers and to explain what he called the German point of view, that is to say the view of some Germans hand-picked by the Soviet security services. When this was rejected, the meeting broke up. Bevin looked flushed and angry as he came away; Molotov ashen-faced. No fine words could now explain away the fact of the cold war, and even the Russians tacitly admitted its existence. A few months later, Stalin imposed his blockade on Berlin in the hope of driving the Western Powers out of the city.

West Germany became the principal beneficiary of this East-West tension. Up to then, she had played a minor walking-on part on the European stage; but now she came to dominate the play as one of the principal guarantors of Western security. The policy of the victorious Western allies had to be adjusted to meet German views and German requirements; and German reunification became synonymous with European security and peace. At the Teheran Conference, Britain, America and Russia had tentatively agreed that it would be wise to split up the Reich and to create a new Roman Catholic State in the heart of Europe, incorporating Bavaria and Austria. Those days had gone; there were other ideas now; and Churchill's 1919 plan to resist Bolshevism with the help of a re-armed Germany was back in favour. Once again, the German problem came to dominate the European scene as it had done for the greater part of the twentieth century. I was brought up under its shadow. I remember, as far back as 1912, that one of my parents' friends, a reserve officer in the Prussian Army, had warned them that a European war was imminent and advised my mother to lay in a reserve of food: sacks of flour and rice and things like that against the shortages that would inevitably arise.

So far as British policy was concerned, the process of adjusting it to the revived German problem was greatly facilitated by the movement of staff in the higher reaches of the Foreign Office. I do not know if successive Cabinets acted deliberately in this matter; but the fact remains that the three men who successively held the highest post in the Foreign Office, i.e. that of Permanent Under-Secretary, were all acknowledged experts on the German problem with years of German experience behind them. William Strang (later Lord Strang) whose appointment was announced late in 1948 had been Political Adviser to the British Commander-in-Chief in Western Germany. Ivone Kirkpatrick who succeeded him towards the end of 1953 came straight from Bonn where he had been High Commissioner; and Frederick Hoyer Millar (later Lord Inchyra) who followed Kirkpatrick also came straight from Bonn, where he had been British Ambassador after the formal ending of the occupation régime. It is not surprising that German views came to be given a high priority in the formulation of British foreign policy; or that Adenauer's prejudices were given a sympathetic hearing. Before the war, and especially in Vansittart's time, the usual sneer was that the Foreign Office was just a hot-bed of pro-French intrigues. It was a sneer that could not have stuck in the post-war period. For the twelve years after 1948, German views must have greatly benefited from the airing they got in Whitehall.

It was under the guidance of these German experts that German re-armament was finally brought about, and Germany introduced into the North Atlantic Alliance. The Germans, at first, were not particularly enthusiastic, at least not officially. The slogan '*ohne mich*' flourished like bind-weed among them. Carlo Schmidt, then Socialist leader, declared that he was opposed to the raising of German units for the defence of Western Europe on the ground that 'ultimately a German army might take control of the German State'. Adenauer himself, as recently as 1954, said it was grotesque that he, of all people, should find himself supporting the creation of a German Army. And in France the hostility to German re-armament on any terms was bitter in the extreme and found expression in all sorts of ways. The French reaction puzzled and dismayed General Eisenhower who had been made Commander-in-Chief with the mandate to plan a NATO force. At a press Conference held in Brussels in 1951 he dealt sharply with French opposition to the Western plans. He told us that if the French insisted on having two Frenchmen to guard every German under arms, he would not want to have any German units under his command. Two years later, even Roman Catholic priests took part in violent demonstrations in Paris directed against what were described as American plans for German re-armament. Bevin also was opposed to the revival of German military power. In September 1950, on the eve of his departure for discussions with the United States Government on defence problems, he told a group of diplomatic correspondents that in spite of growing American pressure he would in no circumstances agree to the re-creation of a German army. That, he told us, was the message he was taking with him to Washington. Within two or three days of his arrival there, he was asking the Cabinet for authority to agree to a German contribution to a NATO defence force. His position had been undermined, not so much by American pressure, which was very strong at the time, as by the news that The Netherlands Government, whose people, unlike the British, had suffered the indignities of Nazi occupation, had agreed to some measure of German re-armament. It had been explained to the Dutch that on the basis of the ground forces then available, Western Europe, excluding Germany, would have to be defended on the Rhine. That meant abandoning a large part of The Netherlands to possible Russian occupation. The longer line, to include the whole of The Netherlands and therefore parts of Germany also, could not be held without a German contribution. Were the Dutch prepared to increase their forces to the point where they would be responsible for the defence of a demilitarized Germany? The Dutch were not. Their opposition to German re-armament crumbled. And Bevin's stand was undermined. I have no doubt myself that he would have had to give way in any case; the Americans had made it plain that they could not ask their people to take on the high cost of a major contribution to the defence of Western Europe unless the Germans were in some way associated with it.

The French Government at the time found it best to give qualified support for the creation of some German military units. Ultimately, they produced the plan for a European Defence Community, in which there would be no separate national forces. the National Assembly finally turned it down because of the British refusal to put British forces under supra-national control along with French and German. In the meantime, the French Government decided upon a cautious diplomatic ploy. They said they would allow the Germans to re-arm in due course after a probationary period, and as a reward for good behaviour in the fields of politics and economics. Then followed a major political gaffe which made the French approach impossible. John McCloy, the United States High Commissioner in Germany, in a public speech, advocated the creation of a German force of ten divisions with its own officers. The inference was that Western Europe could not be defended without the Germans. The moment this statement had been made publicly the diplomatic initiative passed into German hands. Adenauer, one of the ablest politicians of the post-war period, now found himself in the agreeable position of playing the part of a German political leader strongly opposed to re-arming his country, and having re-armament forced upon him by his former enemies. He was therefore able to extract concessions from the Western Powers for doing something that his Right-Wing followers wanted him to do, instead of being asked to make concessions himself in order ultimately to be allowed to restore German military power. French policy in Europe collapsed, and did not recover until General de Gaulle took over in 1958.

Adenauer was rewarded with a three-power declaration, British, French and American, that the Bonn Government was the repository of sovereignty over the whole of Germany, and that only the Federal Government had the right to speak for the German people as a whole. It froze East-West relations; and when the Hallstein doctrine was added it made an active and constructive German foreign policy in Eastern Europe impossible. It underlined that German reunification would not come about as the result of conciliatory gestures by the Government in Bonn, or at the end of a long period of European pacification, but as the inevitable consequence of the strength of the North Atlantic Alliance. Adenauer thus became the King of anti-Communism, with a vested interest in maintaining a high state of tension between

East and West. The greater the tension, the more important he became as the flaming sword guarding Western Christendom. On a later page I hope to describe how General de Gaulle was able to take advantage of this situation and to turn Western Germany into his willing associate, to the point, at times, of alienating not only London, but Washington also. His attitude gave Adenauer's self-confidence an even greater head of steam. When the 1960 Summit Conference in Paris broke down after the shooting down of an American reconnaissance aircraft over the Soviet Union—the so-called U-2 incident—Adenauer was neither dismayed nor shocked. I happened to be in the Bundestag in Bonn shortly after the collapse, and I had the good fortune to hear Adenauer make a statement on the international situation. As I sat waiting in the visitors' gallery, there was a desultory buzz in the Chamber, and a good deal of movement. When the Old Man came in, dressed as he always was in curiously ill-fitting clothes, everybody stiffened. There was an expectant hush as he mounted the speaker's rostrum. He did not speak for very long: all he said, in effect, was that the breakdown in Paris proved the correctness of his Government's policy. This piece of self-congratulation was not challenged. Having delivered it, the Chancellor withdrew.

Kirkpatrick, British High Commissioner in Bonn when the German debate was at its height, produced what he thought was an unanswerable argument in favour of a German army. It was all very simple, he insisted. Unless German industry carried the same burden of taxation as British, whether for welfare or for arms, British industry would find that its costs were higher than German and would therefore be unable to compete upon the export markets of the world. To someone of my own age, familiar with all the pre-war agitation against the arms manufacturers, or the Merchants of Death, as we used to call them before Mr. Wilson's Government appointed a special salesman to sell British arms throughout the world, the Kirkpatrick argument was a little hard to take. After sacrificing many millions of lives in two world wars to snatch all weapons out of German hands, we were now told on the highest authority that British exports could flourish only if the Germans got their guns back. One could put Kirkpatrick's argument in another way: the need to persuade the Germans to spend money on armaments arose out of the need for them to match British expenditure on the forces required to maintain Britain's status as a world power.

Later, when Foster Dulles came upon the scene with his elephantine tactics, the disheartened French became openly resentful. For months French Ministers had been dragging their feet in the negotiations that were supposed to lead to the creation of a European Defence Community in which the national forces of France, Germany, Italy and the Low Countries were to lose their separate identities and come under supra-national control. Most French people with whom I discussed the plan had no great faith in it; and they assured me that it would be rejected by the National Assembly if Britain failed to join. It was suspected by many British officials and politicians that the French had put it forward mainly in the hope of holding up German re-armament. When I saw Mendès-France at work in Brussels, at the 1954 Conference that killed the Defence Community, I had little doubt myself that the Prime Minister of France had come to the meeting to put an end to the monster that the French themselves had created. It had taken a long time for the French to make up their minds to drop the Community; and in the long delays that followed the original decision to invite the Germans to make a defence contribution to the West, Dulles and his closest advisers became increasingly irritable. At a meeting of the North Atlantic Council in December 1953 he lectured European Foreign Ministers in general, and the French Foreign Minister in particular, on the dangers of procrastination. The French, for their part, wanted to know how far the 'Anglo-Saxons' were prepared to go to ensure that France was not left to face a re-armed Germany on her own. They also wanted it clearly established that the British and possibly the Americans would keep adequate military forces in Europe to deter the Russians. At a press Conference in the old NATO headquarters in the Trocadero building in Paris, crowded with reporters, Dulles was severely heckled. He was always unpopular with the press; and he was often roughly handled. I could see that his temper was beginning to get the better of him. He fidgeted uneasily in his chair; his voice became harsher; and a touch of colour crept into his face. The public relations adviser sitting next to him kept tugging at his sleeve in the hope of preventing an explosion. He failed.

When Dulles began to explain the aims of United States policy in the cold war, and of American hopes for European unity, he was interrupted by Harold King, Reuter's correspondent in Paris. Would the United States Government be prepared, King asked, to guarantee the presence of American troops in Europe for the next twenty years as part of a general agreement to contain Russian power? Dulles replied abruptly that no statesman could commit himself for that length of time. King realized at once that he had uncovered a weak spot in the American position and attacked with a supplementary question. 'Why then,' he asked, 'do you expect France to commit herself for fifty years under the proposed Treaty for a European Defence Community?' Dulles took it badly. If France did not adopt the European Defence Treaty, he growled, the United States would have to subject her foreign policy to an 'agonizing re-appraisal'. It was a clear threat; and, to make matters worse, it was made in public. It could mean either that the Americans would be prepared to leave Europe to her own devices if the French did not come to heel; or alternatively, that they would make a special arrangement with the Germans. All sorts of rumours were in circulation at that time about the possibility of a special relationship between Bonn and Washington; rumours that were used even against Macmillan when he went to Bonn to discuss a suitable German contribution towards the cost of keeping forces in Germany. The Germans were furious with the Prime Minister; they thought it presumptuous of the British to claim a great-power role while unable to find the money for the British Army on the Rhine.

What Adenauer particularly resented was the effort that Macmillan appeared to be making to act as mediator between Bonn and Moscow. Adenauer had a way of sweeping mediators out of the way unless he could be assured that they would mediate against his opponents. In the anti-Communist Europe that Adenauer personified, there was no room for honest brokers, middlemen, or touters of compromises. He was as unyielding in his anti-Communism as Foster Dulles himself. Anyone who disagreed with him was regarded as a traitor. When he went to Moscow in 1955, ostensibly to persuade the Russians to release some of the Germans still held as prisoners of war, but in fact to sound out Russian intentions, he sought advice outside the ranks of his own civil servants. He invited Brigadier Hill, a former member of the British secret service, then living at Bad Neuenahr, to call on him. Hill, as I have recorded on another page, had a deep knowledge of Russia and of Russian affairs. Adenauer thought Hill would be the best man to advise him on how to approach the Russians on matters close to his heart; and I am sure that Hill gave him some useful advice. Yet I found his dependence upon an outside source curious. It proved, or so it seemed to me, that the Chancellor was determined to go his own way and to pursue his own ideas without reference to anybody except people of his own choosing. Unsolicited advice offered by honest brokers was something he did not want; and when it was offered by a British Cabinet Minister it made him suspicious and resentful. When Eden tabled his plan for reducing European tension at the Geneva Summit Conference in 1955, the Germans were furious. Eden had proposed that Britain, France, America and Russia should agree upon a scheme to inspect and to supervise the forces stationed on either side of the line that divided Europe, which meant, in effect, on either side of the line dividing Germany. As the West Germans saw it, the Eden plan was a plot to perpetuate the status quo. At the press Conference held at their hotel in Geneva, they made no secret of their hostility. They became convinced at that time that British policy had gone soft, and could no longer be relied upon.

Their suspicions were confirmed when Macmillan and Selwyn Lloyd went to Russia in 1959, on what the British Ministers called a voyage of reconnaissance after Khrushchev's ultimatum on Berlin some months earlier. The communiqué issued at the end of their talks with the Russian leaders made Anglo-German relations even worse because it repeated some of the points of the Eden plan. The representatives of the two Governments, the Moscow communiqué said, 'agreed that further study could usefully be made of the possibilities of increasing security by some method of limitation of forces and weapons, both conventional and nuclear, in an agreed area of Europe, coupled with an appropriate system of inspection'. And in the light of German susceptibilities it is impossible to describe as tactful the comments on the international situation made in the pamphlet presented to the Conservative Party Conference at Llandudno in 1962. 'The European Economic Community as it stands at present is acutely concerned with the Communist pressure at its emotional flashpoint, namely on the borders of Germany and

Berlin. This is natural enough, since Federal Germany is itself an important member of the Community. But it would be a very dangerous thing if the Europe of the future allowed the problems of its Eastern frontiers to become a dominant obsession. Britain and the Commonwealth have always striven to resolve discords and reduce these tensions.' And then the author, Harold Macmillan himself, went on to say: 'As Prime Minister I have done my best to promote personal contacts between the Communist and Western worlds and seek better understanding. *This is one of Britain's main functions*, and I am sure it is a task which we can fulfil more effectively as active members of the European Community than by remaining outside.' As a definition of an ideal foreign policy, it could hardly be bettered. But it sprang from a make-believe world. It lacked three essential ingredients: adequate power, confidence in the Macmillan Government, and credibility. It did not contribute to the establishment of better relations with Moscow; it failed to remove the impressions of British weakness that were so prevalent in Washington and Bonn at the time. Nor was it calculated to tempt the Germans to give ungrudging support to the British effort to join the Common Market.

The widespread impression of British 'softness' provided General de Gaulle with an opportunity that he ruthlessly exploited. He flattered Adenauer by being firmer on the question of German reunification and Berlin than even the old man himself. When the British Government suggested, in 1959, that Western rights of access to Berlin should be given legal definition in treaty form, de Gaulle replied that since definition involved limitation he could take no part in any four-power talks on the subject. The Western rights of access, he insisted, were absolute and unlimited and there was nothing to negotiate about. At that particular point in time, de Gaulle had precisely the same interest as Adenauer in perpetuating East-West friction. Tension kept Adenauer in the limelight as the leader of the anti-Communist resistance movement; it enabled de Gaulle to play the part of a devoted and disinterested friend of the family, strong enough, as Adenauer no doubt reflected, to disregard all the pro-Russian and anti-German prejudices at the Quai d'Orsay. The Franco-German Reconciliation Treaty of 22 January 1963, drawn up and signed in Paris within a few days of the rejection of the first British application to join the Common Market, came as the climax to this triumphant diplomacy. But it was not an unmitigated triumph. In Eastern Europe there was a sharp setback: the good progress of Franco-Polish relations was halted. In Bonn there were hesitations which eventually led the Bundestag to insist upon passing a preamble to the Treaty re-affirming West Germany's loyalty to the North Atlantic Alliance and therefore to the United States. Reports of sharp quarrels between Couve de Murville and Dr. Schroeder, then German Foreign Minister, became more frequent. The position was not restored until Dr. Kiesinger became Chancellor in 1966. Since he took office at a time when British influence was lower than at any time in the post-war period and when economic weakness was crippling what was left of the British capacity for independent action in the field of foreign affairs, it is hardly surprising that Dr. Kiesinger and Herr Brandt failed to give adequate support to Britain's second application to join the Common Market. There were also, in 1966–67, new factors in the international situation: increasing doubts about the direction of American foreign policy, growing fears, as the French put it, that Europe might be dragged into a war not of her own making in which her interests were not involved; and the suspicion that South-East Asia, not Germany or Europe, was the primary American interest. In these circumstances, the Bonn Government had no obvious alternative to the French connection. At least not so long as German reunification retained its high priority in German foreign policy.

In 1962, it was possible for the *New York Times* to declare that President Kennedy was basing his policy on a 'special relationship' with West Germany; on the political unification of Western Europe, backed primarily by United States and West German military power. As seen from Bonn this was no longer true in 1966; a fact that goes part of the way towards explaining the collapse of the Erhard Government. British support for reunification, at this point of time, is irrelevant. That leaves only the French to be relied upon. And when de Gaulle was in Poland in the autumn of 1967 he went out of his way to re-state his support for reunification, in spite of much Polish nagging. But this support is valuable to the Germans only so long as they continue to believe that reunification is just below the horizon. When they no longer do, French influence in Bonn will vanish. This is the great weakness in the French diplomatic position; and that is why de Gaulle is so obviously in a hurry to achieve results, principally as it affects Anglo-Saxon influence in Europe. Once the Germans have made up their minds that they can live with a separate German State, and have thrown the Hallstein doctrine overboard, they will recover their diplomatic freedom. In the meantime, the dilemma facing de Gaulle is that France's relations with Eastern Europe can only move beyond their existing phase at the cost of publicly withdrawing support for German reunification; if he is driven into doing that he will lose German friendship and with it his capacity to dominate his other associates in the Common Market.

These are among the reasons why the French have been so very sensitive about what remains of British influence in Bonn. Some years ago they openly accused the British Embassy there of carrying on anti-French propaganda and anti-French intrigues in the West German capital. Couve de Murville himself seemed at the time to be convinced of British guilt in this matter; and this undoubtedly added to anti-British feelings in the French official world. Its hostility first became vocal when the British and American Governments, in 1958, rejected de Gaulle's proposal for the formation of a three-power club consisting of France, Britain and America to discuss global policy and to agree upon global aims. The French pointed out that since France had world-wide interests in the same way as Britain and America, it would be unreasonable not to include her in the Anglo-American cave in NATO. The argument had no effect in Washington, and still less in London; and de Gaulle never forgave the British Government for it. I believe myself that his every action since then must be seen in the light of this rejection. Since he could not join the club he made up his mind to beat it. Some of the smaller NATO powers considered that Britain made a great mistake in refusing to support the French application. In their view, its implications should at least have been explored. But Whitehall was openly hostile. Officials assured me that if France were to be included in the Anglo-American Club, the Italians would have to be admitted and no doubt the Germans also. If they were, NATO would be divided into two separate tiers that would make fruitful cooperation with the smaller powers impossible. It did not seem to me at the time that this argument had any validity: it ignored the fact that France did have interests outside Europe whereas neither Italy nor Germany had. Finally it all boiled down to the 'special relationship' with Washington, and to the British Government's fear that the French were trying to tamper with it. I do not believe anyone could have defined what the term meant; but I am convinced that every Prime Minister since the Roosevelt–Churchill era has misused it and exaggerated its importance. It is perhaps significant that it does not figure so prominently in the American political vocabulary as in the British. It seems to me that Drew Middleton was near the mark when he wrote in the *New York Times* in December 1962 that 'The British have assumed ever since the Bermuda Conference early in 1957 a right to play an important role in the making of Western policy and to speak in tones more authoritative than those of Bonn or Paris. But the last few weeks have demonstrated that the President of the United States pays equal heed to all voices in making Western policy.' These facts were apparent long before 1962, and it was a tragedy that the British Government of the day did not perceive them in 1958.

Gaullism in the aggressive form we came to know it was the product not only of the refusal to recognize France as an equal with the 'Anglo-Saxons' but also of the French defeat in 1940, of what is thought to be undue American pressure, of doubts about British intentions and good faith, of fears of Germany, of a love-hate relationship to Russia. We may dislike de Gaulle's behaviour; but it should not surprise us. Our politicians have had many warnings of his views and intentions. As long ago as December 1954 he defined his attitude to the North Atlantic Alliance in the following terms: 'In the system known as NATO, France does not control the means by which she can act independently. She has placed her armies, her bases, her communications, directly under an authority that is not hers. She is therefore in a situation of dependence that puts under foreign control all military action, and therefore by definition, all political action in territories that are her own; yesterday and today in Indo-China; tomorrow in North Africa. She has left in other hands the monopoly of atomic weapons, without which a State can only be subservient.'

Those who believe that de Gaulle spoke only for himself and that few Frenchmen agreed with him would be well advised to refer back to the passionate debate in the National Assembly that took place when the Fourth Republic lay dying. The date is 15 April 1958. First there came the angry complaint that the United States, after having 'forced The Netherlands to leave Java, and Britain to abandon Egypt', was now apparently driving France into surrendering Bizerta and Oran. Then a speaker on the Extreme Right declared: 'In the name of what is called peaceful co-existence, the two super-powers have agreed to divide the world into spheres of influence. If our relations with the other members of the Atlantic Alliance are not to be relations between equals, if the Alliance is nothing more than an instrument of American domination over the Western World, then I for my part am willing to run almost any risk to avoid the subjection of my country. I do not want to live as a slave, either Russian or American. If it becomes necessary to leave the Alliance in order to safeguard the future of France, then let us leave it.' This had long been the Gaullist view. It was expressed at the time by a nationalist on the Extreme Right, yet it was calculated to appeal to French Communists also, and to the xenophobia that is never far below the surface in France. 'The national renewal of our policy is not isolation,' Debré, then Prime Minister of France, said in a broadcast in August 1959; 'it is a reaction against alliances which, because of our weakness, entailed our subservience to foreign powers, which do not hesitate to thwart our essential interests. Who would have said, only six years ago, that visits of Heads of State would be carefully organized between Moscow and Washington? To avoid being crushed by agreements between the very great Powers, a nation like France must have the power to make herself heard and understood.'

On the other hand, it would be wrong to believe that de Gaulle and his Ministers have had the vast majority of Frenchmen behind them in the last two or three years. Over large parts of provincial France, people have been critical and unconvinced of the wisdom of their policies. From 1967 onward there could have been a hostile majority against the Government in the National Assembly if only all deputies had had the courage of their convictions, and been unafraid of a premature general election. And while the French word '*gloire*' sounds rather better than the English word 'glory', I am convinced myself that ordinary French people are bored by de Gaulle's patronizing grandiloquence. I have noticed their reactions when his voice comes over the radio or from the television screen: they respond with indifference. On one occassion, in a restaurant in the South of France; on another, in a café in Paris: no one spoke while the General was speaking. But once his discourse had ended, people resumed their conversation at the point where they had left off. In their ears, at least, his words had lost much of their meaning and there was nothing for them to discuss; they were not interested. What kept the General and his Government afloat was not the active support of an electorate that is vigorously alive. It was the fear of change; the belief that after a period of stable one-man rule, Parliament would again become supreme and make and unmake Governments with the irresponsibility that prevailed under the Fourth Republic. So let the inevitable change be put off for as long as possible.

CHAPTER 18

AMONG THE most puzzling things about Khrushchev's foreign policy was his apparent inability to derive much advantage from the difficulties and disagreements among the Western Powers. Perhaps his greatest mistake was to embark upon an armaments race with the United States. This is a race the Russians cannot win. The United States is the first and only country to have both guns and butter; and while the economy has shown signs of strain at times owing to the high cost of the Vietnam war, American civilians have not been asked to tighten their belts to any noticeable extent. In Russia, living standards are still being held back because of the armaments race, and because of the help given to all those countries most likely to obstruct the policies of the Western Powers: North Vietnam, the more Radical States of Africa, Egypt and Syria and Cuba. The evidence suggests that there is mounting pressure by Russian urban workers of all social categories for better living conditions. Dr. Margaret Miller in her book *The Rise of the Russian Consumer*, speaks of 'unacknowledged but irresistible pressures from below' in favour of a 'more rational way of ordering economic activity'. The shoppers I observed in Moscow in 1966 behaved very differently from those I had seen ten years before. Then, they bought whatever was offered to them, no matter how bad the quality and the appearance. In 1966, they were critical and unwilling to part with their money until they got something they thought was reasonably good. In GUM, the department store near the Kremlin, I saw them pick up things from trays on the counter, inspect them, and throw them back with a gesture of disapproval. The Government may eventually be forced to choose between a reasonable agreement on disarmament, coupled with international cooperation in the matter of aid, all in deference to the demands of the Russian consumer, and imposing further checks on living standards at home and in Eastern Europe generally against the present strong current of opinion throughout the area in order to pay for more armaments and military aid. I believe that among the reasons for Khrushchev's erratic policies is that he had to move uncertainly between those two possibilities. The Kosygin–Brezhnev combination has been equally uncertain; although it has been less boisterous about its hesitations. We now know that the consumer in Russia and in Eastern Europe generally was made to suffer for the aid given to North Korea during and after the war. We also know that among the reasons for the Russo-Chinese conflict was the unwillingness of the Russian leaders to pay the bill for the industrial revolution in China. What we do not yet know is the cost of the help given by Russia to North Vietnam and to Egypt. But in the light of past experience, it seems permissible to believe that the hostility of the peoples of Eastern Europe to the pro-Arab policies of their Governments is due, in part, to the fear that it is going to cost a great deal of money, and therefore that it will affect their living conditions.

Khrushchev's policies in 1959 and 1960 were entirely unpredictable. In 1959 we had all those friendly noises from Camp David where Khrushchev had been having long talks with Eisenhower, after the Berlin ultimatum that took Macmillan to Moscow. Then came his genial invitation to the President to visit the Soviet Union. This was followed by his threats and blusterings in Paris after the U-2 incident in the spring of 1960. Those of us who saw Khrushchev on that occasion suspected that when he appeared on the rostrum to address the press, he was acting under duress, and that he was not saying the sort of thing he would have said if he had been entirely free to speak his own mind. He came into the room peacefully enough, followed by Marshal Malinovsky. After a minute or two he was shouting and gesticulating like a peasant at market who has just been offered a derisory price for his chickens. His dirty grey suit hung loosely round his heavy frame; his eyes glittered with spite; his voice was hoarse with anger. The Marshal stood impassively at Khrushchev's side, looking at him from time to time out of the corner of his eye. He gave me the impression that he was there to make sure that Khrushchev spoke his piece. It was, to me, a shocking and frightening experience. But were we right at the time to assume that Khrushchev was speaking under duress and that the Stalinists among his colleagues had put a check on him? Friends of mine in Eastern Europe who felt free to speak their minds told me some time later that all this talk about a Stalinist opposition to Khrushchev was moonshine. They did not deny that the Chinese attitude was a factor; and that there was a point beyond which Khrushchev could not go without risking a possibly fatal onslaught on his ideological credibility. They thought that Khrushchev was finding it increasingly difficult to square Russian Great Power claims with the growing pressure for a better life at home. At the Paris Conference, then, Russian prestige demanded a Grand Show-down; but Khrushchev could not permit himself more than an ill-mannered oral demonstration.

I have little doubt myself that his bad manners played into the hands of his critics, and led ultimately to his downfall. He did not behave as a 'cultured person' should; and some Russians undoubtedly considered that he was letting the side down in the presence of foreigners. His shoe-banging operation in the United Nations shocked not only his East European friends, but also the eminently respectable African and Asian politicians then in New York. I suspect that he had planned this demonstration well in advance and he had gone to the United Nations with the intention to capture the newspaper headlines. Friends of mine who were present in the Assembly at the time—I myself was in Washington and saw his turn only on the television screen—told me that he seemed to have worn a special kind of shoe for the occasion, a shoe that slipped off the foot more easily than any normal shoe could have done. There was not much sign of anger on his face. He appeared to be enjoying himself; there was perhaps a twinkle of mischief in those pig-like eyes.

But it was Scandinavia that saw Khrushchev at his worst. I was in London during his visit to Northern Europe, but I heard a great many stories about him; about his petulance, his bombastic tone of speech, and his endless indiscretions. The fact that he was disgraced shortly after his tour in the summer of 1964 prompted a number of reflections, so I went to Scandinavia to find out for myself. It soon became clear to me that he had behaved abominably. After a banquet in one capital, he was invited into a private room for serious political discussions. His hosts were the Prime Minister and the Foreign Minister and leaders of the various opposition groups in Parliament. There were no discussions. Instead, Khrushchev delivered himself of a long monologue on the stupidity of his colleagues and ex-colleagues and on how he had outwitted them time and again. When he was shown over one of the finest farms in Denmark, he turned to his hosts and said: 'We have nothing whatever to learn here.' He looked bored and was evidently anxious to get away. His statement was widely reported in the Danish press at the time. On the following day Mrs. Khrushchev asked one of the journalists why the papers had reported this particular bit of comment. 'His remarks were silly,' she said, 'and he knows it. He was envious. We have nothing like it in Russia. And when he's envious he says silly things.' On the same occasion, Khrushchev was presented with three Danish heifers and a bull, all prize cattle. The gift made him furious. When the news of his anger was conveyed to Oslo, the Norwegian Government hurriedly changed their plans. They had arranged to give him a new style of plough, said to be the most efficient of its kind. They gave him, instead, two silver candlesticks.

Also during the course of his tour, Khrushchev was asked why he was so opposed to modern art. He erupted into anger. 'They're all homosexuals, those people,' he shouted. 'They should be in prison.' When he was out of earshot, Mrs. Khrushchev turned reprovingly to the man who had put the question. 'Why do you ask about these things?' she said. 'He knows nothing about art. He just loses his temper.' More than once I heard the comment that if Mrs. Khrushchev had been Prime Minister of Russia, the tour would have been an outstanding success. His son-in-law, Adzhubei, made a very unfavourable impression. He seemed to be more interested in the night-life of the Scandinavian capitals than in the political aspects of the tour. And his dependence upon Khrushchev was absolute and undisguised. One senior civil servant with a command of Russian talked to him about Khrushchev's policy of peaceful co-existence, and spoke of Khrushchev's great contribution to the cause of international understanding. Then he said: 'I have no doubt that the policy will be continued after Mr. Khrushchev's retirement.' Adzhubei banged his fist upon the table. 'Retirement?' he asked. 'His departure would be a catastrophe.' Then, after a pause, he added: 'But our friends will know how to keep him in power.' What made Adzhubei so unpopular among senior Party men and officials was that he was used by Khrushchev to carry out diplomatic missions without reference to the Politbureau or the Ministry for Foreign Affairs.

The then Soviet Ambassador in Bonn, Smirnov, was particularly annoyed. On the day of reckoning, Adzhubei, too, found that he had made some powerful enemies.

When the members of the Russian delegation took off from Scandinavia it was reported that they left unpaid liquor bills behind them. They removed several cases of whisky from one country house they had been staying in. Not least shocking, perhaps, was that Khrushchev's small-talk with his immediate entourage was unprintable. His vocabulary, I was told, derived not so much from the pornographic primer, as from the stable, the cowshed and the lavatory wall. His rough country ways were therefore hardly suited to Russia's new status in the world, and it is not surprising that his colleagues in the Kremlin decided to get rid of him. There were people who believed at the time that he had in fact lost his footing some six months before his Scandinavian tour and that he therefore thought he could afford the luxury of indiscretion.

It has been argued that Khrushchev's tantrums were always contrived; that he never lost his temper and that he was never the worse for drink—he only seemed to be. If indeed he had an uncontrollable temper, it is hard to see how he could have survived under Stalin. I am willing to believe that his scene in Paris before the Summit Conference that never was, was partly contrived, but only partly. I am sure he was genuinely angry. I continue to believe that the scene in the United Nations was wholly contrived. But another scene, this time at the Heads of Government Conference in Geneva in 1955, was, I believe, inspired by genuine feeling. Each of the four delegations at the Conference, British, American, French and Russian, had got into the habit of inviting the senior members of another delegation to dinner after the day's work. Sometimes the Russians would have the Americans to dinner; and another evening they would have the British; and then the French would have the Americans and so on. On the night Khrushchev dined with the French, he worked himself up into yet another emotional outburst. All day long the Heads of Government and their Foreign Ministers had been discussing the German problem; and the Western Ministers, as usual, had concentrated on reunification through free elections. When the party left the table for cognac and cigars in another room, Khrushchev seized the French Foreign Minister by the lapel of his jacket and shook him. 'We will never, never, never change our minds about the German problem,' he shouted. 'Never. Do you understand?' I believe there was genuine feeling behind that cry and that most Russians share it. More than any other, it was the German problem that roused Khrushchev to anger and brought out the worst in him. I have been told that he always regarded Adenauer as being insufferably arrogant. The constant nagging of the Poles and the East Germans added to Khrushchev's perplexities. They always wanted him to do something. His Berlin ultimatum in November 1958 was provoked, it was widely believed, by Gomulka, the Polish leader, who was in Moscow a few days before Khrushchev issued his warning to the Western Powers. And I believe, too, that the sudden check suffered by West German diplomacy in its attempts to establish diplomatic relations with Czechoslovakia and Hungary early in 1967 was due, not to any Russian initiative, but to pressure by the Poles and the East Germans on Moscow to act firmly and at once to prevent their own isolation.

The constant repetition by the Western Powers of the importance of free elections in order to determine the kind of government that should exist throughout the whole of Germany infuriated Khrushchev. At the four-power meeting in Geneva in May 1959, the Western Foreign Ministers once again produced all their old arguments about the need for free elections in Germany. A few weeks later, Khrushchev demolished their arguments in the course of a 'Friendship Meeting' in the Kremlin at which the East Germans were the guests of honour. At the Geneva Conference, he told them, the representatives of the Western Powers advocated 'the speediest holding of so-called free elections in Germany. But again they prefer to maintain silence over the fact that five years earlier their Governments solemnly pledged themselves to hold within two years free general elections in Vietnam for the reunification of the country. And what happened? Were the elections held? No.' The analogy is far from perfect; yet the Western demand for free elections in East Germany was no more honest than the Russian demand for elections in Vietnam. It is inconceivable that the Soviet Union could have accepted a process that would have led automatically to the destruction of its principal strong-point in Eastern Europe. The British and American Governments have made a fetish of free elections and this has not helped the cause of East-West diplomacy. In a country without firmly established foundations, or in which the basic social compromises have not been made, free elections are an open incitement to violence and civil war. One wonders how a demand for free elections would have been received by the early Tudor monarchs as they strove to create a more cohesive community upon the ruins left by the Wars of the Roses. Even Léon Blum, whose democratic principles were never in doubt, came to question whether a Parliamentary régime could provide France with a Government suited to the political temperament of the French people.

Looking back, then, upon Khrushchev's tempestuous career as head of the Soviet Government, it seems to me that among his basic errors was that he so often got his timing wrong; and that he moved from cajolery to intimidation without any warning signals. With Stalin, you always knew where you were; with Khrushchev, hardly ever. I have already referred to his many contradictory moves in the years 1959 and 1960. The Western Alliance at the time was in great disarray, and was undergoing a crisis that I think was even more severe than the one that overtook it in 1966 when de Gaulle gave notice that he was pulling out of the integrated command structure. In 1959, it seemed for a time that American foreign policy was becoming more flexible; and the reports that had come out of the Camp David conversations between Eisenhower and Khrushchev were distinctly encouraging. But de Gaulle and Adenauer were busily establishing a common front on the Berlin question. They insisted that if there was to be a Summit Conference at all, and Macmillan had set his heart on it with the full backing of British public opinion, then the Western Powers must stand by the plan tabled in 1955. This particular plan had been rejected out of hand by the Russians at the time; the fact that the French were reviving it with German support was a clear warning to the Russians that they must not expect any results to come out of a four-power meeting. Moreover, de Gaulle refused to attend any Conference until Khrushchev had first paid an official visit to France. This further delay gave time for the tougher elements in Washington to bring pressure to bear upon the Eisenhower Administration. Dean Acheson, one of the most prominent of tough-liners, declared at the time that de Gaulle's firmness on Berlin was 'a service to his allies'.

And he added that Adenauer's 'views of reality and of policy, which very largely coincide with the views of General de Gaulle, will, I believe, constitute an element of strength'. But the time the four leaders had gathered in Paris, the American position had hardened. And suspicions of German good-faith had been re-awakened by the report published in the *New York Times* some time before that West Germany was negotiating direct with Spain for air-force training facilities. In London it was thought that the Americans were unnecessarily bellicose, and that the de Gaulle–Adenauer agreement would put the Western Powers in an impossible position. In France, de Gaulle was determined to develop his alliance with Adenauer without any regard for the international situation as a whole. For British weakness he had nothing but contempt. Moreover, it seemed that the French were not averse to the inclusion of Spain in the Western security system. The three major Powers in the Atlantic Alliance were so far apart in their views that they were not in a position even to begin negotiations with the Russians. If Khrushchev had been a skilled diplomatist he would have welcomed the opportunity to expose Western differences to public view, and to ridicule the contradictions in their policies. But he muffed it; he refused to come to the Conference until Eisenhower had offered a public apology for the U-2 incident. The Western Powers were let off the hook. Not only that: Khrushchev stopped over in Berlin on his way back to Moscow and made what was regarded by many as a comparatively reasonable speech; reasonable that is to say in relation to his truculent attitude in Paris. De Gaulle and Adenauer found themselves in the position of being able to claim that their firmness had saved the day.

Perhaps Khrushchev's most successful *coup* was the erection of the Berlin Wall in 1961. The fact that the Western Powers did not at once intervene led to a sharp fall in Western prestige throughout Eastern Europe and particularly, of course, in Eastern Germany. It seemed to confirm that all the lofty talk in Washington about the liberation of Eastern Europe was as meaningless in the case of East Berlin as it had been of Budapest five years earlier. I myself am unable to support the view that the erection of the Wall was a disaster. On the contrary, I believe it helped to stabilize East-West relations which were constantly being threatened by the flow of escapees from Eastern Germany. If one believes, as I do, that a substantial improvement in relations between Eastern Europe and Western is impossible so long as the disparities between Eastern and Western living standards remain as wide as they are now, then the Berlin Wall served a useful and pacific purpose. It helped to strengthen the economy of Eastern Germany, and therefore of the whole of the Eastern bloc. It was not, therefore, a divisive factor, but an important step towards the goal of European unity. There is much to be said for Richard Crossman's point of view, expressed in an interview on the West German television service on 26 August 1962. 'The Berlin Wall.' he said, 'was a pre-requisite for peaceful co-existence.' And he added that it had prevented a revolt in East Germany that would have resulted in the complete collapse of the Communist system. 'Had there been a revolt the West would have been unable to help and the Russians would have been forced to take over and turn East Germany into another Hungary.' I do not believe as Crossman did that a revolt in East Germany would have been promptly suppressed by Soviet tanks; the danger was rather that the Western Powers would have been driven to intervene in order to save the face of the West German Government, and to preserve the credibility of their anti-Communist policies. We can see now that the Wall in fact stabilized relations between the two parts of Germany; and that in so far as it stopped the flow of refugees, it removed a serious source of friction between them. The man who conceived the plan deserves the Nobel Peace Prize. I am sure that the British Government would be greatly relieved if their experts could devise something as effective as the Wall to stop British doctors and scientists from escaping to the West.

But if the Berlin wall was an undoubted success from Khrushchev's point of view, it was an isolated success. In most other fields his policy was a failure because it was too erratic as I have already suggested. When he came to Vienna in June 1961 to meet President Kennedy, his intention was no doubt to test the fibre of the new man at the White House. Those of us who were in Vienna for the Conference were given to understand that Kennedy had been deeply disturbed by Khrushchev's bombastic ruthlessness; and by his apparent unwillingness to listen to Kennedy's quiet warnings. The President came away, so I was told, with a sombre view of the international situation. Of course, Khrushchev knew that there were people in Washington who had lost their nerve at the time of the Suez operation; and that they were seized with panic when Moscow threatened to intervene. No doubt he thought they would again panic under pressure. The President himself had a blot upon his own record—or so it must have seemed to Khrushchev who in 1956 had had the forcefulness to crush the Hungarian rising—in his refusal to support the plot to invade Cuba earlier in the year. Kennedy failed to make the right impression upon Khrushchev, who was in an ebullient frame of mind after Gagarin's successful flight into space and back some months before. I was told at the time that the head of the Soviet Government was full of self-confidence and bounce.

When the Western Powers failed to prevent the erection of the Berlin Wall in August, Khrushchev must have felt sure that he had taken the measure of the new Administration in Washington. I myself did not believe that the Western Powers could have done other than acquiesce in the Wall, and later events have served only to strengthen my opinion. But one sees how it could have misled Khrushchev into believing that if the Western Powers were prepared to tolerate this overt act at a sensitive spot in the Western security system, with all the risk for them of a catastrophic loss in prestige that it involved, they would be prepared to accept almost anything. The Cuban confrontation followed as an almost inevitable consequence. Kennedy's sharp and determined response must have come as a most unpleasant shock to Khrushchev. After all, his report on the Vienna talks must have convinced his colleagues that Kennedy was no tougher than Eisenhower; and that the new men in Washington were not only soft but inexperienced. In the event, Washington was unexpectedly tough; and the Russians, not for the first time, had to retreat. Khrushchev was checked by the intelligent and restrained use of power; just as Stalin was checked in Persia shortly after the war, and in Berlin in 1948. But Stalin got off the hook rather more gracefully than Khrushchev did and his reputation did not therefore suffer to anything like the same extent, if it suffered at all.

It is hard to recall now how promising they seemed, the early days of the post-Stalin régime. They gave us, among other benefits, the Austrian Treaty after years of deliberate Russian sabotage, and the armistice in Korea. But confidence was still lacking. When I was in Moscow on the occasion of Macmillan's visit early in 1959, I was asked by a senior official at the Ministry for Foreign

Affairs whose acquaintance I had made during the war, why Soviet relations with Britain had failed to improve in spite of all that Khrushchev had done. He pointed out that he and his colleagues in the Ministry could not understand the motives that inspired British foreign policy, with all the risks that it involved for Britain. The Soviet Union and the United States, he said, were countries of great size and with enormous resources. They could afford to make mistakes. They might be costly mistakes, but Moscow and Washington would survive them. They had the resources to put them right. But Britain was just a small group of islands off the Eurasian mainland. It had no noteworthy resources of its own. One or two bombs would put an end to the British chapter in history. Yet here was Britain following in the wake of the United States, supporting all that was foolish and dangerous in American foreign policy. She was running an appalling risk in so doing. Was this fact not apparent to every Minister, every politician, every man and woman in the British Isles? All this was said to me with the greatest earnestness. I replied that it all turned on confidence: if Soviet propaganda became less venomous, if Moscow were to make some attempt to understand the Western point of view; if Soviet Ministers would only concede that previous Soviet Governments might have handled East-West relations with rather more tact, then we could perhaps make a fresh start. He asked me to explain what I meant. I answered that if Khrushchev had denounced Stalin's foreign policy in the same vigorous terms as he had criticized his other follies and excesses, many influential people in the West might have been prepared to believe in the possibility of better days. My friend finished his glass of vodka and moved off to talk to someone else.

This Macmillan visit, incidentally, gave rise to a curious misunderstanding. When the Prime Minister and Selwyn Lloyd announced that they had made arrangements to visit Moscow they said they were going on a reconnaissance trip, or more colloquially, to spy out the land. This business about spying out the land, and above all the word 'spy', caused great offence in Moscow; and I was told that the coolness of the Soviet press to the visit was due, in part, to the use of this word. Macmillan was able, in due course, to put the right gloss on things; although this did not prevent Khrushchev from having a short diplomatic indisposition during the course of the visit. It is curious that a

Government that finds it desirable to commemorate the fiftieth anniversary of its intelligence service, and which treats defectors from the Western secret services with such honour and deference, should be so sensitive about the use of the term 'spying out the land'.

When Kosygin took over from Khrushchev, the manner became more restrained, more diplomatic perhaps, but the basic policies were in no way affected. Those Western leaders who have met the Soviet Prime Minister have been impressed with his practical and unemotional approach to current problems. Whether all these East-West contacts have done any good is another matter altogether. I have the gravest doubts about the wisdom of these constant visits to Moscow by British Ministers; I think they debase the currency of international diplomacy. I flew to Moscow when Wilson went over in the summer of 1966; and, so far as I could see, about the only thing he did achieve was to annoy some of the exhibitors at the British Industrial Fair there for failing to visit their stand at the time that they expected. George Brown's quick trip later in the year, delayed by bad weather, was no more useful. The Soviet leader knows that the British Government cannot influence American policy in South-East Asia. If they were to criticize it, they would lay themselves open to a rebuff that would make Washington even less likely in future to pay attention to British views in other areas. And if the Soviet Government is going to make is concession, it is not going to use the British Government as a go-between or mediator, especially in full view of all those television cameras for which politicians of all parties have such a compulsive affection. I believe that British Ministers would serve their country's interests far better by staying at home until they had succeeded in restoring the economy. So long as sterling is under suspicion, British influence in the world is not going to count for very much. I have found no one in Western Europe who regards this constant flitting between London and Moscow and between London and Washington as other than evidence of weakness. The need to travel has become a sort of *tic douloureux*.

CHAPTER 19

THE SUREST indication that Soviet power is no longer regarded as a serious threat by the Governments and peoples of Western Europe is to be found in the state of the North Atlantic Alliance. Its members were at cross-purposes as long ago as the year 1960, as I have recorded on an earlier page, in spite of Khrushchev's bellicose words on Berlin. Some sort of unity was restored as a result of the Cuban confrontation in October 1962, but in so far as it highlighted the capacity and determination of the United States Government to go it alone, it also underlined the relative impotence of other members of the Alliance when faced with what appeared to be the ultimate crisis. It drove them into re-examining their policies and aims. The reactions varied widely throughout Western Europe: some people were shocked by the American attitude; others were heartened by Kennedy's firmness. I was in Bonn within a week or two of the affair and was able to discuss it with one or two Social Democrat members of the Bundestag, whose party was then still in opposition. I asked them if the failure of the United States Government to consult Bonn in advance had been resented. 'On the contrary,' was the answer. 'We consider that the Americans behaved wisely and correctly. If they had consulted each and every Government in the Alliance about the desirability of standing firm against the Russians, we should all have laid ourselves open to Moscow's blackmail. The Russians would amost certainly have warned us that if we gave approval in advance to American actions, they would be compelled to take reprisals against us. How many Governments in Western Europe could have resisted such pressure, especially if the public got to know that it had been applied? Consultation in advance would have paralysed the United States Government. The deterrent would have lost all credibility. This would have been an ever greater danger to world peace than the

Cuban affair itself.' In France, as we know, de Gaulle was quietly philosophical. When Dean Acheson conveyed Kennedy's message to him he said: 'I am in favour of independent decisions.' In the eyes of German Social Democrats, then, American leadership justified itself by the way it handled the confrontation with Khrushchev. In France, it provided de Gaulle with the best possible argument in favour of independent decisions by national Governments, and above all by the national Government of France.

His independent decision in 1966 to withdraw from the integrated command structure in the North Atlantic Alliance, brought Western disagreements into the open. His action came as the culmination of a series of moves that had gone on for years and whose purpose was to force his partners in the Alliance to fall in with French views, and to ensure that France attained that equality of status with Britain that she had formally lost in the various defence agreements incorporated in the revised West European Treaties of 1954. His first move was made in 1959 when the French Mediterranean Fleet was withdrawn from the NATO command, and was put on the same footing as the British Mediterranean Fleet. Next, in 1962, there came his refusal to return to NATO the three French divisions withdrawn from Germany for service in Algeria. They were stationed in France instead. It was whispered at the time that these units were not altogether reliable in the political sense, and that they needed a period of re-acclimatization and re-indoctrination on French soil. In 1963, he withdrew the French Atlantic Fleet, leaving only five submarines under NATO control. In 1964, French representatives were withdrawn from the NATO Channel Committee. In 1965, the French announced that they would take no further part in any NATO exercise that did not accord with French strategic thinking. So when de Gaulle announced that France would pull out of the integrated command structure altogether, his demolition job was rounded off.

It is not surprising, then, that morale in NATO has been low for some time. Yet it would be wrong to put the whole blame for this upon the French. What they have done is to precipitate developments that were inevitable because of the failure of other Governments in the Alliance to adapt themselves to the political and military circumstances of the time. The importance of NATO was bound to decline when the military threat appeared to decline. If the continued existence of a Russian threat is to be used as an argument for condemning the French Government for withdrawing from the command structure, then it can also be used to criticize other NATO Governments for cutting back their military commitments in Europe. This was a point that was put with the greatest emphasis by Couve de Murville, the French Foreign Minister at the time when the dispute was at its height. As for the sagging morale in the Alliance, the British and American Governments cannot escape some share of the blame for it. They failed to recognize in time that conditions had changed; and they did not undertake the necessary re-examination of the aims and purposes of the Alliance. During that very critical period in the late spring of 1966 they did no more than lecture the French. At the Ministerial Council of NATO held in Brussels at that time, the then British Foreign Secretary and his Minister of State were warned by their friends not to push their homilies too far, lest it injure British prospects of getting into the Common Market. Even the Americans were shocked by the stiffness of the British attitude and found themselves, at times, acting as mediators.

If the Foreign Ministers on the Council had paid more attention to Article 2, things might have turned out rather differently. This article calls for 'better understanding' among the parties; and it commits them to 'eliminate conflict in their international economic policies' and to 'encourage economic collaboration between any or all of them'. Article 4 insists upon the need for political consultation; and Article 12 makes it possible for the parties to the Treaty to review its terms at the end of ten years: that is to say, in 1959—at the very time when de Gaulle was making his first move against NATO control over French military forces, and within a few months of the rejection by the British and American Governments of his proposal for a Franco-British-American policy grouping in Washington. Where the Alliance has failed, then, is in the field of political consultation; and in its ability to adapt itself.

In all the years since 1949, only two Foreign Ministers have made real and persistent efforts to turn the Ministerial Council of NATO into an effective political forum. They were Lester Pearson, then Canadian Minister for External Affairs; and

Halvard Lange then Norwegian Foreign Minister. Both were among the original signatories of the Treaty; both saw in it something more than a military alliance; and both feared it would fall into a decline, once Russian pressure was relaxed, if political consultation did not become a reality. Every Secretary-General of NATO, and almost every one of its Foreign Ministers has maintained as a matter of course that political consultation was steadily developing, and that everybody was becoming more and more impressed with its range and depth. Their statements were about as true as the claim made by a commercial advertiser that his product is the best in the world. If those concerned had taken the public more into their confidence, something might perhaps have been achieved. But they preferred, so it seems, to lull people to sleep. Even the military terminology became suspect after the Lisbon Conference in 1952. It was reported officially from the Council meeting that the Allies would make available in Europe 50 divisions of troops by the end of 1952; and journalists accredited to the Conference were encouraged to write that there would be 100 divisions by the end of 1954. Nothing like this strength was ever achieved, and the figure was soon deflated to something between 25 and 30 divisions. Since then I have found it hard not to regard as humbug any figure put out by NATO headquarters purporting to give the size of the military forces in the Alliance. Later, as military budgets were cut, and people began to question the existence of even 25 divisions, the term 'trip-wire' became fashionable. It was used to describe the military units that would be permanently on duty to alert major forces if a Russian incursion into the NATO area did take place. I was told that it really meant that there were no effective forces available; but that the politicians liked the sound of the term since they thought it would encourage people to suppose that the situation was well in hand. The outburst of self-righteous anger that followed when de Gaulle began his onslaught upon all this humbug was inevitable.

There were people who believed that the Council would be well advised to pay more attention to the political problems of the future and rather less to soft-soaping the public. Among them, as I have already noted, was Halvard Lange. He is a man of courage and integrity, but he was too diffident to act on his own initiative in the Council. In Pearson, he found a compatible partner. And Pearson had the special advantage that he was as well known and as respected in London as in Washington. It is not generally realized how much we all owe him for his constructive and imaginative policies. It was the Canadian Government, after all, that induced Washington to play an active part in the defence of Western Europe through the North Atlantic Alliance. De Gaulle appears to have forgotten that the Prime Minister of Canada at the time was a French Canadian. It was a black day for the Alliance when, in 1957, Pearson went into domestic politics. Lange remained on the Council until 1964, when the Norwegian Government suffered defeat in the year's general elections. Then he, too, disappeared from the international scene.

I had the good fortune to be in Canada in the spring of 1959; and I spent a couple of afternoons in the House of Commons in Ottawa to get the feel of things. Pearson at the time was leading the Opposition. His handling of the House and the way some of its members treated him made a deplorable impression upon me. It was impossible to resist the conclusion that Pearson the international statesman was altogether out of his depth in the Canadian domestic field. His bow tie, his lisp, and above all his sense of humour were dreadful handicaps. It made me squirm to see how easily he was disarmed by that political mountebank, Diefenbaker. It seemed to me that Canada had not gained by Pearson's involvement in domestic politics; but that international life had become a great deal poorer. If only he had accepted the offer of the post as NATO's Secretary-General, the spirit in the Alliance might have been better than it became. He had always wanted it to be dynamic and capable of adapting itself quickly to changing conditions. 'The Atlantic Alliance,' he told the House on 8 April 1959, 'might find its most important task in the next ten years in building cooperation among its members.' The *Toronto Globe*, in a leading article published on the same day, showed that the more perspicacious of Canadian newspapers were of the same mind as Pearson himself. Indeed, it was while he was Foreign Minister that the Canadian press came to develop its strong interest in international affairs, and to give its support to policies that until then were regarded as utterly beyond Canada's scope. A word or two from the *Globe*'s editorial will show how far ahead Canadian thinking had moved in relation to both London and Washington. 'NATO has failed to produce a true partnership. There has been too much domination—military, economic and political—by the United States. This is NATO's great failure—a failure which has led to a suicidal dependence on atomic arms and to a stagnant diplomacy.' De Gaulle at his best and least discourteous could not have expressed it more succinctly. And I find it hard to believe that the Gaullist crisis in NATO would have arisen if Pearson had spoken with a clear Canadian voice in the Ministerial Council.

The Department of External Affairs in Ottawa was largely his creation. It was permeated with his liberal and generous spirit; and when he left, some of the zest went out with him. It acquired immense international authority under his leadership, in spite of the gravitational pull of the United States, and in spite also of the perverse determination of so many Canadians to regard themselves as the citizens of a small power. The *esprit de corps* in the service, in Pearson's day, had few parallels; many of the men in it had a true sense of vocation; they knew that they were doing something more than a bread-and-butter job. When Diefenbaker took over as head of the Government, he brought a deeply suspicious mind with him. I was told that any Foreign Service officer seen in Pearson's company ran the risk of falling under a cloud. So Pearson found himself isolated from his old friends. And since he no longer had access to official papers, he was cut off from all his former sources of information: an unusual and rather frightening experience for a man who had held high office in the public service for many years.

I found a clearer view in Ottawa, in 1959, of the dangers of Gaullism than in Washington or in London. The people I spoke to, French Canadians among them, did not believe that there was anyone who could influence de Gaulle. They feared that he might one day pull out of the Alliance, even if a change in French policy in Algeria made it possible to restore the three French divisions in Algeria to the NATO command. They were apprehensive, too, of Gaullist influence upon German national sentiment. All this was quite plain in Ottawa some ten years ago; it was not so plain in London or in Washington. And if the problem came up in the North Atlantic Council at any time, the official spokesmen were remarkably successful in ensuring that it did not come to the knowledge of journalists. I suspect that if the Pearson-Lange combination had been at work, public opinion would have been alerted far sooner, and remedial action taken in NATO in good time.

Is it too facile to argue that if Pearson had had his way in NATO, and if de Gaulle's plan for a Three-Power directorate had been accepted, Britain's relations with France and therefore with the Common Market would have taken a different turn? The result would have been a diminution of American influence in NATO, and a consequential decline in the Anglo-American connection. This would have fitted in with de Gaulle's views, and also with those of other members of the Alliance. Where British policy-makers erred after the war, it seems to me, was in insisting that the road to stability in Western Europe lay through Franco-German reconciliation; just as they erred in giving the highest priority to German reunification by insisting that the peace and security of the European Continent were to be achieved through German reunification rather than the other way round. Both these errors had far-reaching effects on British relations with France. I believe myself that the future of Europe turns upon Anglo-French relations above all. These should have had the highest priority after the war.

Anglo-French interdependence, and therefore the inevitable quarrels between them, have deeper roots in history than Anglo-German or Franco-German. It is hardly possible to open a school textbook of English history without coming upon some reference to France, and of the influence of France upon English and British affairs. But you have to turn over a great many pages before the word Germany occurs, or even Prussia. When Chesterton was writing about the Battle of the Marne in his book *The Crimes of England*, he recalled the Battle of Crécy. 'The English went forward through the wood that is called Crécy, and stamped it with their seal for the second time. The Empire of blood and iron rolled slowly backwards towards the darkness of the Northern forests; and the great nations of the West went forward; where side by side as after a long lovers' quarrel, went the ensigns of St. Denys and St. George.' Anglo-French relations have a quality that cannot be defined. The two countries have always been rivals, always seen European history from a different angle, always got in each other's way. Yet they are inseparable. There is an almost lesbian element about the friendship between those two well-developed females, Britannia and Marianne. Their sympathies, like their quarrels, tend to become highly emotional, and often neurotic. And yet a Europe that is not founded upon Anglo-French agreement, would be a desolate and meaningless Europe of *dépaysés*.

At one time, de Gaulle had this vision of the need for Anglo-French understanding. In 1947 he told a gathering of British and American correspondents in Paris that among the conditions for a European settlement was 'a real and sincere agreement between Britain and France'. Churchill, on the other hand, gave a higher priority to Franco-German reconciliation. 'The first step in the re-creation of the European family,' he declared in Zurich in 1946, 'must be a partnership between France and Germany.' Who can doubt that de Gaulle was a wiser prophet than Churchill? It is true that de Gaulle appears to have betrayed his dream, as he has betrayed others in his search for French national glory. But it seems to me that successive British Governments since the end of the war must bear part of the blame for the change of mood in Paris; and for their failure to get on closer terms with Western Europe.

Some of the reasons are to be found, as I have already suggested, in the British attitude to NATO. Others again are contained in the British insistence upon maintaining the so-called special relationship with the United States, even to the extent, at times, of subordinating European interests to it. Still others must be sought in the strange kind of romantic imperialism to be found among Labour politicians. Herbert Morrison, during his short spell as Foreign Secretary, regretted that the days of Palmerston had gone and that it was no longer possible to send a gunboat to discipline the Government of Persia at the time of the oil crisis. The Wilson Government, if the Ministerial statements made at the time are anything to go by, came within an inch of using naval power to force the Egyptian blockade of the Gulf of Aqaba in 1967; but the rapidity of the Israeli advance got them out of that particular dilemma. To these politicians, and to others as well in the post-war period, the Imperial connection has mattered more than the problem of Europe. Successive Governments have suffered under the delusion that British influence in Europe must rest upon Imperial power and world-wide commitments. The precise opposite is the case. Above all things, British security demands a strong European base. Without it, Britain will not be able to play even a minor part in such global affairs as are left to her by the United States.

Looking back over the whole of the post-war period, it seems to me that Britain has never enjoyed greater popularity, and therefore greater scope for European leadership, than on the day when Bevin grasped with both hands the opportunity offered by Marshall Aid. Up to that time, the general impression had been that Britain stood rather on the same level as the United States, determined, like the United States, to remain aloof from the housekeeping details of European life; sharing out, on equal terms with the rich Americans, and on a global scale—even if it meant borrowing dollars for the purpose—the bounties of economic aid, and relief under the UNRRA umbrella. With Marshall Aid all this came to an end. Britain came down to the level of the other European nations; her problems were now seen to be the same as theirs; and her ability to solve them no greater. She was in the same queue as they were: at the head of it, no doubt; but nevertheless standing about with the rest of the down-and-outs. She no longer stood on a pedestal far above the heads of all the others, in the rarefied air of equality with the United States. Churchill contrived a miracle when he was accepted as an equal in Washington. But it was a miracle; those who followed him tried hard to stay in the old familiar place but they failed. So when Marshall Aid was offered and accepted with alacrity by all except the Russians and their unfortunate satellites, it was seen that Britain, at last, was no longer drawing herself apart. There was a warmth in West European feelings that have never been exceeded. Almost any British plan for a European settlement would have been received with enthusiasm in those days. Britain, it was hoped, would stay with them and lead them all into an era of unity.

The mood changed when the Attlee Government decided it was important to get out of the queue as quickly as possible, and, by becoming a nuclear power, to get back on terms of equality with the United States. The MacCarran Act had made it impossible for Washington to communicate nuclear secrets to London in spite of the British contribution during the war, so a fresh start had to be made. From that time onwards, British popularity tended to decline, not so much because of the bomb, but because its production drew British energies away from Europe and into the greater world beyond Europe. I confess that I have never really understood those politicians who have argued in favour of both the H-bomb and the special relationship with the United States. One or the other would seem to me to be adequate. But I must also admit that I became half-convinced of the need for the British nuclear programme after seeing Attlee in the Cabinet Room at No. 10 Downing Street on the eve of his departure for Washington early in December 1950. He had asked some of my colleagues and myself to call on him so that he could tell us about the background to his trip. There had been a good deal of speculation at the time about the possibility that the Americans might be contemplating the use of the atom bomb in Korea, and Attlee had been urged to warn Truman of the danger of precipitating a third world war. Attlee was his calm unemotional self on that dark Sunday afternoon when he received us. And I, for one, came away deeply impressed with his quiet determination to assert the British point of view and to ensure that it was given full weight before the soldiers took major political decisions—such as the decision to use the bomb. Was it the British nuclear programme that persuaded Truman to pay attention to British warnings? Or was it the personality of Attlee, and the high reputation that the British Government still enjoyed in Washington? Perhaps both questions must be answered with an affirmative. I am sure that de Gaulle would say that it was the nuclear weapon that turned the scale. So when he speeded up the nuclear programme devised by the Fourth Republic and was, in consequence, denounced for his dangerous nationalism, although he was only doing what the British had done before him, he became bitterly resentful.

All British Governments since 1945 and up to the conversion of Macmillan in 1962, and the delayed conversion of Wilson in 1966, have suffered from the delusion that a great-power policy was possible for Britain. All have tacitly assumed that it was not possible for France; or, to the extent that it was possible, irrational. The point was rubbed in by Eden's refusal to consider British membership of the European Defence Community; or rather by his triumph in piloting into port the revised West European Treaties (the so-called Paris Agreements) after the rejection of the Defence Community by the French National Assembly. Under these agreements, the French finally acquiesced in German re-armament on condition that some part of Britain's national forces were stationed on the mainland of Europe. All

French and German national forces, on the other hand, came under the control of an American General. This arrangement undoubtedly maintained Franco-German equality; but it also stabilized and emphasized British superiority and British separateness. And it was this that the French found so hard to take; although they took it at the time.

Another tombstone on the road to an Anglo-French break was the quarrel in the Organization for European Economic Co-operation and Development. I was in Paris for what proved to be one of its final meetings in December 1958 before it was transformed into a wider but looser body. Never before or since have I seen Couve de Murville so angry. His lips were tight and his hand was trembling as he came out of the Council Chamber. David (now Lord) Eccles, then President of the Board of Trade, who has a well-developed capacity for making remarks that raise blisters on the skin at a distance of fifty yards or more, had given of his best. Those who had heard him told me later that he had used words as a matador used darts. I suspected at the time that he had just been having his bit of fun; he knew, by then, there was nothing much he could do in the way of persuading the French to accept an industrial free trade area without compensating advantages in the matter of farm produce, so he did not mind a storm. It was not until much later that I discovered he had acted under instructions. He had been asked to get the French to clarify their position. He succeeded. The British Government's attitude at the time prompted a number of reflections among those not directly involved in the battle, and they were not all favourable. In the spring of 1962, the Belgian Foreign Minister said openly something that he had long been saying in private. 'I prefer,' said Spaak, 'a politically integrated Europe of the Six to a commercial magma of seven, eight or nine.' By that time, of course, Spaak and his friends must have known that de Gaulle would always resist political integration in so far as it limited French sovereignty; what he had in mind, I suppose, was that the British Government could not count upon the support of the Five if they sought an easy way into the Common Market by deferring to French views in the matter of integration.

Nevertheless, the Six were making such rapid progress in other fields that it alarmed the Macmillan Government. Early in 1960 the Prime Minister flew to Washington in the hope of getting

American support for British attempts to check the progress of the Six towards political unity. According to *The Times* on 31 March, he warned the Americans that 'should France and Germany get on the road towards a unified Western Europe, Britain in the long run had no other choice but to lead another peripheral alliance against them. He added that in the time of Napoleon Britain allied itself with Russia to break the French Emperor's ambitions.' Embarrassed Foreign Office officials did all they could to take off the edge of this report. It could not be true, they said. If the words had actually been spoken, one of them added hopefully, it would be wise to assume that Macmillan had addressed the Americans, not as the head of the British Government, but as Chancellor of Oxford University; not as a politician, in short, but as an historian. On the following day, those who feared the worst had their fears confirmed. The *Daily Telegraph* observed that 'reports of some frank speaking by Mr. Macmillan to the United States Government in Washington about the dangers of a split in Europe were confirmed by the Foreign Office yesterday. The Prime Minister referred to Napoleon and the disastrous results that flowed from the division of Europe caused by the Napoleonic wars.' It left us all wondering how the substance was divulged of the Prime Minister's very private remarks to members of the United States Administration. What happened, it seems, was that his warnings made some Americans so angry that one of them deliberately communicated them to the press, in the knowledge that it would embarrass the British Government. After all, ever since the end of the war one of the major objectives of American foreign policy had been to promote European unity in one form or another; and here were the British up to their old game of trying to block it. Anger was perhaps a natural response.

I was in Belgrade some weeks after this explosion, and I found a good deal of sympathy among officials there for Macmillan's point of view. What they foresaw was that if Britain were excluded from the movement towards the unity of Western Europe, Germany would be bound to become the predominant partner in it. They, too, saw West Germany as the main power factor in this kind of Europe, and they did not like it. But they resented Macmillan's words about the division of Europe. 'You always refer to the division of Europe as if it were something new,' they said. 'You do not think beyond the Common Market and the European

Free Trade Association, and you see Europe divided between these two groupings. When we speak of the division of Europe we mean a division that goes back to 1945. And when we refer to Europe, we mean the whole of Europe, not just a Western corner dominated by Germany and France.' Once again, it seemed to me, Western remarks had stirred Eastern grievances in that they carried the implicit assumption that the Europe that mattered lay west of the Elbe. In his book on Suez, Hugh Thomas gives a striking example of this British attitude of contempt towards the countries of Eastern Europe. The Yugoslav Ambassador had called on Kirkpatrick, then Permanent Under-Secretary, to inquire about developments in the Suez crisis. 'The U.K.,' Kirkpatrick is said to have replied, 'is not accustomed to receiving advice from small Balkan countries.'

Some months after his visit to Washington, Macmillan went to Bonn in the hope of persuading Adenauer to slow down European integration from the inside. Professor Hallstein, then President of the Common Market Commission, was moving too quickly, Macmillan insisted, and it was time to call him to order. It was believed at the time that Macmillan had succeeded, and that he had persuaded others to take the first step towards the elimination of Hallstein—an operation that de Gaulle finally carried out. The Prime Minister's initiative did not add to the British Government's popularity in Brussels; it disheartened their friends in the Low Countries; and it did not soften up the French as Heath was to discover in 1963. What it did was to sow doubt about British good faith and British intentions. The threat of a *renversement des alliances*, so often attributed to de Gaulle, has a distinctly unpleasant sound when translated into English.

It is easy to be critical when looking back upon the zig-zag trail of British foreign policy after the war. A deeper study may well reveal that the alternatives then were not so apparent as they are now; or, alternatively, that we were all at fault in over-estimating British power, and therefore in failing to see the need for a solution of the British problem throughout Europe rather than through what was still known as the Empire. A comment that in Continental eyes illustrated to perfection the British attitude to Europe was made by Lord Chandos and appeared in *The Times* on 25 September 1957, as a contribution to the debate on whether or not Britain should join the European Atomic Energy Community

(Euratom). 'If we join Euratom,' he wrote, 'our whole research programme would have to be submitted to a consortium, including the other six nations who are members. It is difficult to overestimate the crippling effects. There is no substance in the argument that we might cut ourselves off from European research and development. A nation cannot cut itself off from something which it has.' I have no doubt that the politicians who failed to pursue what may be called a European policy reflected the national mood, and certainly the mood of the older generation. This is a defence that can equally well be made for Neville Chamberlain's policy of appeasement, as I have suggested on an earlier page, but it will not be accepted by those who demand of their Ministers that they lead public opinion rather than follow it. I believe myself that the higher reaches of the civil service were at least as short-sighted as the politicians. Those who had the imagination to look beyond their immediate problems were few and far between. 'I often wonder', R. A. (now Lord) Butler told the House of Lords in May 1967, 'why we did not take part earlier in the discussions about the Common Market. I believe it was due to our Ministers and our Government Departments, including the Treasury, the Foreign Office and the Board of Trade, not taking the Messina conversations seriously, and their being frightened about the word "federation".' It is an understatement to say that the Messina conversations that led ultimately to the Common Market were not taken seriously in London. Some of the key Ministers in the Attlee Government were hostile to them; they were against the idea of a closer British association with Europe. When Churchill came back into office in 1951 he was clearly reluctant to pursue the ideal he had himself outlined in the speeches he made while Leader of the Opposition. Eden was of the same mind as his predecessors in office. He demonstrably dissociated himself from the deliberations of the Council of Europe in Strasbourg. Among senior civil servants, there were several who took an active stand against the European idea. Kirkpatrick on behalf of the Foreign Office argued forcefully not only against the danger of exposing British political life to corrupt Continental practices, but insisted that the main purpose of European unity as sponsored by the French was to induce other countries, and notably Britain, to shoulder burdens they should be carrying themselves. It is one of the ironies of history that de Gaulle came to use precisely the same argument against Britain in 1967. The justification for Kirkpatrick's statement lay in that de Gaulle himself had said in July 1947 that among the four conditions necessary for European unity was the 'rehabilitation of France'. Another opponent was the former British Ambassador in Washington, Roger Makins (now Lord Sherfield) who, like Dawson of *The Times* thirty years before, valued the American connection above all else, and who considered that too close an association with Europe would endanger it. The conversion of Gladwyn Jebb (now Lord Gladwyn), Britain's Ambassador in Paris in the critical years, to the belief that Britain must join the Common Market in her own interests is rather more recent than is generally supposed. Senior men in the Treasury, the Board of Trade and, above all, the Ministry of Agriculture, were almost apoplectically hostile. Some of them made it their business to convince the politicians that Continental Europe was a cesspool of underpaid factory workers, religious bigots, illiterate peasants, income-tax evaders, and corrupt politicians. Not, of course, that Labour politicians needed much convincing in the early post-war years. They knew it. None of them, so far as I knew, made the much more pertinent comment that democratic institutions are so fragile in France and Germany that it would be unwise to entrust the political leadership of Western Europe to them. A British leavening would seem to be essential, in Britain's interest as much as in Europe's.

The Maritime States on the North Atlantic seaboard, Norway, Denmark, The Netherlands and Belgium, still look to Britain for a lead. They would regard a Franco-German condominium in Western Europe as a disaster. But before that lead can be given, the debate in Britain about British European policy will have to be lifted from the economic to the political level. Macmillan failed to take his party into his confidence about the political implications of the Common Market when the debate was at its height in 1962. Wilson did no better in 1966 and 1967, although he added a heavy dose of technology to the economic case for British membership. So the suspicion persists in Western Europe that the essential foreign policy decisions have not yet been taken in London. It remains true, as Dean Acheson remarked some years ago, that Britain has lost an Empire and not yet found a role; and the evident impotence of British foreign policy over the past forty years or so, and the repetitive stop-go misadventures in economic policy are due, it is believed, to the failure to re-examine and re-define the basic requirements of British political and military security and economic prosperity. Those people in Western Europe who are most disposed to sympathize with the British point of view consider that because of this lack of precision there has been something unconvincing about British policy in recent years: in terms of East-West relations, as we have already seen; in relation to France and the Common Market; and with respect also to the European Free Trade Association, where the Government's attitude has been brutal as well as unconvincing. I do not believe any British Cabinet Ministers have ever been so sharply attacked by foreign political leaders as were Patrick Gordon Walker and Douglas Jay, then Foreign Secretary and President of the Board of Trade respectively, when they arrived in Geneva in the late autumn of 1964 to explain their reasons for breaking the EFTA treaty by the imposition of a 15 per cent surcharge on all imports. Those heads of delegations to whom I spoke on that occasion assured me that they would have been fully prepared to make considerable sacrifices in order to help Britain. After all, it was in their best interests that Britain should be so strong. But the Government's action was inconsiderate and high-handed; it proved to the other members of EFTA, or so it seemed, that Britain would ride rough-shod over the rights of small European countries. When the British Ministers came out of that long and embarrassing session in the early hours of the morning, they looked as if they had been roughly handled. But this mattered much less than the fact that the British reputation in Europe had suffered another setback.

Some fifty years ago, another American, as distinguished as Dean Acheson, found the British scene just as disconcerting, and just as puzzling as it seems to be today. President Wilson's special envoy, Colonel House, had come from Berlin to London in June 1914 to warn members of the British Government of the dangerous forces that were on the move in Europe. He found, he told the President, 'an utter inability to grasp the realities of the European situation'.

BIBLIOGRAPHY

1 P. N. Ure: *The Origin of Tyranny*. Cambridge University Press, 1922.
2 H. G. Wells: *The Work, Wealth and Happiness of Mankind*. Willian Heinemann Ltd.
3 Survey of International Affairs 1931. Oxford University Press for the Royal Institute of International Affairs.
4 Harold Nicolson: *Diaries and Letters 1930-1939*, edited by Nigel Nicolson. Collins, 1966.
5 Anders Nygren: *Den Tyska Kyrkostriden*. C. W. K. Gleerup's Förlag, Lund, 1934.
6 Erik Boheman: *På Vakt*. P. A. Norstedt & Söners Förlag, Stockholm, 1964.
7 Antonina Vallentin: *Poet in Exile*. Victor Gollancz Ltd., London, 1934.
8 G. Gathorne Hardy: *Norway*. Ernest Benn Ltd., London, 1925.
9 J. K. Galbraith: *American Capitalism*. Hamish Hamilton, 1957.
10 Paul Reynaud: *La France a Sauvé l'Europe*.
11 Georges Bernanos: *Les Enfants Humiliés*. Gallimard, Paris, 1949.
12 Colonel Beck: *Derniers Rapports*. Baconnière, 1951.
13 Nora Waln: *Reaching for the Stars*. The Cresset Press, London (undated, but pre-war).
14 Robert Murphy: *Diplomat Among Warriors*, Collins, 1964.
15 Kenneth Pendar: *An Adventure in Diplomacy*. Cassell, London, 1966.
16 Nicolas Berdyaev: *Towards a New Epoch*. Geoffrey Bles, London, 1949.
17 A. Ciliga: *Au Pays de Mensonge* and *Sibérie*. Librairie Plon, Paris, both 1950.

18 Elliott Roosevelt: *As He Saw It*. Duell, New York, 1946.
19 S. Mikolajczyk: *The Pattern of Soviet Domination*. Sampson Low, 1948.
20 Frances Perkins: *The Roosevelt I Knew*. The Viking Press, New York, 1946.
21 Viktor Rydberg: *Uppsatser, Barndonsminnen*. Tal M. M. Bonniers Förlag, Stockholm, 1924.
22 Konrad Adenauer: *Memoirs 1945-1953*. Weidenfeld and Nicolson, London, 1966.
23 Burton J. Hendrick: *The Life and Letters of Walter Hines Page*. Heinemann, London, 1923.
24 Margaret Miller: *Rise of the Russian Consumer*. Institute of Economic Affairs, London, 1965.
25 G. K. Chesterton: *The Crimes of England*. Palmer & Hayward, 1915.
26 Hugh Thomas: *The Suez Affair*. Weidenfeld & Nicolson, London, 1966.

INDEX